LOVING Without Losing YOUR SELF

Bonnie Kreps

LOWELL HOUSE
Los Angeles
CONTEMPORARY BOOKS
Chicago

For Lise

We are like sculptors, constantly carving
out of others the image we long for, need,
love, or desire. Often against reality,
against their benefit, and always, in the end,
a disappointment because it does not fit them.

Anaïs Nin

Grateful acknowledgment is given for use of the following:
Excerpts from *The Token Woman* by Marge Piercy.

Library of Congress Cataloging-in-Publication Data

Kreps, Bonnie.
[Subversive thoughts, authentic passions.]
Loving without losing your self / Bonnie Kreps.
p. cm.
Originally published: Subversive thoughts, authentic passions. 1st ed. San Francisco : Harper & Row, c1990.
Includes bibliographical references and index.
ISBN 0-929923-77-4
1. Love. 2. Sex role. 3. Interpersonal relations. I. Title.
BF575.L8K73 1992
155.3—dc20 92-112
CIP

Lowell House
2029 Century Park East, Suite 3290
Los Angeles, CA 90067

Publisher: Jack Artenstein
Executive Vice-President: Nick Clemente
Vice-President/Editor-in-Chief: Janice Gallagher
Director of Marketing: Elizabeth Duell Wood
Manufactured in the United States of America
10 9 8 7 6 5 4 3 2 1
Originally published under title: Subversive Thoughts, Authentic Passions: Finding Love Without Losing Your Self

All of the people and examples I refer to actually occurred and are accurate. However, I have changed the names, locations, and identifying details.

Contents

Acknowledgments

Taking on the subject of love from a position that goes against the cultural grain can be a daunting exercise. My task would have been far more difficult and a lot less enjoyable without the involvement of a large variety of people, from close intimates to complete strangers. I thank my friends, who over several years let me pull out my tape recorder or notebook whenever they made an interesting remark about love—which was often. And I thank the many people who volunteered to be interviewed, often within minutes of first meeting and always with candor and generosity. I almost feel I should thank the airlines of North America as well. It's wonderful how freely people will reveal intimate details on even a short flight when you tell them you're writing a book about passionate love. I've deleted or altered names and circumstances to insure that no one's privacy is invaded.

This is my first book. Many people helped me with everything from advice on launching myself as an author, to suggestions for material I should include, to lengthy discussions about major ideas, to insightful commentary on the chapters as they appeared. I particularly thank my sister, Anne Koedt, who first suggested that I should write books, who became my first editor, and whose feminism has inspired me since the first days of the women's movement. My thanks also to my father, Bob Koedt, for his unfailing generosity to me in all phases of writing my book. And to: Margaret Atwood, James Barber, Beverly Burnside, Elaine Dewar, Stephen Dewar, Joanne Edgar, Ursula Franklin, Alison Leslie Gold, Paul Grescoe, Maryon Kantaroff, Rodney Kreps, Ellen Levine, Wendy Mathison, Norm Miller, Haida Paul, Birte Peschcke-Koedt, Richard Reid, Anne Wilson Schaef, Ann Snitow, Edie Stinnett, and Johanna Stuckey.

The single most important influence on my overall mode of thinking is probably the work of Kenneth Burke. Its stunning diversity and originality illuminated for me the world of symbolic form and taught me the joys of perspectives by incongruity. I thank Bert O. States, my graduate school mentor, for introducing me to this work. It informs my entire book.

My research was done in Vancouver, British Columbia, and Jackson Hole, Wyoming. I especially thank the staff of the Vancouver Public Library's sociology section, the Teton County Library, and the Valley Bookstore. Not only were they very efficient, but they also had a cheering habit of putting little notes with wry editorial comments on some of the more florid eulogies or romance that I needed to look at.

Among the people who made the publication of this book possible, I especially thank the following: my editors, Yvonne Keller and Dinah Forbes, for offering the best in criticism as they helped me bring my manuscript to its final shape; executive editor Jan Johnson for steering me through many a turmoil; Terri Goff for initiating me into the art of copyediting; Steve Anderson for being so readily available to deal with yet another detail; and Glenna Goulet for typing the final manuscript and for her encouragement when it was most welcome. Douglas Gibson, publisher of McClelland & Stewart, made a separate Canadian publication of my book possible. I thank him for that, since I am a Canadian. Clayton Carlson, publisher of Harper & Row, cheered me on from near and far from the beginning and often seemed to know what I really wanted to write even before I knew it myself. I thank him for a completely felicitous working relationship and for inspiring some of my favorite parts in the book.

I further thank the Explorations Program of the Canada Council and also the Ontario Arts Council for financial assistance that enabled me to start this project with maximum freedom.

And I thank literary lawyer Marian Hebb, who deftly and with much appreciated humor guided me through both Canadian and U.S. contract negotiations before I had an agent. For becoming my agent I thank Faith Hornby Hamlin, with whom I propose to work happily ever after.

One's working environment becomes of major importance when one is fairly shackled to a desk for months stretching into years. So I thank Mardy Murie for giving me, in the historic homestead on her ranch, not only a well-loved home but also the perfect place in which to write a book.

Three people were especially important to me in the writing of this book, as they were intimately connected with the entire process. The book is wiser, kinder, and more vital than it would have been without their participation. My very deepest thanks, therefore, to:

- My mother, Inger Koedt, with whom I worked out many an idea during hikes and ski tours. You may picture us, arms gesticulating with or without ski poles, as we arrived at yet another stupendous-feeling insight on the messy business of love.
- My friend Jon Deak, who took time from his busy schedule as a composer and member of the New York Philharmonic to become my responding diary. That diary is twice as long as the manuscript, and it became the ground from which the figure of the book arose.
- My daughter, Lise Kreps, a lucid and original thinker about love who bravely and innovatively is living out the farthest reaches of the territory explored herein. I dedicate this book to her.

Moose, Wyoming
January, 1992

Thinking About Love

We live in unprecedented times, times that are ripe for thinking some truly new thoughts about love. What people say when they are madly in love also applies to our era: "It's never been like this before." A compendium of recent technological and social factors, foremost among them humanistic psychology and the women's movement, have brought us to the point where women no longer are cast as economic dependents and subservients of men, and men no longer as providers and protectors of women. With the crumbling of these old, restricting roles comes a new freedom for the two sexes. No longer are we required to meet facade-to-facade through the artifice of sex roles. For the first time in recorded history, we can begin to seek authentic selfhood—to be true to who *we* feel we are, as a unique and irreplaceable self. From this base we can at last begin to meet each other face-to-face as authentic beings. If we take advantage of it, this momentous development in our time can kindle a transformation in our love lives.

We can begin to create new images of the self and new images of the self in relationship and to think of love as a passionate, intimate relationship between two peers where both people are empowered. Where one person does not exist "for" the other but is seen as a separate and equally important self, alike and yet his or her own, to be valued for just that. Where each person is enhanced instead of constricted by being intimate with the other. And as we create these new images of love, we can trust that they will begin to come alive in our experience.

What this kind of loving requires is two autonomous persons. The fully autonomous woman is a being who so far exists more in aspiration, as someone to strive to be, than in actuality. When I use the term in this book, I therefore mean any woman who is *striving to explore and determine her own identity according to her own reality,* instead of according to "her man" or society's notion of a "real" woman. She is a person who is seeking a viable relationship with her self and a direct relationship to life.[1]

The autonomous woman is quite visible today, truly a sign of the times. What of the autonomous man? He does not exist in great numbers, being generally focused on "measuring up" as a "real" man instead of on gauging his worth by his own standards and reality. "Measuring up" promises a man self-sufficiency but instead robs him of his self and leaves him with what two male experts on stress rightly call a chronic sense of personal inadequacy. For men who want to leave this con game in order to seek authentic selfhood, the autonomous woman is a valuable ally and mate, because she will not undermine such a shift in consciousness.

How does one become autonomous? Put another way, how do you gain an authentic self—and then not lose it in love? To me, autonomy means the continuing exploration of one's self, while holding that self accountable to everything that is not oneself. In such a scheme, autonomy and relationship are inherently connected: you can't have one without the other. If you're autonomous, you take responsibility for your self, and you leave others free to be themselves without pushing them around with your needs, desires, or demands. This is what Anne Wilson Schaef calls honoring your own process, and it makes you capable of genuine love. You don't use the other person to meet your needs, and so you have the option of actually *relating* to him or her. Whereas if you don't honor your own process, as she fondly puts it, you puke it on other people.

This conception of love between two people means that if you don't include your self in the equation of loving, you are not capable of love. But if you don't include the other's self, you also are not capable of love. Here, women traditionally err in the first part and men in the second. Women tend to deny the self, while men deny the other in the activity of loving. In popular parlance this translates into the often-heard claim that women love "too much" and men "too little" or not at all. In other words, to the extent that women and men do this, they both love poorly.

This new image of the self in relationship offers both self-affirmation and self-transcendence. Jessica Benjamin calls it becoming alive in the presence of an equal other. The subjective experience of this kind of connection is that we feel, "Here is a person with whom I am more alive, more of a person, and in better contact with myself." It produces a surge of passion and feels illuminating, expanding, and joyful. A love relationship based on such a union offers us enduring mutual passion as it encourages and supports us in engaging life at its fullest and most direct.

How many of us know the kind of love I'm talking about from our own lives? Most of us don't, not fully. Though we talk of it longingly, look for it eagerly, and may even experience it fleetingly, it seems to elude us with depressing consistency. Why? What stands between us and the experience of this vision of love? I say the culprit is the Myth of Romantic Love.

The Myth tells us that the path to True Love is to "fall madly in love": "Boom!" you're "swept off your feet," and you're supposed to go with it even though you "don't know what hit" you; "it's magic," your "head is in the clouds," you "can't get him/her out of your mind," and you just *know* that this is "the real thing." And so forth. The language of romance says that True Love strikes like this: (1) Something happens to you over which you have no control. (2) You're not supposed to have any control (that would spoil the magic). (3) You are in some essential way not yourself (that, too, is part of the magic). What are you supposed to do about it? (4) Where's the altar? Because (5) this "crazy feeling" is how you *know* you've found True Love and are going to live happily ever after.

The Myth of Romantic Love is a lie. It lies about women and men, and it lies about love and passion. The Myth is built on the sex-role stereotyping of people into "real" men and "real" women, an arbitrary confinement of the human spirit that has divided humanity against itself and poisoned our love lives. Unconfronted and unanalyzed, the Myth continues to alchemize the so-called battle of the sexes (which really is the battle of sex roles) by calling the uneasy union of its more or less real enemies, "the attraction of opposites." By designating only its own brand of love as True Love and by calling romantic passion the only passion in town, the Myth runs steady interference in the lives of people who genuinely want to love each other.

Ask yourself why the "great" love stories almost always end with the death of the lovers (in each other's arms, preferably), and why romantic fairy tales also invariably end, "And they lived happily ever after." I think they end that way because they have to. And they have to because the story of romantic love and the story of authentic love are two different stories. The writers of classic romances like *Tristan und Iseult* know this, the writers of romantic fairy tales like *Sleeping Beauty* know this, and the writers of formula romances like *Harlequin* know this. Why don't we all know it in our personal lives?

Because the power of myth is so great and so hidden. Myth operates in the form of a simple and striking symbolic story based on a potentially unlimited number of largely unconscious associations. Like what happens when a smell hits our nostrils and we're suddenly transported into the state of mind and feeling we associate with it, a myth hits us with associations that are so immediate and complex that they are beyond our volition. They just happen. This is why the most telling characteristic of a myth is the power it wins over us, usually without our being aware of it. Therefore, it should not surprise us that "falling madly in love," as per the Myth, is involuntary in its most significant aspects.

What I'm saying is that, with respect to love, the Myth of Romantic Love casts a spell on us. I call it *sparkledust.* Basically, this spell amounts to a loss of authentic connection to our self, to our lover's self, and to reality. But for the power of the Myth, we could see what our friends see when they say, "I don't know what you see in him/her." And we would realize that "I can't get him/her out of my mind" amounts to the kind of obsession psychologists tell us is caused by partial reinforcement, one of the strongest known causes of behavior. Like "he loves me, he loves me not," it is based on uncertainty. While under its influence, a pigeon pecks at the rate of 6,000 times per hour for an unpredictable reward of grain. How many times an hour do we think about Him or Her when we've "got it bad"? With the pigeon, we demonstrate it nicely: the result of partial reinforcement is that behavior is sustained over long periods of time with very little return. I call it the tyranny of romantic love. And I say that the Myth of Romantic Love is our most socially endorsed addiction and this is why we find it so hard to "just say no" to its blandishments.

Can we break the spell? Can we take back our passion from the Myth that has misappropriated it? Certainly. Allow me to introduce you to a union of passion and authentic selfhood to which you can say, "Yes!" I call it *aspiring passion.* Aspiring passion is authentic passion at its best. It dazzles your mind with reality instead of dazing it with illusions; it illuminates the core of your being with direct perception, instead of obscuring it with mystification. It's a passion that makes you feel more truly yourself instead of like someone else. And as a path to love it has the further advantage that it doesn't stop when you "settle down" into a love relationship. Disenchantment and boredom don't set in because, unlike the romantic passion, aspiring passion is of essentially the same nature as authentic love. If this sounds like having your cake and eating it too, it's probably because we've been duped by the Myth of Romantic Love.

It is, I think, a misuse of romantic passion to insist that it be the path to love. When we do insist, we are forced to develop the quick alternate vision George Eliot talks about—so that even while we "rave on the heights" we can still hope to see the "wide plain where our persistent self pauses and awaits us." With aspiring passion we don't have to create such a split in our self, because here it is our persistent self that is aroused. It doesn't have to pause and await us, because it is the core of this passion. We become more ourselves from going with it, whereas the result of going with the romantic passion (and a great part of its appeal) was described by Romeo: "I have lost myself; I am not here; this is not Romeo, he's some otherwhere."

You can't really have an intimate relationship with someone who isn't there—with an absent self. No wonder the romantic passion self-destructs. You may feel, "I want you. I want you now, yesterday, and always." But scientific research, people's experience, and what we call our great love literature all tell us that the prognosis for this passion is an average maximum lifespan of three years.

If we use aspiring passion as the path to love and meet self-to-self as authentic beings, I think exactly the opposite can happen. Here, love is based on an authentic connection between two distinct and separate selves who are present to each other at a deep level. Such a connection has a very high emotional impact and is inherently passionate and erotic. Genuine contact with a familiar yet separate other is like electricity: it produces a palpable surge of excitement as the mind and senses are aroused and tremble in unison. The distinctive feeling that characterizes this passion for me is its affirmation. It says, "Yes!" to myself, to the other, and to life—all in the same breath. The passion comes from feeling the universe open up, offering more possibilities for being, because of the interaction with the other. Love based on such a passion is grounded in authentic selfhood and yet ever self-renewing as it responds to the growth of each lover. It offers us the best, and perhaps the only, chance we have of "living happily ever after" together.

I think it's very important that we change the way we move into love. Choosing a mate is probably the single most serious choice we make in terms of the subsequent quality of our life. "Falling" into such a choice doesn't do justice to the consequences at hand. "Just *knowing*" isn't good enough; we need to know soberly and wisely before we commit ourselves. Fortunately, this kind of knowing is precisely what fuels aspiring passion. This is why I advocate the romantic passion as the path to *love a la mode:* a delicious treat at its best, but you wouldn't make a meal of it any more often than you'd gorge on ice cream as your one and only dinner fare. And it is why I advocate aspiring passion as the path to authentic love.

Shifting from the habit of "falling madly in love" to the newness of moving into love by way of aspiring passion has its own excitement. The overall feeling is one of beginning to use new muscles that we always have had but haven't used because of the way we've lived; and as we begin to use them, we can do things with our body we never could do before. The psychological muscles also exist, and my aim in this book is to look through the camouflage of the Myth of Romantic Love in order to find them—and then to see what love might look like when more of us begin to flex them.

Thinking these new thoughts about love, I've become convinced that it is, after all, possible to be wholly oneself as a woman and also find love with a man. And that if men take the chance to be wholly themselves instead of the partial human being called a "real" man, they can also love wholeheartedly. That in an authentic love relationship the self is not lost but instead heightened through the passionate connection to the other and the pleasure of engagement.

Our old divisions are the product of old scripts for women and men which we no longer have to endorse or follow. They keep us forever searching for "True" love and all too often frustrated with what we find. We can continue to live our love lives in the customary manner prescribed by the Myth of Romantic Love, or we can begin to write ourselves some new and better scripts for loving. Scripts that are more self-affirming, more vital, and ultimately more genuinely passionate. For the first time, the choice is truly ours.

This book is the story of a journey. It charts my own attempt, as a woman seeking autonomy, to find a voice in the complex matter of love in our time and then to make that voice public. My hope is that my book will fortify all women who seek to become autonomous persons and lovers. My hope is the same for men. So that any woman or man who decides to think some new thoughts about love and to put them into action may have my exploration as a companion on their path.

I TO THE CASTLE–
Playing "True Romance" in the Name of Love

1. Once Upon a Time

I used to stare surreptitiously at women on the subway who were reading Harlequin romances. Day in and day out, there they were, oblivious to rush-hour crowds, reading as many as fifteen different romances per month. Day in and day out, there I was, commuting to my job in public affairs television and also to the headquarters of what became Canada's founding radical feminist group. The year was 1968, and I had just completed my first film, an analysis of sex-role stereotyping and its effect on women called, "After the Vote: A Report From Down Under." The romance readers fascinated me. If the covers of their many romances were any indication, the world in which they submerged themselves with such avid regularity looked to me like the very world I was fighting against: the world of masculine and feminine sex roles, with its conquest-and-surrender love.

If you had told me then that one day I actually would try to live out what in the romance trade is known as the Ideal Romance—the perfect expression of the romantic fantasy—I would have scoffed in total disbelief. Nevertheless, that is what I did (and so, I was surprised to discover, do many other women like me). I had made a concerted attempt to star in my own real-life Ideal Romance. That means I tried to act like the ideal heroine. And *that* means I performed on myself an extraordinary change of character which I now would label something like a nonsurgical prefrontal lobotomy, but which I then thought ecstatically of as "finally doing it right!"

For all its copious versions, the Ideal Romance has an unvarying plot, and the ideal hero and heroine invariably possess some key characteristics that are essential to the unfolding of this plot.[1] The hero is your standard super-masculine stereotype: hard, forceful, dominant, inexpressive, contemptuous of women.

In romances, this adds up to "romantically grim." The action turns on the character of the heroine, and for this job she has an intriguing mixture of traits—one or two of which she must repudiate in order for the happy ending to come about. She is attractive to men, especially because she is alluring without being aware of it. She is also innocent and inexperienced, and she has an extraordinary capacity for nurturance. And (this is the part she gets rid of at the turning point) she has either an unusual intelligence or a fiery disposition, or both.

In the unvarying plot, the heroine gets herself into a number of scrapes from which she extricates herself with resourcefulness—until she meets the hero. He pursues his important work among men while trifling with women—until he meets the heroine. Upon meeting, they are initially either wary of each other or outright antagonistic—until the hero suddenly and inexplicably declares his tender and eternal commitment to her. She responds by promptly reinterpreting his previous negative behavior toward her. This romantic reinterpretation makes him into Mr. Right, and he becomes the only thing that matters in her life. As whatever she previously was so devoted to (work, adventure, learning, etc.) fades in oblivion, she becomes increasingly passive and dependent on him. The action fades out on this note. This is what romance writers generally tend to mean by "and they lived happily ever after."

What I have just described is the romance trade's version of the perfect expression of the romantic fantasy. It is also a good, if banal, description of the promise (to women) of the Myth of Romantic Love. In the three stories that follow, you will see three otherwise intelligent and feisty women try to act like the ideal heroine—and find out the hard way what lies behind the fantasy, especially for the autonomous woman. Ultimately, of course, you can't live a fantasy in the midst of reality. But you can give it a darn good try, and that's what we did. At around age forty, we were somewhat late bloomers in the romance game. We had two factors going for us, though: the determination which we previously had applied to our work now turned to True Love, and our consummate abilities at the romantic skill of reinterpretation.

Sparkledust

I met my Mr. Right when I interviewed him for an article I was writing. I distinctly remember thinking three things about that first meeting: one, that he looked quite sexually attractive to me; two, that he also looked suspiciously "new agey-cagey" (my catchword when I don't altogether trust the apparent openness and lack of pushy masculinity of the "new male"); three, that as he saw me as a well-known feminist and I candidly answered his questions about this, he probably would consider me too strident for further involvement. But he surprised me: He invited me for dinner, wanted a sexual involvement, and in no time at all declared himself in the dashing and importunate manner of the hero in an Ideal Romance. I now know what "he swept me off my feet" feels like: out of control while thinking, "This must be love!" Before you could say, "How romantic," I had left my own apartment and moved into his.

The terms we use for romance are very apt. I certainly went around with my head in the clouds. Mostly, I think, because I was convinced that, after a number of wrong ways—which included a marriage—I was finally doing it *right*. "Right" being having a real, seal of approval, love relationship with a man—at last. The relationship was right, he was Mr. Right; therefore whatever he did was somehow also right. At worst, it was charming in its difference from what I normally would have liked. Since he wanted many things I didn't want—marriage, my taking his name, big house, big income, and so on—I had ample opportunity to practice my skill at romantic reinterpretation. I drew the line at most of it then, but in the following five years I became less and less able to draw such lines, and I lived more and more in a manner I never had liked before and don't like now. Yet I felt throughout it all that I had hit the jackpot.

My body knew better. It put on twenty-five pounds and started to develop the precondition for glaucoma—or, as a friend coined it after I was once again back to myself, glowcoma. I did carry on with my work, but I found it increasingly difficult to concentrate. I managed to finish a complex film with a close coworker, who told me afterward that she had begun to worry seriously about the strain I clearly was under and of which I was unaware. I do remember a constant desire to change in some profound way that I could not pinpoint, except that I increasingly felt I should be more serene. With time, it became an insistent mental command: Be Serene. I now find this an interesting unconscious statement in view of one meaning of serene: to render free from anything that perturbs.

I was still trying hard to be serene when the end of my Ideal Romance came with his sudden pronouncement: "The spark is gone." No warning, no explanation then or later; I was, simply, *out*.

In shock, I fled. It is not pleasant when all one's fantasy chickens come home to roost in one fell swoop. The pain was excruciating. During the first week of my sanctuary I had nightmares every night and woke devastated by what I had dreamt. Each dream turned out to be a variation on the same theme: My former Mr. Right would be in the midst of activities that symbolized our private universe. He was always with other people and always disregarded completely my agonized and uncomprehending presence on the sidelines. I was exiled from humanity as one can be only in a dream.

Every day I skied and tried to face the rubble of my fantasies. And every day a phrase from Woody Allen floated recurrently through my mind. It was one of those wry Allen comments about sex, to the effect that a good thing about masturbation is, at least you know you're in bed with a friend. Why, I asked myself while chuckling every time it came around, why am I continually thinking of this phrase? When the answer hit home, I stood stock-still on my skis as the world imploded with the force of my insight. Suddenly my dreams made complete sense. They were trying to tell me the truth of my situation. Wake up, they said, you're not in bed with a friend, and you never were in bed with a friend. I knew then that it was true; I know it now.

My pain was soon replaced by curiosity. This shift was set in motion by a friend's comment. When she heard about my sudden expulsion from True Love she said, "Of course I empathize deeply with your pain, but what I most of all want to say is: Welcome back." This made a deep impression on me. What had she seen over the years and felt unable to tell me? *Where had I been?* To avoid going there again, I resolved to find out.

My first hint of an answer came from a woman I met while I was on my daily ski tours of personal reclamation. When she eventually heard a bit about my situation she said, "Oh, you mean *sparkledust*." I raised my ski poles in pleasure over her term and asked where she got it. "I coined it myself," she said, "from *A Midsummer Night's Dream*—Shakespeare knew a thing or two about romance—and also from my own romantic excesses, which are numerous, believe me!"

Sparkledust. A perfect name for the potion that figures centrally in the play. Made, says Oberon, from the little flower that was hit by Cupid's arrow and turned purple with love's wound. And whose effect, if put on sleeping eyelids, is to make "or man or woman dote upon the next live creature that it sees."

When the Ideal Romances of two of my closest friends ended in as abrupt and shattering a fashion as mine, and within a few months of it, I began to think seriously about writing this book. What is going *on* here? I wondered. Are we all crazy or is something else at work—or both? Seeing my friends was like seeing myself from the outside. I had considered neither of their relationships a good one, both men below par, and both friends mistaken to have started the relationships and increasingly deranged while in them. I reluctantly concluded that we were three of a kind.

The first of the two to hit the end was my actress friend. I have known her since 1968, when we became involved in feminism. We are long-time intimates and deeply attached to each other. She had worked her way through university, earning honors in a difficult double major, and had then gone abroad to study and work. By the time she returned to Canada and we met, she was an established stage actress. She was also a fine pianist, an expert fencer, a gourmet cook, and a first-rate friend.

It is a fair summation to say of her that she excels in everything she tries—except love. Though she had excellent taste in male friends, I never particularly liked the men she got romantically involved with. And her behavior with them! I used to gape in stunned fascination when we'd be out for dinner with her "latest." She would turn from talking with me in the intense and lucid fashion that is her trademark and, in midsentence as she turned to her lover, her voice would rise an octave and come out in near baby tones while her posture changed to a sort of undulating mincing.

I was filming a documentary where I needed a group of people for an audience, and she had agreed to join. She arrived late, with her usual fanfare, which she toned down instantly when she realized that the camera was rolling. But not before she had advanced upon me with outstretched left hand, on whose third finger glinted an enormous diamond. "We're engaged," she announced in a stage whisper and managed to add that they were getting married in the full regalia of her parents' church. I was aghast as I returned to the camera. Like me, she had found Mr. Right at last, and everything they were doing was perfect. They were buying the perfect house together, where she would set up a studio and he would carry on his work as a fashion designer, and where they would live. He was *wonderful,* a *total* feminist, interested in the same things she was, so open, so intuitive, so genuine, and on and on. I realized how my friends used to feel when I went on like that, because as I listened to her I didn't know whether to gag or weep or laugh. I had dinner with her and "Him," hoping for the best, and walked away feeling worse.

The end of her romance was far more spectacular than mine. They had lived together for a year and had made a down payment on that dream house. The date of the big wedding was nearing when she went to the hospital for exploratory surgery. It turned out that she had to have a complete hystere eight hours after that operation, he walked into room, made a scene, and walked out on her.

Some time before the beginning of the three Ideal Romances under scrutiny here, I drank wine with friend number two. She was nursing the wounds of a recent divorce, in a restaurant that used to be "theirs" and that she with my help was reclaiming as "hers." She was the very image of a modern career woman: a lively, highly visible woman in a profession at which she generally was acknowledged to be superb. Over the years I had seen her make far-reaching decisions with the swift equanimity that denotes full mastery of the circumstances. Yet there she was, sighing into her glass as her eyes glazed over with memories of lost romantic splendor. "It was Camelot, Bonnie," she mourned in nostalgic tones. Then she shook her head as if to clear it of mists and proposed a toast, "No more sucky behavior with men!" A worthy aim. We toasted. But the banner of what was to come had been raised with that one word, Camelot. Her next Mr. Right was about to arrive on the scene.

I didn't like him. I found him vain and pompous and intensely competitive in the most boring manner. He also tended to emphasize, by his general superficiality, her temptation to live out various fashionable images of the trendy set. It was what we might call a conventionally stormy romance, and I had hopes that it would blow itself out—so I was shocked when she phoned for what she called my blessings on their marriage. That Ideal Romance lasted three years, during which time I watched her behave more and more liked a subdued version of herself at home, while carrying on in a more and more anxious fashion with the work whose success so threatened him. The end, when it came, was sudden, explosive, and final on all counts.

Five months later, after I had gone west to write a book that would try to take a sober look at romance, I received a special delivery letter from her informing me that she had meanwhile gone east and once again Committed Romance. And *this* time he really *was* Mr. Right, she announced ecstatically, as I would know when I saw them and could observe immediately in the enclosed newspaper column, with photo. In florid prose that column broke the news of their "whirlwind" transatlantic courtship and of her secret marriage abroad to the "mystery man" the previous month. I stood in my sagebrush field and laughed out loud at life's delicious ironies. Then I studied the photograph. She, of course, looked radiant (uh huh, back in Camelot); he, to my happy surprise, looked like a very nice person. Maybe he really is, I thought, but with her method of choosing it'll be ten parts luck to one part sense.

Breaking the Spell

So. What's wrong with us autonomous women? Are we all crazy, or is something else going on—or both? I think both. Our craziness is the result of our attempt to reinvent womanhood in a culture that prescribes a very different role as the proper one for women. A "real" woman is still generally socially endorsed; an autonomous woman is not.

The autonomous woman is looking with new (read: independent and questioning) eyes at love, at men, at work, and she is making some new choices which her unprecedented options now make available to her. Since this means that she is tampering fundamentally with a value system that has existed essentially intact since biblical times, she is stepping not only into new territory but often into real hostility. We who choose this route therefore soon learn to start each day with a mental "Damn the torpedoes, full speed ahead!" To challenge traditional ideas of womanhood and the institutions that give them power is exciting; it is also stressful. And so, as study after study tells us, we pay a price in terms of ailments like headaches, insomnia, ulcers, and colitis. But we pay a further, and to my mind bigger, price: We are more highly at risk than other women to make complete fools of ourselves in love. For though we may achieve the feat of walking as autonomous women in a man's world, we do so with an enormous Achilles heel. That Achilles heel is called Romance.

Above my desk hangs a postcard from a friend who has twenty books and numerous writings behind her. It says, "Dear Bonnie: Hang in. I can't wait to read your book on love. *Everyone,* including me, writes on that subject through a wall of crud. Fondest, May." A wall of crud. You know how right she is when you try to say something sane and unmuddled about love and see how far you get before you become depressed, infuriated, weak from laughter, and certainly perplexed. All of us talk about love through a wall of crud, and I think the reason is that the Myth of Romantic Love has little or nothing to do with genuine love. In short, the Myth casts a spell on us with respect to love, a spell I call sparkledust, and this sparkledust explains the existence of the wall of crud.

Our culture considers love a "woman's subject." Women are expected or even supposed to talk about love, men are not. Women are also expected to be the custodians of love: to dispense it, to nurture it, to care about it. And our most important function as custodians of love is to love men. A "real" woman and certainly a "good" woman is a woman who loves—baubles, bangles, babies, and especially big boys who are "real" men. Enter the autonomous woman. In this scenario, her arrival is viewed like the arrival in Oz of the Wicked Witch of the West. She is a subversive thought incarnate, her very existence an invitation to break the spell.

Everything the autonomous woman stands for challenges our culture's main unwritten law. The one that says: Men first. Sex-role stereotyping defines man as the standard and woman as the Other. A woman is a "real" woman to the extent that she is different from (and usually less than) a "real" man. That's why she looks up to him and traditionally finds her true identity as Mrs. John Doe. *Vive la différence!* Her destiny is to maintain it. An autonomous woman seeks her own identity as defined by herself and not as an adjunct to "her man." She may or may not end up with John Doe, but if she does it will not be as Mrs. John Doe.

That "may or may not" regarding John Doe is another subversive thought exemplified by the autonomous woman. It challenges one of our culture's main hidden assumptions. The one that says: All women are happiest when coupled with men. Therefore anything women are doing when not coupled with men, even if it feels like happiness, is actually unreal happiness. Most women are tied into this mental knot to a degree. We make ourselves crazy trying to get into a relationship with a man and then telling ourselves this is happiness, even if we feel miserable. Meanwhile when we do things in life while not in a relationship with a man it doesn't seem like real happiness, even though we are having a fine time.

Fortunately, more and more women are beginning to question the assumption that real happiness equals being involved with a man. I think what's happening is that the visibility of autonomous women is lowering women's inhibition against looking at love with our own eyes. This phenomenon is being charted, among other places, in two of the three *Hite Reports*—which may be characterized as a record of the increasingly subversive thoughts expressed by an increasingly large number of increasingly autonomous women.

In the first *Hite Report,* on female sexuality, 3,000 women speak about how they feel about sex, what they like and don't like, how they see their own sexuality.[2] Since what they say often contradicts what experts tell us women "are" sexually, we are left with an invitation to this subversive thought: Perhaps female sexuality should be reevaluated, and with it the whole idea of sex?

The second *Hite Report,* on male sexuality, performs the autonomous function of treating men the way the first report treats women: as *a* group instead of as *the* group, which sets the standard for sex.[3] This report, in which men talk about not only their sexuality but also love, supports many women in our view about relationships with men. It leaves an invitation to this subversive thought: Perhaps the virtues of "real" men should be reevaluated, on behalf of both women and men?

In the third *Hite Report,* on women and love, 4,500 women find their love relationships with men more or less wanting.[4] They speak of moving those relationships away from the center or even out of their lives; they speak of defining themselves on their own terms; they question a masculine value system that is centered on competition and even aggression, and consider alternatives based on their own life experiences. We are left with the invitation to the biggest subversive thought of all: Perhaps it is better for women's lives and for life on this planet if we no longer put men first? That thought alone, if it spreads far enough, will change the face of love forever. It will also foment a cultural revolution.

The power of the *Hite Reports* lies precisely in their subversiveness. The fact that personal vituperation aimed at Hite all but drowns out legitimate discussion of her work should therefore surprise no one. It's merely an indication of her remarkable gift for inviting us to think subversive thoughts and thereby move out of the spells cast on us by unexamined myths.

The emergence of a significant number of women who seek autonomy is a momentous sign of the changes that will be required in our time—changes in our most habitual ideas about our relationship to our planet and to each other. As that fine scholar of profound processes, Northrop Frye, writes, "These changes are so revolutionary that they force us into re-examining the assumptions underlying those habits . . . to re-examine the myths which make up our customary vision of life."[5] I can think of no better place to start than with the source of our culture's most powerful myths. That is, with patriarchy.

2. The Prince

Patriarchy is usually defined as a form of social organization in which the father or the eldest male is recognized as the head of the family or tribe and in which descent and kinship is traced through the male line. Or, simply, as government by men. But there is more to it than that.

From women's vantage point patriarchy is more aptly seen as a social system in which women are defined solely in terms of their relationship to (more powerful) men. Our traditional titles for a woman demonstrate this truth in their careful delineation of her status—either *Miss* (not with a man) or *Mrs.* (with a man; or once with one, but he departed)—and in the meaning of "marrying well."

It's clear that patriarchy primarily is a sex class system where women are categorized as an inferior class based on sex. But this division obscures the larger truth that, although the patriarchal system does indeed subordinate all women, it also subordinates most men. It is really government by *a few* men. Patriarchy, in short, is a dual system. It is the institutionalized system of male dominance in which (1) all women are subordinated *and* (2) a small elite of men further subordinate other men and appropriate for themselves a vastly disproportionate share of power and wealth.

The essence of patriarchy is control, which is not always manifested in the actual seat of government, but rather in who controls the means of production. This is why we can have the seeming contradiction that currently exists in the United States: a country with a representative government, but simultaneously a country in which 86 percent of the net financial worth is held by 10 percent of its families.[1] Only rank naivete would believe that there is no connection between those who control a nation's wealth and those who run its government. This is why the Democratic fund-raiser Terry McAuliffe could say of the 1988 U.S. elections, "There are three ways to win an election. Money, money and money."[2]

Patriarchy has been with us for so long that it has come to be seen as inevitable—given in the nature of the human animal, even in the laws of what many call God; and therefore not only appropriate but right. As we'll see, however, it is not inevitable—a happy fact, since it certainly isn't right. It would be a demoralizing statement about human nature and a very strange one about Divine Power that a system so rigid and destructive should be the best we can come up with. Dare we hope that the demise of patriarchy is in the offing? I think so. And I think that the initial impetus for this demise is coming from women. Enough of us no longer must depend economically on a man (even if we choose to live with one), and this reality is inviting us to reexamine the age-old myths that make up the customary vision of women.

In short, women are now beginning to think their way out of patriarchy. What of men? I think men remain largely seduced by the differential payoffs offered them by that system. They are oblivious to their true condition, in the manner of Marshall McLuhan's famous observation, "I don't know who discovered water, but it certainly wasn't a fish."

Patriarchy: Form Follows Function

When I say that form follows function, I mean that the particular shape of patriarchy follows directly from what that system is supposed to *do.* What is the purpose of patriarchy? Or, going to the heart of the matter, why has it been necessary to categorize women arbitrarily as the inferior sex, and to maintain this categorization with such vigilance? I say "arbitrarily" because, as the authors of a book on sex differences put it, "If there were in fact basic personality differences between the sexes that insured the higher status of one sex, controls on female behavior would not be necessary. No law states that dogs and four-year-olds may not run for public office; when we find such laws against women . . . we must ask what they accomplish."[3]

What they accomplish is to keep women down and men in line. The purpose of a system like patriarchy is authoritarian control. We see this purpose enacted most often in the form of a hierarchy of power maintained by the threat or actual use of force that keeps the elite on top. But you can't go around constantly holding a gun to the head of every person who might see fit to disobey the ruling order; so successful authoritarian systems are those in which the people who are to be controlled eventually aid and abet in their own subordination—or at least enough of them do that the rest cease to be a serious problem. In this sense, patriarchy as it has evolved in Western civilization has been an immensely successful system. Keeping women down has had many direct benefits to men since the female sex first was categorized as the inferior one. But there have been other, more subtle and indirect, benefits accruing to patriarchal powers from the subordination of women. These benefits are psychological, and they have been exacted most successfully from men. In defining woman as the Other—essentially different from and inferior to man—patriarchal ideology divided humanity against itself. This most basic of all schisms is the prototype for the others that follow. The "battle of the sexes" with its *Vive la différence!* is the fundamental model for setting up the outsider—who easily becomes the enemy, usually the scapegoat, and *always* the means of uniting the in-group in the service of the powers that be.

On the principle of divide and conquer, patriarchal ideology thus divided men from women and thereby conquered them both: because the creation of woman as Other brought with it another creation, patriarchal man. He is the species of human being who is caught between the carrot and the stick and therefore effectively controlled. The carrot is the distant promise of patriarchy's Three Ps: power, prestige, and profit. The stick is the Myth of Masculinity, which keeps men in line with the threat, "If you don't behave *like men* you will be sissies, wimps, and fags"—which is to say, *like women.*

To avoid this terrible epithet men pay a high price. They give up their autonomy. To be a man among men is first and foremost to be unlike women. But it is also to "measure up" by fitting into the competitive treadmill of the patriarchal hierarchy in the largely futile attempt to come out "on top." As a method of acquiring wealth, the average man's chances would be better in Las Vegas. Stripped of its Horatio Alger myth the existential reality for patriarchal man is: To be is not to be; it is to fit in. As Sam Keen rightly observes in his book on the psychology of enmity, "This submersion is equivalent to the abdication of the self as a moral agent, the surrender of control to a force outside ourselves."[4] There are few autonomous women in our society. There are even fewer autonomous men. But then it never was the aim of patriarchal ideology to favor autonomous people, since patriarchy and personal autonomy are mutually exclusive.

Patriarchy: Before and After

Fortunately, it appears that before what we call our "history"—which really is the history of patriarchy—there was another much longer, and at times very different, history. This hidden past lasted for thousands of years, when social structure was based more on autonomy and cooperation than on hierarchy and control, when power was not equated with power *over,* when wealth was more equitably shared, when peace rather than war reigned, and when neither sex subordinated the other but lived in partnership. If this seems hard to believe, it's because we've all been fish in patriarchal waters for much too long.

Thanks to several modern developments we are now the beneficiaries of discoveries that the British archaeologist James Mellaart, who made many of them, calls a veritable archaeological revolution.[5] This archaeological revolution tells us that the beginnings of what we call Western civilization are much earlier than we thought. Sumer was apparently not our "cradle of civilization"; instead, there were several such cradles located in the Near East and Old Europe, all of which date back millennia earlier than Sumer, to the Neolithic. In fact Catal Huyuk, flourishing 8,500 years ago in what now is Turkey, is one of the earliest known large towns of Western civilization.

These Neolithic sites have a lot to tell us about our hidden past. They tell of a variety of art-loving and apparently peaceful peoples who lived in what appear to have been egalitarian societies where male dominance was not the norm. Nor, it appears, was war. American archaeologist Marija Gimbutas has uncovered many fascinating details from her extensive studies of Old Europe, her name for the first European civilization. She reports, for example, that Old European sites show a characteristic absence of heavy fortifications; they are noteworthy for their beautiful settings, their excellent views of the environs, but not for their defensive value. And—almost unbelievable in our time—in his excavations of Catal Huyuk and Hacilar in the same region, Mellaart found no signs of damage through warfare for more than 1,500 years.

The high point of this prepatriarchal culture was the place where it came to an end: the island of Crete. The story of the culturally advanced civilization that was Minoan Crete began around 8,000 years ago, and it ended with the fall of Crete to invaders 3,200 years ago. When archaeologists discovered Crete they were dumbfounded. "From the start," reports the Greek archaeologist Nicolas Platon, who spent more than fifty years excavating the island, "amazing discoveries were made." They included vast multistoried palaces, villas, and farmsteads; districts of populous and well-organized cities with harbor installations; and networks of worship with planned burial grounds. Excavations also uncovered the remains of a unique art form that depicted what the British scholar Sir Leonard Woolley has called the most complete acceptance of the grace of life the world has ever known.[6]

The fall of Crete marks the end of an era during which a severe pattern of disruption in the form of natural disasters and human invasions struck the ancient world. A growing number of radiocarbon dates made it possible for Gimbutas to trace several waves

by her husband. This last condition is straightforward: Here, clearly defined and given divine sanction, is the first law of patriarchy.[12] The law is still with us today. A leading current Christian apologist for the subordination of woman to man puts it this way: "It is entirely a matter of law and order and compliance with divine command."[13]

The scientific remything of women as the inferior sex was developed in classical Greece. Here, notably in the work of Aristotle, we see the biblical classification of man as Absolute and woman as the inferior Other turned into scientific doctrine.[14] In the creation of human life, says Aristotle, the male seed is the active agent and will naturally reproduce itself in its own image: that of a healthy male child. The female seed, lacking "the principle of soul," can produce only a "departure from type." All female children are in the category of a departure from type. Thus women are inferior to men because they are born inherently defective. Or, as Aristotle concludes, in the phrase that was to reverberate into the future, "The female is, as it were, a mutilated male."

The influence of Genesis and of Aristotle (who many centuries after his death was known, simply, as "the philosopher") has been so immense as to be invisible. The remything by religion and then by science produced the Bible's fallen Eve and Aristotle's woman as mutilated male, and finally established patriarchy not only as an actuality but also as an ideology. With these two symbolic constructs built into the very foundation of what became the symbol system of Western civilization, the subordination of women came to be seen not only as normal but also as natural and therefore right.[15]

This influence is reflected in any number of pronouncements by any number of the most hallowed thinkers from then to now. Here is Thomas Aquinas, the thirteenth-century Italian philosopher who was canonized by the Roman Catholic church, practically paraphrasing Aristotle more than fifteen centuries later:

> Woman is defective and misbegotten, for the active force in the male seed tends to the production of a perfect likeness in the masculine sex,

while the production of woman comes from a defect in the active force, or even from some external change, such as that of the south wind which is moist.[16]

This influence allowed the nineteenth-century German philosopher Immanuel Kant to add to his *Principles of Justice,* "Of course, I exclude women, children, and idiots."[17] And it is reflected in this statement by Charles Darwin, the nineteenth-century founder of the theory of evolution and natural selection: "It is generally admitted that with woman the powers of intuition, or rapid perception and perhaps of imitation, are more strongly marked than in man; but some, at least, of these faculties are characteristic of the lower races, and therefore of a past and lower state of civilization."[18]

We in the twentieth century are witnessing what may be the most dangerous remything in 5,000 years of established patriarchy; namely, the purportedly scientific claim that "man" is by nature aggressive. This claim, if left unchallenged, amounts to a final vindication that a male-dominant and violent society is "natural." In times like ours, where Star Wars are a real possibility, it may also prove to be final vindication that the annihilation of our world is "natural."

The substance of this concept is stated by Robert Ardrey, author of *African Genesis* and *The Territorial Imperative:* "The human being in the most fundamental aspects of his soul and body is nature's last if temporary word on the subject of the armed predator. And human history must be read in these terms." We do not, as Ardrey did, need to go all the way back to our australopithecine ancestors to see that history tells us nothing of the kind. Taking Ardrey at his male pronoun, the history of our hidden past tells us that even men did not live as armed predators in the thousands of years when peace reigned. The male as "a predator whose natural instinct is to kill with a weapon" may be patriarchy's last word on men, but it is not nature's last word and never was.[19]

What human history really tells us, if we look back beyond the creation of patriarchy, is that human beings, if given enough time and inducement, can *learn* to become violent. It's true that recorded history roughly coincides with what Sam Keen calls the era of *Homo hostilis,* but that's because recorded human history roughly coincides with *Homo patriarchus.*[20] Patriarchal man, using the word "man" specifically, is a product of the history of patriarchy. In learning to become dominant and violent he learned to become different in the most fundamental aspects of his soul and body from the type of man who preceded him in our prehistory.

Since *Homo patriarchus* is harmful to his own well-being and now directly threatens the well-being of all species and of our globe, it is imperative that we heed the message brought to us by our hidden past. Our failure to unlearn what we have learned under patriarchy can have calamitous consequences for human existence – as it already has had for human love. Let's begin at the beginning: by remything the remything that distorted us all in the first place. That is, with the myth of man as Absolute and woman as the Other in its most recent version: the Myth of Masculinity; its counterpart, the Feminine Mystique; and with the myth that joins them, the Myth of Romantic Love.

The Myth of Masculinity

Quite a bit is known now about what the framing of Eve has done to women. What about its effects on men? Certainly, male privilege puts men first in line for patriarchy's Three Ps. Equally certainly, it gives the average man the diffuse but comforting knowledge that no matter how low he feels on the totem pole among men, there is always the whole other half of humanity who as a group is lower; and whose members are supposed to service him. But the result of dividing humanity against itself has also been to divide individual human beings against themselves. Because in order to fit into the patriarchal model of man and woman, each person has to deny part of his or her humanity in the attempt to be masculine or feminine. Is the average man in pursuit of masculinity the "master of his fate," the "captain of his soul"? No. He does not have "Invictus" inscribed across his manly chest but, more often than not, "Feed My Adequacy."

Books about men talk a lot about masculinity these days. The concept clearly preys on men's minds. But futzing about with definitions of masculinity isn't really going to help men—who are not, as one book has it, caught between old and new modes in "the paradox of masculinity" but are trapped on the horns of an inevitable patriarchal dilemma.[21] The two horns go like this: (1) Truth is the first sacrifice we made in order to belong to an exclusive group; and (2) mental health is an ongoing process of dedication to reality at all costs.[22] The pursuit of masculinity as opposed to femininity *in any form* is harmful to men. It may get a man into the exclusive group of "real" men where he can feel superior to women and wimps and fags. But there is a price: in thus sacrificing truth and reality, he must also sacrifice a part of his whole human self. As psychologist Lawrence LeShan writes, "The price of rejecting a part of oneself . . . is anger against the self, self-loathing, anger against others and, at bottom, a blind rage against the universe, which, we feel, forced us into this position . . . *No one* who feeds only part of his being escapes unscathed."[23]

That most men still pursue masculinity is clear to anyone who looks around. The loss of autonomy engendered by this pursuit, and the hostility that goes with it, explains why the author of the nine-year study *How Men Feel* (about women's refusal to remain subordinate) can say that only 5 percent to 10 percent of men come close to accepting women as equals, while the rest express their feelings of anger, fear, and envy through overt and covert hostility.[24] Ask yourself why he found that "it is the combination of competence and sexuality in women that men seem to find so terrifically threatening." An autonomous man does not feel threatened by this combination in a woman, because an autonomous man's sense of self is not precariously balanced on women's willingness to be less than whole human beings.

We can deduce from this sorry state of affairs that (1) 90 percent to 95 percent of men are still caught up in the pursuit of masculinity; (2) 90 percent to 95 percent of men are therefore more or less hostile in general and specifically toward women; and (3) 90 percent to 95 percent of men are not autonomous.

How can men regain their autonomy? They can join women and start to think their own way out of patriarchy. They can begin to take back their personal power from patriarchal attitudes and institutions by examining the Myth of Masculinity for what it truly is instead of accepting masculinity as natural and desirable.

Like other patriarchal myths, the Myth of Masculinity is a lie. It promises men personal power while robbing them of just that power by seducing them into "measuring up" instead of gauging their worth by their own individual standards. And, since the game is rigged so that only a very small minority of men will ever come out "on top," the flip side of "measuring up" is "feed my adequacy"—a state of being that, in its dependency on feeders, is the very antithesis of autonomy. The truth is that the Myth of Masculinity robs men of their self-reliance, not to say of their peace of mind. This is why two male experts on stress can claim that the birthright of every American male is a chronic sense of personal inadequacy.[25]

One of the most famous essays of early radical feminism is Naomi Weisstein's "Psychology Constructs the Female."[26] In this lucid and witty analysis of psychology's shabby role as the police force of the mind, Weisstein (herself a Harvard- trained psychologist) documents how "psychologists have set about describing the true nature of women with a certainty and a sense of their own infallibility rarely found in the secular world." When women began to liberate themselves from the psychological construct Betty Friedan so superbly named the Feminine Mystique, men were still largely sleepwalking in the fond belief that they had nothing to be liberated from. Thus they overlooked the fact that, in true patriarchal fashion, the construction of the female was the adjunct to the construction of the male which preceded it—that before the Feminine Mystique came the Myth of Masculinity.

Two nagging questions underlie the set of ideas about the male sex role that has dominated the academic sciences since the

1930s, writes psychologist Joseph H. Pleck. The two questions are: What makes men less masculine than they should be? and What can we do about it?[27] The "we" in question being largely psychologists, and what they did about it was to get busy constructing what a recent book on men calls the myths that control American manhood today.[28]

According to the line of thinking that produced these myths, it is not psychologically sufficient for people to be aware that they are males and females. They can't live simply as human beings, because they have an innate need which, if not satisfied, will make them psychologically maladjusted. This need is to validate or affirm their biological sex by having sex-role identities (which are measured by sex-typing tests).

The questions in the sex-typing tests used by psychologists to assess sex-role identity run along these lines: "I prefer a shower to a bathtub." A man who is not psychologically maladjusted will mark "shower," thus validating his masculinity over and against a psychologically healthy female, who validates her femininity by marking "bathtub."[29] In this fashion did psychology set out to measure patriarchy's division of humanity against itself and to call it health. To see this confinement of the human spirit is to appreciate the term "shrink" and to understand why William James turned his back on the field he helped to found, calling psychology a "nasty little science."

It's nice to be able to report that not all psychologists followed in this tradition. Therefore when we ask, How does a man show that he is as masculine as he should be? we have some answers available that do not endorse the product. One way, described by two male psychologists, is to follow our culture's blueprint for manhood:

1. No Sissy Stuff: the stigma of anything even vaguely feminine
2. The Big Wheel: success, status, and the need to be looked up to
3. The Sturdy Oak: a manly air of toughness, confidence, and self-reliance

4. Give 'Em Hell: the aura of aggression, violence, and daring[30]

"Measuring up" to this blueprint starts pitifully early. Psychologist Ruth Hartley cites some telling research studies which indicate that the small boy is already aware that something is expected of him because he is a boy, and tries hard to act accordingly while still in kindergarten.[31] He tries, but he often fails, because the demands for appropriate behavior aren't spelled out but are usually expressed in terms of what he should *not* do. By trial and error he comes to recognize this vaguely as anything that is regarded as "sissy." The small boy thus finds himself faced with demands to do something that is not clearly defined to him, something based on reasons he can't possibly appreciate, and which is enforced with threats, punishments, and anger by those who are close to him. This situation gives us practically a perfect combination for inducing anxiety. Small wonder, then, that "feed my adequacy" should be the adult male's general request to the world.

As he grows up, the average man's quest for manhood takes him into the arena of competition where men rank themselves and each other according to criteria of masculinity. Here, in the early years, males are ranked according to physical strength and athletic ability.[32] That this is serious business is reflected in this man's memory of being a teenager: "I used to get pissed off a lot when we played ball whenever someone showed any signs of having fun, if that seemed more important to the kid than winning."[33] Later in life, men's ranking focuses on success with women and the ability to make money.[34] The bases for evaluation may change, but the importance of establishing a ranking of worth among men remains.[35] What do men enjoy about competition? A thirty-six-year-old advertising executive explains it this way:

> I get to show off with men—I mean, I can strut my stuff, let myself go all the way. I really get off on that; it's exciting. It doesn't make much difference whether it's some sport or getting an account, I'm playing to win. I can show off just how good I am. Maybe they don't like to lose, but I get respect for winning.[36]

I get respect for winning. Here we have the core of the method whereby men end up aiding and abetting in their own domination. Competition is the glue that binds men to the patriarchal system. It produces a performance ethic that says to men: You are worthwhile *because* you perform well—regardless of what you perform *at.* Whatever it is, you get to strut your stuff and collect your masculinity points. The performance ethic equates winning with worth, with moral good. That is a very dangerous equation. If it doesn't matter whether you win at sports or at getting an advertising account, does it matter whether you win at producing harmful toys, or "scoring" with women, or polluting the biosphere, or exploding nuclear weapons? Where do you draw the line? With a performance ethic, you don't. This is the kind of ethic that makes you end up saying, in the slogan of current bumper stickers and T-shirts: "The one who dies with the most toys wins!"

Such an ethic stands a good chance of producing moral fools and imbeciles, because in cutting out all the means to the overriding end of winning, it is not an ethic at all. What it *is,* is a way of controlling men by fooling them into serving goals that ultimately are not their own. Pleck illustrates to a T my point about patriarchy's subordination of men by way of the Myth of Masculinity with his observation that, "By training men to accept payment for their work in feelings of masculinity rather than in feelings of satisfaction, men will not demand that their jobs be made more meaningful, and as a result jobs can be designed for the more important goal of generating profits."[37]

The Myth of Masculinity takes a terrible toll on men. Not only do they lose their autonomy in the quest to "measure up," they become more and more like automatons in the process. An automaton is an apparatus that automatically performs certain actions by responding to preset controls or encoded instructions. I'd say that describes a "real" man pretty well and is why one of the most perceptive and compassionate books about men, by a man, can be called *The Male Machine.*[38] Psychologists have found what many of us know: that masculinity is associated among other things with being anxious, aloof, emotionally unresponsive, and dull.[39] Here is how various men talk about these traits and their effect on men's lives. Their competitiveness creates such an obstacle to openness between men that there is no real emotional give-and-take: "If others know how you really feel you can be hurt, and that in itself is incompatible with manhood."[40] A man even feels uneasy about trying to help a friend in trouble by offering an emotional insight because, "It would catch him off his guard; it would be something he hadn't already thought of and accepted about himself and, for that reason, no matter how constructive and well-intentioned you might be, it would put you in control for the moment. He doesn't want that; he is afraid of losing your respect. So, sensing he feels that way, because you would yourself, you say something else."[41]

Why are masculine men so boring? Because being anxious, aloof, and emotionally unresponsive makes a person boring. And because feeling he has to be "on top" no matter how boring he is makes a person more boring. Masculine men numb one's mind because they must always be on "send," even when they have little or nothing to send. As one man said of those times in his life, "When I was talking I used to feel that I had to be driving to a point, that it had to be rational and organized, that I had to persuade at all times, rather than exchange thoughts and ideas."[42]

Hearing such revelations from men about the emotional reality of being masculine in our culture always gives me a sense of eeriness tinged by sadness. It feels like being taken through a strange, yet familiar, zoo. I had the same feeling when I was scouting for material for a film on stress. Under the rubric "men and stress" I needed locations where we could film men *en masse* as they go about the daily business of being masculine. On the first day I stationed myself at lunch hour near Vancouver's court building. This proved an excellent vantage point from which to observe the anxious posturing of men as they try to "measure up." Lawyers straight from the ritualized combat of that masculine temple, the courtroom, were particularly rewarding to study.

They acted out exactly what this lawyer was talking about: "There simply was no room in my ideal image of a human being for anything but confidence and control."[43]

The next day I went in search of Management Man. A male friend who was of that world took me through several large bank and insurance office buildings. Here I saw the scenario described in *The Corporate Eunuch* (note how the title is yet another reference to masculinity or the lack thereof):

Naturally he is very busy. . . . He reads research reports. He eyes flow charts. He runs meetings. He attends seminars. He generates projections. He plans strategies. He formulates budgets. And yet some days he does not really feel that he has accomplished a damn thing. . . . Still, it is absolutely necessary for the manager to maintain a facade and a steady flow of articulate self-confidence. The firm jaw, the crisp collar, the taut crease, the decisive, forceful finger on the telephone dial. He must be in uniform and in character at all times, ready for the cry, "This looks like a job for Management Man!"[44]

"In uniform and in character at all times" is exactly what I saw in the hundreds of men I observed. How pathetic. These men resembled nothing so much as grey-and-charcoal-pinstriped ants. How *can* men stand to look and act so relentlessly alike? This is living?

To make matters even worse, if that's possible, men must live in their world of anxious automatons with the sword of Damocles hanging over their heads. For they can lose whatever they have managed to "measure up" to in the single blow of being labeled a homosexual. All it takes, according to one man, is "almost any sign of behavior which does not fit the masculine stereotype."[45] How powerful is the threat of being called homosexual?

Nothing is more frightening to a heterosexual man in our society. It threatens, at one stroke, to take away every vestige of his claim to a masculine identity—and to expose him to the ostracism, ranging from polite tolerance to violent revulsion, of his friends and colleagues.[46]

I asked some male friends with a variety of sexual backgrounds if the situation really is as bad as this. They all agreed with my gay friend who, when I read him the quote over the phone, said, "I think that's true. Most men aren't comfortable enough with themselves to take gay-baiting as something to brush off. And because most men feel that way, it *isn't* something to be brushed off." Gay-baiting is the ultimate irony of the patriarchal creation of women as the Other as it plays itself out in men's lives. Here we see the basic truth that the creation of any out-group always boomerangs back on the in-group, because it inevitably creates the closet from which the specter of that Other can step out and undo whoever defined it so. The list is endless: Racist whites must live with the fear of finding a black in the family lineage; "Aryan" Germans in terror that the Nazis would similarly find a Jew; Moslems afraid of being declared Infidels and subjected to a Holy War; Americans at risk of being hounded by the likes of Joe McCarthy, and so on. But the most fundamental and also largest in-group that has terrorized itself by its creation of the out-group is the male sex, in which men since the time of that creation have been kept in line by the threat of being seen as "effeminate" and ultimately as "queer." What fools we are to let our lives be blighted in this manner. How far we've come from the ubiquitous joy of living that scholars tell us characterized Crete.[47]

Can You Be Masculine and Also Loving?

If the Myth of Romantic Love lies about men, it also lies *to* them. The Myth says to men: Be a "real" man and the world is yours: you'll get your Three Ps, gorgeous women will fall all over you and feed your adequacy, "your woman" will devote herself to you, and you'll live happily ever after. Does the Myth say anything about love? If we mean love in the sense of mutual caring between two intimates, forget it. That's not part of the deal.

The question of whether a "real" man can love begins to look absurd after our tour through the zoo world of masculinity. No, you can't be loving if you can't be open enough to let others know how you really feel. Or if you can't help another man who's in trouble because both of you would see that as putting you in control. Or if "staying cool" means being emotionally unresponsive. Or if communicating means always being on "send." Or if winning is how you prove your worth. That way of being is not how you become loving; it's how you end up saying things like, "The word 'tenderness' throws me off. I associate it with mothers or with artists; it is not a manly characteristic."[48]

A large and varied number of psychological studies in the area typically called "sex typing as it relates to the expressive domain" demonstrates what everyday experience confirms: Masculinity and emotional expressiveness are virtually mutually exclusive. The author of *The Total Woman* baldly states the result for men: "Your man, like so many American males, may be like an empty cup emotionally."[49] Joseph Pleck, writing in *The American Man*, makes the point that in the traditional male-female relationship men experience their emotions vicariously through women.[50] Women know from our intimate relationships with men as fathers and lovers that this is true. It is we who all too often are the intermediaries between them and their children, we who pour emotional oil on troubled waters, who interpret other people's feelings to them because they as a rule don't hear them directly, and who explain their feelings to other people for the same reason. We, in short, who help men express their emotions and often even express their emotions *for* them. And how could it be otherwise? In the patriarchal set-up, which delegates "hard" characteristics to men and "soft" ones to women, men get to compete and women to emote. In hard competition emoting is a handicap, and anyway it's sissy.

It's clear that the socializing process that makes boys into "real" men is an obstacle to men's intimacy with women. It's difficult to be loving if you are emotionally mute. When we add to this obstacle the sexual training of adolescent males, the situation begins to look pretty hopeless for men who want to be loving with women. The training is described this way by the author of *Being a Man:*

> By convincing a girl to have sex—to "make" them, to get them to "put out"—we gained status among our male friends, and we could think of ourselves as accomplished males. We either "scored" or we "failed." Our guideline for behavior never was to become emotionally committed. We tried to get as much as we could while giving as little of ourselves as possible. The goal was to be a "cocks-man" who could screw myriads of girls (or could say that he did) without ever having to love any of them—to be a member, as we said, of the "Four F" club: find 'em, feel 'em, fuck 'em, and forget 'em.[51]

I had never heard of the "Four F" club until I read his words (possibly because I was born and raised in Denmark), but I soon heard plenty. On the slightest pretext—at parties, on airplane rides, by copying machines, in laundromats, grocery stores, bank queues, and so forth—I started asking men if they had ever heard of the "Four F" club. Of the many men of various racial, economic, and ethnic backgrounds I asked, only two had never heard of the "Four F" club. All the others knew of it instantly when I asked my question. They hadn't all "joined," but they had all felt pressured to do so. (There was a single variation of this theme. One man called it the "Three F" club. When I asked which "F" his club had left out, he replied, "Find 'em, fuck 'em, and forget 'em." Efficiency rears its head even in adolescent practices at "measuring up.") This kind of training in the objectification and conquest of women, pervasive as it seems to be, does not exactly predispose the average male toward caring intimacy with women.

How can you love at all if you need other people to express your emotions for you? How can you love women if you have been taught to think of them as an inferior and even contemptible sex? How can you love an individual woman if you are threatened by her combination of competence and sexuality? Must she be either incompetent or sexually unattractive to you for you to feel drawn to her? You're supposed to be emotionally and sexually intimate, when you've been trained to be just the opposite, *and* with one of your worst epithets? Help!

Help is on the way. But, as we might expect from the Myth of

Romantic Love, it is help that is mystified and therefore no help at all. The Myth lies to men, because it robs the "real" men it promotes and endorses of their chance at authentic love. What it gives them instead is romance, which is not at all the same thing and only adds fraud to robbery.

The Prince's Horse: Romance

I say that romance is the Prince's horse because the man who wants to be masculine and also loving is faced with two daunting problems, and romantic love promises to solve them both. This promise is seductive because if he wants to be masculine a man is *supposed* to be a lover, since success with women is one of the major ways he earns masculinity points. The Myth of Masculinity says: "Real" men are supposed to be ready to "come through" at all times. Masculine men say: "When I meet a good-looking woman and I don't make her, I have a small but very real sense of failure, I feel diminished as a man."[52] But women are among his worst epithets, and anyway he's rotten at intimacy, so how can he "score" in this arena? If he's human enough to want something more than "scoring," how can he overcome her inferior status as a potential beloved and his own inferior capacities as a potential lover? Solution: Romance in the form of True Love with the One and Only, as promoted by the Myth of Romantic Love.

Romantic love and the masculine man as lover were made for each other. Romance is to him what the phone booth is to Clark Kent. No doubt this is why men are FILO (first in, last out) of romance, while women are LIFO (last in, first out). The FILO/LIFO reality is completely contrary to what the Myth of Romantic Love would have us believe, but there it is. This contrast illuminates the Myth's function of mystification, nicely stated here by one heroine who did not fall for it: "Romantic, in my lexicon, means unreal; glossed over with a false attractiveness to entrap those who will not see through the gloss to the truth beneath."[53]

Romantic fairy tales emphasize the Princess in their happy

endings. She reaches her fulfillment when she climbs onto the Prince's horse and they ride off to live happily ever after in his castle. But what's true for the Princess is also true for the Prince. The whole story is that he, too, is swept away by romance; for it is he, after all, who is the rider even as she is the passenger. The horse also takes *him* to the Castle—which, as you may agree later, is not a healthy place to be. The Myth of Romantic Love defrauds men because it glosses over the fact that it does not solve the masculine man's problems with love. It actually intensifies those problems by renaming them and calling its mystification True Love. Meanwhile, it locks the romance-smitten man even more firmly into the masculine stereotype that is at the bottom of his problem in the first place. This vicious cycle goes a long way toward explaining why so many men are FILO in romance.

How can a man get "brought down" by one of his epithets and still call it love? He sighs, "I don't know what hit me" but "'S wonderful! 'S marvelous!" Contrary to all expectations, it's "the real thing." In fact, as so many love songs declare, "It's Magic." And so it is. Magic is the *modus operandi* of romantic love because magic, as Denis de Rougemont reminds us, persuades without giving reasons and is perhaps persuasive to precisely the extent that it withholds reasons.[54] Magic lifts his beloved out of her regrettable category of inferior epithet and makes her special, thus worthy of loving. Magic also makes *him* special. It lifts him out of masculine limitations in loving by converting those very limitations to the qualities of love's Superman.

How does the Myth of Romantic Love work this alchemy for the masculine man? It takes his distance and aloofness and calls them romantic idealization—a process of abstraction that, in enabling him to see the object of his passion as perfect or more nearly perfect than she actually is, saves him from having to deal with her directly. Romantic idealization also lifts her out of the hated category of epithet and makes her "not like other women." About men's misogyny Mark Gerzon argues that, "In fact, men have far more complex and contradictory feelings about women. We may despise them, but we also worship them."[55] I argue that to worship and despise women at the same time is not contradictory but merely flip sides of the same misogyny, because worship in this case is a means of not relating to what you in fact despise. You put the woman to be worshiped up there on the pedestal in order to get her away from you as a real and vital presence. And calling it romantic idealization is how you hide that truth from yourself.

How about the masculine man's emotional unresponsiveness? Romantic love masks it by giving him the mantle of romantic lover who "sweeps her off her feet"–which is not an emotional give-and-take but merely a take. It looks like responsiveness because he is so completely focused on her, but it is really another opportunity for him to be "on top" and on "send." By the same token his dullness is not noticed because both he and the woman who thinks she's supposed to be "swept off her feet" will see him as dashing rather than boring and needy. Their lack of communicative give-and-take will likewise go unnoticed while they are in this state. La Rochefoucauld was speaking of them when he said, "Lovers never get tired of each other, because they are always talking about themselves."[56]

A masculine man's inability to admit to being vulnerable, which would preclude real intimacy, is also deftly bypassed by the romantic euphoria that makes him feel "on top of the world." That is, impervious to life's vicissitudes. That is, invulnerable.

Then there's the matter of feeling so terrifically threatened by the combination of competence and sexuality in women. Here, too, romantic love comes to the aid of the masculine man because a romantic heroine is, above all, passive. In romantic fairy tales, in fact, she's often comatose. That's nonthreatening. Romantic poetry goes fairy tales one better. When I mentioned the comatose aspect to a friend, she laughed and said, "dead virgins." Dead virgins? "I have a friend who was doing her Ph.D. thesis on romantic poetry. She found that most of it consisted of odes to dead virgins." That's *certainly* nonthreatening.

Even in the everyday world of the twentieth century the same message comes through with respect to what makes a woman romantic. For example, I have been inundated lately by mail-order catalogs for women's clothing. I've noticed that whenever a section is headed by the word "romantic" the models are predominantly very young and blond; their clothes are pale pastels, usually pink, and festooned with lace; and the copy is full of words like "gentle," "delicate," "pretty," "feminine," and "sweet-as-can-be." Let's face it: A successfully romantic woman is *neither* competent *nor* sexual, never mind the combination. Her competence must be flawed, and her sexuality must be only of the responding kind. In sum, a successfully romantic woman is, above all, a woman who is nonthreatening because she feeds a masculine man's adequacy where it counts the most: by giving him the feeling of "measuring up"–in or out of bed. Joseph Pleck, whose book *The Myth of Masculinity* is a landmark of its kind, has written of men and masculinity that men create and foster hierarchies of competition, and that women function as rewards for that competition and as refuges from it.[57] With the conquest and surrender of a successfully romantic woman, a masculine man gets both his reward and his refuge.

I don't mean to speak unkindly of the masculine man's problems with love. I see his predicament as extremely unfortunate. His conditioning makes him a sitting duck for what in my opinion is the worst kind of love, and it makes him more or less stuck with that kind of love to the exclusion of a better kind. He, far more than women, is driven by romantic compulsion. Since this reality is so contrary to his own belief, I'll note here that it is a reality which not only was predicted by feminist analysis of sex role conditioning but later supported by study after study in psychology and social psychology.[58]

The evidence indicates that over a lifetime men fall in love more often than women; that men fall in love much sooner in a new relationship than do women and cling more tenaciously to an obviously stricken love affair than women, who more often than men decide when an affair should end; that men feel more depressed, more lonely, and less free after a breakup than women and are three times as prone as women to commit suicide after a disastrous love affair. And—the final twist—though the masculine man is driven more than women by romantic compulsion, it is women who experience more intensely the euphoria and agony of romance. I call that a bad deal. It's the deal brought by the Myth of Masculinity, which trains and requires men to "validate" their masculinity by behaving in ways that make authentic love impossible for them.

Does the experience of love depend on one's sex-role orientation? The question is posed in a rather elegant study by three psychologists, who answer it as I do: Yes.[59] They conclude that there effectively are two kinds of love for two kinds of people. To the extent that you favor traditional sex roles of masculinity and femininity, your experience of love will tend to be in the romantic mode. To the extent that you don't, you are free to seek a love based on what I would call authentic passion and intimacy instead of the pseudo-intimacy of the "attraction of opposites."

The Myth of Romantic Love stands in fundamental opposition to personal autonomy. If masculinity locks men into the Myth of Romantic Love and robs them of a chance at genuine love, the same is true for femininity and its results for women and love. This truth is being dramatically illustrated by the autonomous woman's singular difficulties in the Land of True Romance. Since it stands like a double whammy on the path to love, there's no way around this Myth. Let us therefore take a concerted look at how it works, where it gets its great power, and how it reveals itself in head-on collision with the love lives of autonomous women.

3. The Myth of Romantic Love

"My Lords, if you would hear a high tale of love and death . . ." Thus begins *The Romance of Tristan and Iseult,* often called the world's greatest love story, and a fine opening it is.[1] Already we feel the spell a myth can cast over us, as this particular myth has done for the eight hundred years since Thomas of Britain wrote down its earliest known version around the year 1185.[2]

Of all the myths that make up our customary vision of life, this one is among the most powerful. Its legacy, whether we recognize its distinctive contours or not, lies deep in the heart of what we call romantic love: the precipitate ecstasy of love at first sight, the "exquisite anguish" of thwarted passion, the rapture of a union that lifts us out of humdrum reality and into an exalted state of being—all hail from the Tristan myth. The myth's residue is evident, for example, in the lament of this woman I interviewed, who told me that her husband was "a wonderful man but not a romantic figure" and then went on to say:

I don't understand the recurrent romantic fantasies that I plunge into. I finally saw a therapist about it. She suggested that I was using the fantasies to distance myself psychologically from my husband. I thought, This is a very uncomfortable idea. I know that it *does* distance me from him. I can now be with him physically and know I'm not there emotionally. I'm somewhere else, and I'm telling myself that the person I really care about is somewhere else. And yet I *know* that the person I fantasize about is totally inappropriate. But I cannot deal with my obvious need for something more exciting, more thrilling, than what I have in my life.

I go for a walk at night and I've had a couple of glasses of wine and I smell the perfume of the flowers, and *that* seems to embody what I want. Something stirring—and ungraspable. Something you can't have.

Tristan and Iseult: Myth in Action

What actually happens in the world's greatest love story? Here's the plot of *The Romance of Tristan and Iseult*:[3] We're in the time when legend has it that King Arthur and his knights sat at the Round Table in Camelot. Tristan, our hero, is an orphan. His mother's brother, King Mark of Cornwall, takes Tristan to grow up in his castle at Tintagel.

When he is of the age for knighthood Tristan kills the Morholt, the Irish giant who has come to exact his tribute of Cornish maidens and youths. Mortally wounded by the Morholt's poisoned barb, Tristan takes his sword and harp and begs to be cast adrift in a boat without sail or oar. The boat lands in Ireland, whose Queen alone knows the secret of the poison from which Tristan is dying. Unfortunately, she is the Morholt's sister. Tristan therefore does not disclose his name or how he came by his wound while Iseult, the Queen's daughter, nurses him back to life. He returns to Tintagel.

A few years later Tristan is sent on a quest. King Mark wants him to find the woman from whose head a bird has brought a golden hair, because he is determined to marry her. A storm causes Tristan once again to land in Ireland, and once again he meets Iseult. The golden hair is hers. They set sail for Cornwall so she can become Queen, but not before she tries to kill Tristan upon learning his identity. On their voyage they drink, by mistake, a love potion brewed by her mother for Iseult and King Mark. Suddenly, they are madly in love and fall into each other's arms. But Tristan, still bound in duty to his quest, brings Iseult to King Mark. She marries him. Helped by a clever ruse, Iseult's maid (who mistakenly gave the lovers the fateful potion) expiates her guilt by taking Iseult's place in the nuptial bed on the wedding night.

A series of tricks by other knights at King Mark's court eventually (despite splendid countertricks by Tristan) persuades the King that the Queen and Tristan are lovers (they are). Iseult is handed over to a hundred lepers, and Tristan is sentenced to burn at the stake. By a fantastic feat he manages to escape execution and then rescues Iseult from the lepers. The lovers hide in the Forest of Morrois. One day in the forest King Mark happens upon them while they are asleep. But Tristan has put his drawn sword between himself and Iseult, and the King supposes this to mean they are innocent of adultery. He goes away without waking them, leaving his own sword in place of Tristan's. The lovers stay in the forest, where they lead a life "harsh and hard."

At the end of three years the love potion wears off. Immediately, Tristan repents his betrayal of the King, and Iseult wishes she were Queen again. With the help of the hermit Ogrin, Tristan offers the King peace and says he will surrender Iseult. King Mark promises forgiveness, and the lovers return to Tintagel, where they part. But not before Iseult vows that she will rejoin Tristan if he makes a sign, for "neither tower, nor wall, nor stronghold" shall stop her from doing his will. They have several secret trysts.

New knightly adventures carry Tristan far away from Iseult, and he eventually comes to believe she no longer loves him. He thereupon marries another Iseult, "for her name" and also, as they say, in name only, because he still sighs for Iseult the Fair.

Finally, Tristan is once again dying from a poisoned wound. He sends for the Queen of Cornwall, who alone can save him. As her ship draws near, Iseult hoists a white sail signifying hope. But Tristan's wife, tormented by jealousy, tells him the flag is black. Tristan despairs and dies. Shortly thereafter, Iseult arrives. Seeing him dead, she lies down beside him and embraces him. Then she dies, too.

What? you may well exclaim. *This* is the story that fuels countless passions? It is. Can anything testify better to the power of myth than the fact that a story as silly as this doesn't just generate laughter? (In some cultures it does, a significant fact that should not be forgotten.)

When stripped of its mythic spell, the story of Tristan and Iseult is plainly preposterous. The motivation that seems to propel its plot raises more questions than it answers. For example: Why has Tristan placed the sword of chastity between himself and Iseult in the forest, when they already are lovers and do not expect King Mark? Why does Tristan keep restoring Iseult to the King? Why doesn't he take her at her word and give the sign that she vows will make her join him? The plot abounds with obstructions to their being together. When external circumstances bring on these obstructions, Tristan leaps (often literally) into actions to overcome them and gain his beloved–only to turn around and devise obstructions of his own when nothing external separates him from her. Why? The most obvious answer is: Because he doesn't really want Iseult.

What? In the world's greatest love story the hero doesn't want the heroine? Who's kidding whom? To find out, let's try this subversive question: What *does* Tristan really want?

He wants to search for Iseult, he wants to fight for her, to yearn for her, suffer for her. He even dies for loss of hope of seeing her again. But he doesn't seem to want to stick around much and actually care for her. The tortuous path of the plot now begins to make sense. What Tristan really wants is not Iseult but *to be in love with Iseult*. There is quite a difference between the two, and his choice is clear. His desire is not to love but to be ravished by Love. He wants to live branded by the pure flame of a grand passion and, ideally, to die for it. For this solitary quest he needs the dream of Iseult, not the reality, and therefore her absence more than her presence. And Iseult is the perfect heroine, who helps the hero with his quest. She fulfills Tristan's passionate dream of her by staying mostly out of his way before she, too, dies for love.

What we have in *The Romance of Tristan and Iseult* is romantic love in the classic version codified by the Courts of Love in twelfth-century Provence. This society produced the intensely romantic tradition known as Courtly Love (or *donnoi*), which became the template for later Western models of romantic love. When the troubadours sang of love, they sang of this: "Of *donnoi* he knows truly nothing who wants fully to possess his lady. Whatever turns into reality is no longer love."[4]

There are many would-be Tristans in our world, and not a few Iseults. What separates us from the lovers in this myth is not our desire for this passion but how far we are prepared to go for it. Tristan's and Iseult's actions are not really different in kind from ours, they differ only in degree. They are actions writ large, illuminating the hidden truth about romantic passion (if we know how to look for it), thus performing the function of myth.

This kind of love is indeed such stuff as dreams are made of, but it's not much good for moving into intimacy with a real person. It may be attractive and compelling, it may promise ecstasy and even deliver on that promise; but as the basis for a long-term and deepening love relationship it is doomed to failure. The society that produced the Courtly Love tradition knew this: Romantic love was not expected to lead to marriage, it was seen as *opposed* to marriage. I agree, broadening the statement to include love relationships other than marriage.

I also agree with Johanna Stuckey, the Canadian scholar who wrote a refreshingly forthright treatise on passionate romantic love: This kind of love is by definition unrealistic, irrational, and short-lived.[5] And, as she told me in an interview, the hints are right there in the words of the stories:

> If you really look at our great love stories, you'll find that their language tells you so much about romantic love. For instance, it happens *to* you, outside your will. There's always some external force like an arrow, a potion, a drug, or a plant. Also, you're often *miserable* when you're "madly in love": images of disease, of wounding; fire images like spark, flame, scorched, branded run all through the literature.

As we saw in *Tristan and Iseult*, this kind of love doesn't last. As Stuckey says, either the love dies or, more usually, the two lovers die (in each other's arms, preferably) and are crystallized forever in that state of being in love. Why? "Because that's their only way to make sure that it does continue forever. Why do you think the fairy tales always end, 'And they lived happily ever after'?"

Well, I could put the answer bluntly—and I will. They end that way because they have to. And they have to because the story of genuine love and the story of romantic love are two different stories. The writers of great romances know this, the writers of romantic fairy tales know this, the writers of formula romances know this. When we all know what they know, our love lives might finally take off to somewhere worth going.

The Power of Myth

It's no accident that, even in our scientific age, the most powerful influence on our love lives should come from myth rather than science. One scientific study of sexual conduct offers an unexpected example of what I mean. Its authors write that underlying all human activity there exist metaphors or informing imageries, commonly unnamed until they lose their potency, that shape our thoughts and our behavior. Their major premise is as follows: "What is suggested here in an untentative way is that it is the sociocultural that gives sex its meaning and it is the myths of the society that give it its power."[6] Let me rephrase that equally untentatively: It is our sex role stereotypes that give our prevailing idea of love its meaning, and it is the Myth of Romantic Love that gives this idea its power. Without the Myth to define the situation, name the actors, and plot our behavior, we couldn't count on anything we call romantic to happen.

Why is myth so powerful? Because it is built of simple and striking images that work on us without our being aware of it. The world of myth is a world in which actions are portrayed at or near the conceivable limits of human desire. It is a world of grand emotions and grand actions, a world of the extraordinary. It is a world of archetypes—of typical or recurring images that resonate deeply within us. The Garden of Eden is an archetype; so is the cowboy, so is Sleeping Beauty. The most powerful archetypes are those which are most deeply rooted in common human experience—like archetypes based on food and drink, the quest or journey, and the fulfillment of love.[7] Archetypes work largely by unconscious association. This aspect of the power of myth isn't hard to understand, once we realize that the associations we make are so immediate and complex that they are beyond our volition. They simply happen. This kind of power is akin to the enormous effect a certain smell can have on us. We may not even be aware of having noticed the smell, but suddenly and inexplicably we experience the total state of mind and feeling we associate with it. Thus with myth.

We can make two basic responses to the power of myth. The first, unhappily, is the more common one: We silence the myth. This happened even to *The Wizard of Oz,* which was banned in New York City during the McCarthy era, no doubt because its archetypal elements were used to satirical and antiauthoritarian effect.[8] The other response, and the one we'll take here, is to defuse the power of myth by uncovering its unconscious aspects so that we can make conscious choices about them. In other words, let's think some subversive thoughts about the Myth of Romantic Love.

For example, we can think of being "madly in love" as a privileged mode of understanding (which most of us do), or as the impoverishment of a mind obsessed by a single image; as an ardent beatitude, or as a voluptuous destruction of the self by the self; as a magnificent and desirable disaster, or simply as a disaster.[9] Personally, I favor the latter string of choices. I agree with de Rougemont that desire loses its absolute hold over us the moment we cease to deify it.[10] And we cease to deify it when we haul out the assumptions snuck up on us by the Myth of Romantic Love, take a good look at them, and decide if we like them. Then we can look the Myth knowingly in the eye and say either, "That is what I want!" or else, "No way!"

Fairy Tales as Myth

Princess: "Ah! was that you, my Prince, my lips who prest!"
Prince: "She wakes! she speaks! and we shall still be blest! You're not offended?"
Princess: "Oh, dear, not at all! Aren't you the gentleman who was to call?"[11]

Who among us will not know that this, even dressed up in the unaccustomed doggerel of an 1840 Covent Garden pantomime extravaganza, is the denouement of *Sleeping Beauty?*

In high myth like *Tristan and Iseult* the study of archetypes is fairly complex. To get a clearer view of archetypes as they relate to our ideas of love, we turn now to the extremely conventionalized literature of popular fiction. For, as Northrup Frye points out, we can almost define popular fiction as "literature which affords an unobstructed view of archetypes."[12]

The primary feature of conventionalized literature, and the source of its appeal, is that the reader knows what to expect. The familiarity we rely on comes from the fact that the organizing ideas of each type of conventionalized literature remain constant. Formula fiction mysteries, for example, have murder and order as their organizing ideas: whatever may happen to dumbfound us, we know that there will be at least one murder near the beginning, and that it and all subsequent murders will have been solved by the end. In fairy tales the organizing ideas are chastity and magic: chastity will be pursued by evil, chastity will be saved by good, chastity will itself be rewarded–and magic will be used at key points.[13]

Chastity is embodied in the character of the heroine. She is the "sought-for" person, the inert center of the action that swirls around her. While all the other characters in classic fairy tales may be either male or female (villains are often female, even heroes are occasionally not male), the "sought-for" person is always female. In studying fairy tales as myth, I'm going to concentrate on three stories that are central to the fairy tale tradition: "Sleeping Beauty," "Snow White," and "Cinderella." The three "sought-for" persons for whom these tales are named are archetypal romantic heroines.[14]

What are the major elements that make up these stories?

- In "Sleeping Beauty" the principal characters are: the villain (an old fairy, female); the helper (a young fairy, female); the princess (victim of the villain–a beautiful young woman, who sleeps); her father (the protector–who tries to protect her, and fails); the hero (a valiant young Prince–who succeeds, and becomes the new protector).

- In "Snow White" the principal characters are: the villain (sorceress–who is murderously proud of her beauty); the princess (victim of the villain–a beautiful young woman, who is comatose); her father (the protector–who does not even try to protect her); the helpers (seven dwarves–who try to protect her, and fail); and the hero (a young Prince–who succeeds, and becomes the new protector).
- In "Cinderella" the principal characters are: the villains (stepmother and stepsisters, not beautiful, who are jealous); the heroine (victim of the villains–a young woman, both beautiful and good, who becomes a princess); her father (the protector–who does not or cannot protect her); the helper (the fairy godmother–who helps her to become a princess); the hero (a young Prince–who makes her a princess and becomes the new protector).

What does it take to be an archetypal romantic heroine? In "Sleeping Beauty" the princess has "all the perfections imaginable." What are they? She is young, she is beautiful like "a little Angel," she has manners that charm, but she sleeps through most of the significant action. When she awakes it is to a fait accompli: her Prince has come, and she accepts him with love. Meanwhile, the Prince certainly gets to act: He is "all on fire" from just hearing about her, rushes into the "fine adventure" of rescuing her because "a young and amorous Prince is always valiant"; he is in love with her before he has even seen her and falls to his knees "trembling with admiration" when he does, declaring that he loves her better than he does himself.

In "Snow White" the princess is young and the "fairest in the land." She is a child of seven when she enters the state of suspended animation in which she retains her beauty while growing into the young woman who will open her eyes to gaze at the Prince and say, "Where am I?" and who will find the answer,

"Thou art safe with me," satisfactory. The Prince wants her even when he believes she will never leave her glass coffin, and his first words to her end with, "I love you better than all the world; come with me to my father's palace, and you shall be my wife."

In "Cinderella" the beautiful young heroine is not a princess, and she is not asleep. Her "unparalleled goodness and sweetness of temper" make her the placid recipient of vicious treatment meted out by those who should be good to her and even makes her protect the father who does nothing to protect her because "his wife governed him entirely." Her reward is even greater than Sleeping Beauty's or Snow White's. She not only gets her Prince but becomes a Princess into the bargain.

Now, then, what have we here? I'd say we have an unobstructed view of archetypal masculine and feminine behavior as it, according to the Myth of Romantic Love, will magically culminate in the archetypal romance. Nowhere is de Rougemont's observation about myth more appropriate than in fairy tales: "A myth makes it possible to become aware at a glance of certain types of *constant relations* and to disengage these from the welter of everyday appearances."[15]

And these are the "constant relations": In a real romance the woman is the desired one, the recipient of the man's desire. He is the agent, the one who acts, she waits and receives. He sweeps her off her feet; she is swept away. It says that his passion is based on an image of her rather than on knowledge of her, that therein lies the magic, and that this is True Love. It says that "real" life for a woman begins with the arrival of the man who will love her in this special way. It says that the reward for being a "real" woman is not *real* life (no archetypal romantic heroine gets to go out and actively engage the world, she always rides to the castle and is never heard from again) but True Love—that is, protection *from* real life. These three fairy tales offer us a template we can use to make ourselves more aware of the deeper patterns that may lie beneath the welter of emotions we experience when we "fall madly in love." When we say, "I don't know what hit me," this template can tell us.

It is not only fairy tales that talk this way. In our day patriarchal women who advocate a "Romantic Revival" do it, too. Here is the author of *Fascinating Womanhood,* talking like the denouements of all three fairy tales as we've just discussed them:

> When a man loves with all his heart there is a stirring within his soul. At times it is a feeling approaching worship for the woman. At other times he is fascinated, enchanted and amused. It has been described by some men as a feeling almost like pain. It can cause a man to feel like biting his teeth together. Along with all of these thrilling and consuming sensations, there is a tenderness, an overwhelming desire to protect and shelter his woman from all harm, danger and difficulty of life. These feelings cause him to pour out his romantic love in words to her or to someone he trusts.[16]

This kind of love is also the love that is enshrined as True Love in the formula fiction of romances.

The Ideal Romance: Stereotypes in Action

The descent from high myth to the Ideal Romance is essentially the descent from archetypes to stereotypes. An archetype moves us up and out of ourselves. Its potentially unlimited power of association opens a world of possibilities for us, so that we experience a continually growing unity. The plot line may be as silly as the one in *Tristan and Iseult,* but in the action of high myth there is always an element of grandeur, a transcendence of the commonplace that leaves us feeling enlarged.

With formula fiction it is otherwise. Here, instead of transcendence we get reduction and fixation. Instead of being moved beyond the commonplace we are bolted to it. And the bolts that hold us down are stereotypes. A stereotype is an unvarying form or pattern having no individuality, as though cast from a mold. Stereotyping creates its mold by declaring that the part is the whole. It isolates a behavior trait that has been fixed by current cultural prejudice, holds it up, and declares it the whole human being—as in the "wily Oriental," the "childlike black," the "money-grubbing Jew." And also as in the "real" woman and the "real" man. Stereotyping is a process of diminishment. Insofar as it's accepted by an individual, it's a diminishment of the self; when it flourishes in a culture, it becomes an instrument of oppression. And, as will shortly become apparent, when it is the basis for literature we get a depiction of human actions that is soul-crunchingly banal.

It should come as no surprise that the highly conventionalized literature of formula fiction is based solidly on stereotypes. To see how a "real" man is supposed to act in our culture, read adventure fiction; to see a "real" woman in action, turn to romance. The apparent realism of formula fiction stems precisely from this stereotyping of human experience. But it is solipsism, not reality, that we actually are getting. This fiction seems realistic, not because it's based on life, but because it confirms what we already believe or want to believe. We are locked inside the stuffy chamber of the lowest common denominator of what already is taken for granted. Therein lies its excruciating (or comforting) banality.

Romances offer their many millions of readers that delicious mixture of the familiar and the unexpected which is the hallmark of formula fiction. The comforting familiarity comes from the fact that romances are individual versions of a general pattern defined by a set of stereotypes. A romance may take us to distant lands or ancient history, the plot may titillate us with anything from adultery to reincarnation to the "new woman," but the underlying pattern never varies. The heroine will meet the hero, obstacles will be overcome, and the hero will get the heroine. Men in formula adventure fiction may take on the world (and usually, it seems, attempt to kill it off, enemy by enemy); the great quest in a romance heroine's life is one thing and one thing only: Finding Mr. Right (and having him marry her).

The amazing popularity of romances is perhaps not so amazing when we consider the deeper secret of their appeal, which is evident behind the seductive marketing of this kind of fiction. Here, for example, is the motto (complete with dots) from the back cover of Harlequin romances: "Harlequin is romance . . . and you can never have too much romance." This is the promise of the safe fix: the drug that will give you your predictable high without making you an addict. It ignores the fundamental truth of addiction, that it is the *need* for the predictable high which makes you an addict—regardless of the means used to produce that high. The sense of addiction is concisely stated by Robert Warshow in his classic essay on the formula gangster film: "Originality is to be welcomed only in the degree that it intensifies the expected experience without fundamentally altering it."[17] This is also the essence of the formula for romances and is, I think, the primary reason that a so-called "light" reader of Harlequins reads an average of between twelve and sixteen of them per month.[18]

"Formulas," writes John Cawelti in his study of formula fiction, "enable the members of a group to share the same fantasies."[19] The fantasies offered by romances tell us a great deal about the Myth of Romantic Love. They are the fantasies of the second chance—as exemplified here by the Harlequin *Clouded Waters:*

> The feud between the Montagues and the Capulets was like a childish squabble compared to the long-standing quarrel between the Dane and Baird families. It had already ruined the romance between Marian Dane and Adam Baird. But now Fate had brought them together again. Were they being offered a second chance?[20]

Is this a rhetorical question or is this a rhetorical question? A second chance is *precisely* what romances offer their readers. The chance to rewrite the great love stories (which unfortunately tend to end in the death of the lovers) and make them come out right; the chance to avoid forever the "end of the romance" by reconceptualizing marriage as an endless romantic courtship; the chance to legitimize the most perverse behavior with men by making it the will of destiny; the chance to believe that you can submerge yourself in the identity of Mr. Right and still remain yourself; the chance to believe that you can have it all—Mr. Right, economic security, an exciting sex life, *and* your career (if you still want it). The chance, in short, to enjoy the Myth of Romantic Love as cheaply as possible instead of foundering painfully in the actual attempt to live out its inherent contradictions.

Nothing shows me more clearly that the Myth of Romantic Love is a lie than its close match with the world of romances. Ask yourself this: If you have to read formula escape literature in order to see the Myth in happy action, what does this say about its connection to reality?

The convincing portrayal of the world that surrounds each individual romance gives it a verisimilitude, as Janice Radway notes in *Reading the Romance,* which persuades the reader that the romantic action not only is plausible but, like the already known ending, also inevitable.[21] Those of us who actually try to live out this action know better.

How to Be a Romantic Heroine

Here I am going to draw some parallels between the perfect expression of the romantic fantasy and the reality of the autonomous women who, as I did, try to emulate it in their lives. I think it's a useful exercise, because when I asked myself that post-romantic question, "Where had I *been?*" I found many of the clearest answers in the Ideal Romance. I saw that, like Cinderella's stepsisters in their attempt to get to the Prince's castle, I had found it necessary to take a knife to myself in order to star in my Ideal Romance. The plot line of this quintessential romance fiction etched into my mind the contours of where I had needed to wield the knife in order to fit the role. And it made me understand a great deal better, with some compassion for my mutilated self, the powerful forces that lay behind my bizarre behavior while I was in the Land of True Romance.

So here we go. What shall we call our Ideal Romance? *Moonstruck Madness? The Fulfillment? Dreamtide? Made for Each Other? The Wolf and the Dove?* or perhaps *Miss Hungerford's Handsome Hero?* These are but some of the titles from the Ideal Romances in Radway's sample, and they do rather set the mood.

We'll have no trouble choosing the plot, because all Ideal

Romances have the same plot: The heroine meets the hero, and they recognize the attraction they feel toward each other fairly early in the story. The action then concerns the gradual removal of barriers until the happy moment when they unite, usually in matrimony. Note that the obstructions we observed in *The Romance of Tristan and Iseult* are as crucial to the Ideal Romance as they were to the myth. This fact alone should clue us in to the realization that we are dealing once again with romantic love and not with the kind of love that is based on mutual caring and intimacy.

The plot of an Ideal Romance unfolds in thirteen unvarying steps. They are the steps that will lead the ideal heroine along her quest until the moment of its crowning success when she becomes Mrs. Right. We'll take them one at a time and see what they tell us about romantic love and the autonomous woman.

1. *The heroine's social identity is destroyed.* The heroine is often involuntarily removed from her home turf (in contrast to the hero, who usually is in his element). The heroine's social identity may be destroyed in a number of ways, but they always amount to her removal from a familiar realm and her ensuing feeling of emotional isolation. The close connection to Sleeping Beauty, Snow White, and Cinderella is clear. And, as with them, it is the arrival of the hero that will restore her identity when he becomes her protector.

Look closer, and you will see the similarity to many autonomous women in our culture. We are in the process in effect of destroying our own social identity by violating the stereotype of the "real" woman, and many of us certainly experience emotional isolation because of this choice. The solution offered fairy tale heroines and the heroines of Ideal Romances is also, albeit in less romantic terms, the one often offered us: "All she needs is . . ."

2. *The heroine reacts antagonistically to an aristocratic male.* This is a sensible reaction, considering that the reputation of an ideal hero is usually a trifler with women at best and sometimes an outright aggressor against them. But lurking underneath this rational antagonism toward someone who treats you and your sex badly

there is a concomitant attraction that is as perverse as it is fatal. It has to do with exactly what makes a man attractive to women in Ideal Romances. Radway's extensive analysis of everything from the Regency to the gothic to the historical to the contemporary romance concludes that they all characterize their romantic heroes with words like hard, mocking, indifferent, moody, masculine, magnetic, fierce, ruthless, and overbearing. Miss Hungerford's handsome hero sums it up: He is "romantically grim."

Now ponder the connection of those two words and the expectation that it will be attractive to women. This is a very serious question for women today. As long as we can accept that "romantic" and "grim" belong together in the language of love, we are reinforcing the worst aspects of the masculine stereotype in the grossest way. We are also dooming ourselves to fall in love with men who are destructive to us, as well as to an unending round of passionate romances instead of caring relationships.

The conquest and surrender mentality inherent in "romantically grim" is full-blown in this quote from Harlequin's *The Devil's Mistress:* "Women always looked at Alex Brent like that. . . . His lean, hard body held a menacing sexuality, an implicit threat of sexual violence which attracted women like iron filings to a magnet."[22] With this kind of hero it's no surprise that Fate often has to take a hand in bringing about the heroine's acceptance of him—Fate, aided by her romantic skill of reinterpretation. Otherwise, it's just possible that she would see him not as "romantically grim" but instead for what he really is: hazardous to your health when he isn't merely tedious.

To get to this point is to know the sweet liberation of being beyond our most socially endorsed addiction. It is a rare and blessed state for women in our culture. I know very few women who reach it, but more and more of us are seeing it as a desirable goal and as a necessary precondition for autonomy, as for love, and this is a fine development.

3. *The aristocratic male responds ambiguously to the heroine.* Ambiguity is the ideal hero's stock in trade with women. Heroines, meanwhile, are described as being "transparently honest."[23]

This puts our ingenuous heroine in the debilitating state of trying to decipher the hero's mixed message. But the reader is given more information and therefore knows the truth, which the heroine will only gradually discover—namely, that the hero's ambiguity is a *good sign.* His unreadable actions are really the product of emotional turmoil prompted by his feelings for her. In short, if reinterpreted correctly, his ambiguous behavior toward her is really proof of his love for her.

4. *The heroine interprets the hero's behavior as evidence of a purely sexual interest in her.* This is a reasonable interpretation, since the ideal heroine is always extraordinarily beautiful and since the ideal hero's "love-crazed taking" of the heroine is the romance's standard masculine reaction to her beauty. However, since this interpretation is incorrect in an Ideal Romance, this error by the heroine serves two useful purposes: (1) It adds to the obstructions, which are essential to the passion of romantic love; and (2) it sets up a good case of guilt in her so she'll be that much more ready to reinterpret the hero's inexplicable behavior when it really counts. One gets the sneaking suspicion, from both romances and one's own excursions into the Land of True Romance, that the "magic" of romance is in reality a euphemism for one's consistent mistrust or denial of one's own good sense.

5. *The heroine responds to the hero's behavior with anger and coldness.* Good going, there, heroine! Could this be the beginning of sense and sensibility in her? We hope in vain. This is her *last* intelligent and autonomous action. From now on it's downhill all the way.

6. *The hero retaliates by punishing the heroine.* The hero's ambiguous behavior notwithstanding, his right to punish the heroine for misunderstanding his behavior is never questioned in romances. This right is part of his masculinity, as is his method of punishment, which often runs along these lines: "Without giving her a chance to speak again, he crushed her roughly closer, and as she lifted her chin to protest, drove his mouth down on hers in a kiss that explained everything without words. It was a punishment in itself."[24]

This sex-as-punishment includes rape. Rape does not occur in all the Ideal Romances examined by Radway, but when it does it occurs in Step 6. Moreover, the ideal hero is always exonerated. Whether he kisses women into submission or actually rapes them, he is portrayed as unlike the men who rape as an act of aggression against women. *He* rapes because he misinterprets the heroine's actions or because he finds her irresistible. In either case the responsibility lies with her. The politics of misunderstanding in Ideal Romances are a wonder to behold. If she misinterprets him, it's her doing. If he misinterprets her, it's also her doing. And still *he* is the master who is in control.

It is, of course, but a short step from a hero's "romantically grim" masculinity being measured in terms of "hard," "mocking," "indifferent," and "ruthless" to having it measured by his sexual violence. A short step and a very disturbing one.

7. *The heroine and hero are physically or emotionally separated.* More of the obstacle course without which romance could not flourish.

8. *The hero treats the heroine tenderly.* This is the pivotal step in an Ideal Romance and the most revealing one. It is also, as we shall see later, the step that can turn even the strongest autonomous woman into a Reverse Sleeping Beauty. Here, a small hint of humanity in the hero's otherwise terrorizing masculinity suddenly blooms and *voilà*—we have a gentle hero. This amazing shift is never explained in the narrative. "No action on the part of the hero or, for that matter, on the part of any other character can be said to cause or explain the magic transformation of his cruelty and indifference into tender care. The abrupt transformation simply takes place."[25]

9. *The heroine responds warmly to the hero's act of tenderness.* How does she manage this feat of mental gymnastics? At first she simply ignores the enormous inconsistency with his previous behavior and responds to the miracle in good romantic heroine fashion by promptly accepting it without question.

This is where the ideal heroine's stock personality traits begin to turn against her. She can respond warmly to this seeming impossibility because she invariably is open and ingenuous, and because she invariably possesses an unusually compassionate, kind, and understanding nature. This compendium of otherwise admirable traits now gets added to the underlying conviction of every romantic heroine that, "It really is love that makes the world go around. Without it you are nothing, absolutely nothing."[26] This prepares her for the pernicious step she takes next.

10. *The heroine reinterprets the hero's ambiguous behavior as the product of previous hurt.* This is really serious. Radway says that the activity of reinterpretation is essential to the achievement of a final rapprochement between the heroine and hero, and we autonomous women might well say the same about our own rapprochements. I have yet to meet a woman who does not possess at least a measure of the romantic skill of reinterpretation.

My own version of Step 10 began to become apparent to me shortly after I had understood my former hero's pattern with women enough to know that there would posthaste be a replacement of me. It was only a matter of who. Once I got that far the answer was obvious. She was in place within a week of my precipitate exit, as it turned out, and must herself be a near genius at the romantic skill of reinterpretation. I mentioned my new understanding and my presumed successor's name to my mother, who instantly responded, "She's probably saying, 'Poor Neddie, he's never been *really* loved before.'" Her tone was unmistakably ironic. My heart sank. "Did *I* use to say that in my time?" I asked, knowing the answer before it came. "I'm afraid so," she laughed.

What can we say about all this depressing feminine behavior? How does the romantic skill of reinterpretation enable the heroine to say, "He's never been *really* loved before"? The previous hurt suffered by the hero of an Ideal Romance is always suffered at the hands of the "calculating women" who infest his past and who, we may safely assume, are deficient at the romantic skill of reinterpretation. Thus the hero's entire previous behavior—his inability to express any emotion that is not at least ambiguous and usually "grim" or even vicious, as well as his previously exclusive preoccupation with women as "tools for achieving sexual release"—is not a revelation of his character at all. It is really a testimonial to "his inescapable and intense need"—for *her.* This telling scene from *The Black Lyon* is a good case in point:

The Earl of Malvoisin's eyes reminded her of a dog she had seen once. The dog had been caught in a trap, his leg nearly cut in half, and the pain had made him almost mad. It had taken a long time for Lyonene to soothe the animal and gain its trust so that she could release the iron jaws of the trap, and all the while the dog had looked at her with just such an expression of wariness, pain and near-dead hope as did the man who stood before her now.[27]

I wish I could deny that I recognize this pivotal moment in my own Ideal Romance. The man who possesses the skill of looking like the Earl of Malvoisin has a bright future in romance. This is the magic moment when the hero of your romance is going to open up to *you* because he, who had never been *really* loved before, finally has the opportunity to be loved by the Right woman. However others have failed at this moment in his past, *you* will not fail him now—or ever. He is truly yours from here on in.

Of course it's sheer arrogant nonsense, as most of us discover soon enough. But it's also far worse than nonsense. By blaming other women for his behavior, you set yourself up as "savior." This step gives you a gratifying sense of being capable of succeeding where other women have failed. This gratification is gained directly from your betrayal of those others in particular and of all women in general. Not a pretty picture. In your smugness you may not notice the catch: If the two of you don't live happily together ever after, it's now *your* fault.

11. *The hero proposes/openly declares his love for/demonstrates his unwavering commitment to the heroine with a supreme act of tenderness.* This is where he validates your feeling that he truly is yours forever because you alone can transform him. Your reward is that he assumes the role of your protector—as he does in the classic fairy tales and in this typical example from *Pathway of Roses:* "It's all right, my little one," he crooned, stroking her hair. "You're safe now, and with me you always will be safe!"[28]

The message from romances is, "If men would only speak, they would say, 'I love you.'"[29] And if they don't speak, it's your own fault, since they *are* capable of speaking if (and only if) transformed by the right woman. This is a message most women believe to some extent. It is the complete message of books by patriarchal women who advocate a "Romantic Revival"–*Total Woman* and *Fascinating Womanhood* being classics of the genre. That men don't see the message as a clear statement of feminine contempt for their sex continues to astound me.

12. *The heroine responds sexually and emotionally.* The heroine's unique combination of womanly sensuality and mothering capacities, having already magically remade the hero, now remake *her.* The key word here is *responds.* For the romantic heroine who falls in love no longer fights male mastery but is instead thrilled by it.[30] Sexually, whether she lies "trembling, waiting for him to make her complete" and "he [comes] to her then, gently, tenderly, patiently," or she is forced by his "love-crazed probes," she is inevitably "awakened" and quickly overcome by her body's "uncontrollable" response. Emotionally, she now renounces her former ways of fiery independence and finally becomes "all woman."

Here's an absolute gem on this theme, dots of ecstasy included, from *Wait for the Storm:*

> "Rad . . . Rad!" It was a threnody of joy. "I'm glad I was able to give you so much."
>
> "So much and so much, my darling." He held her very close. "You're perfect. You give all the time, and it makes you so strong and sure and generous . . . all woman. My woman."[31]

13. *The heroine's identity is restored.* Her "awakening" is complete. The magic transformation from "strong" to "all woman" has taken place. By means of giving (to him) all the time she has become perfect. She is now all woman. His woman. Even if she is a "new woman." For she has achieved the ultimate goal of every romance: an oceanic merging with a nurturant, heterosexual lover–who still is "all man." The final proof that her identity has been restored is that she becomes Mrs. Right.

This magic transformation from "strong" to "all woman" is what I call becoming a Reverse Sleeping Beauty. The autonomous woman is not "awakened" when she achieves that oceanic merging with Mr. Right, she falls asleep—to who she is, to who he is, to reality. *Why* she falls asleep and then works so hard to stay asleep is the question we will take up in the following two chapters, where we explore how and why she develops the Magic Button which, when pressed by Mr. Right, brings this peculiar reverse twist of magic upon her.

4. The Princess

"Every man I meet wants to protect me," says Mae West in one of her movies. "Can't figure out what from." To ask men who want to protect women, "What from?" is very naughty, since it threatens to expose masculine protection for the racket that it is. Like everything else in True Romance, the masculine desire to protect is mystified: It's called chivalry.

The notion of chivalry is a loaded one for women. What kind of man, for example, is likely to want to protect you? Certainly not a wimp or a sissy; nor would he be an equal, a man who thinks of you as a peer. No, the man who wants to protect you is most likely to be a masculine man, and the degree to which the desire to protect is uppermost in his relationship to women is the degree to which he is a "real" man. What does a "real" man want in the way of a woman? Certainly not an autonomous woman. He wants a "real" woman: someone who needs/wants/likes his protection.

Let's ask some central questions and see where they take us. Do women want to be protected? Yes, says the author of the best-seller, *The Cinderella Complex*. What from? From independence. Women don't want autonomy, we don't want a direct relationship to life. What we want is just what all those men kept offering Mae West. Here's Colette Dowling:

> It is the thesis of this book that personal, psychological dependence—the deep wish to be taken care of by others—is the chief force holding women down today. I call this "The Cinderella Complex"—a network of largely repressed attitudes and fears that keeps women in a kind of half-light, retreating from the full use of their minds and creativity. Like Cinderella, women today are still waiting for something external to transform their lives.[1]

Dowling says her book became a best-seller because it "struck a chord" among women. I think it's more correct to say that the book became a best-seller because it hit a nerve—the raw, exposed nerve of women who know the price of being uppity. We know that the problem for today's woman is not her fear of independence but a well-founded anxiety about the results of her autonomy. For those of us who aspire to autonomy soon find that we also get a few other things along with it, and foremost among them is the sharp disapproval of men. I call this anxiety The Annie Oakley Complex, after the fictionalized life of the sharpshooting woman who found that "You Can't Get a Man with a Gun."

The Annie Oakley Complex

Women's autonomy is threatening to all men who are influenced by the Myth of Masculinity, the degree of threat experienced by a man following directly from the degree of influence by the Myth. An autonomous woman, by her very existence, says two things no masculine man wants to hear: "Don't count on me to feed your adequacy," and even worse, "Don't count on me to let you keep winning." Such words and especially actions are no-no's in the masculine/feminine game, as this man's reaction typifies:

> No, I don't want my wife to throw the game when we play tennis. She should play as hard and as well as she can. Things just got uncomfortable when she started beating me regularly, so we stopped playing. She doesn't have anything else to do all week except go to those damned tennis lessons, you know.[2]

A community organizer who spent a number of years as a nun spoke to the core of the Annie Oakley Complex:

> I remember that sometimes men pursued us, and in the convent that never happened. We were sort of shook up by the fact that someone was trying to make eyes at you, trying to get a date, oh, wow! Some of our gals decided they wanted to get married so they had to relearn behavior they hadn't used for years.[3]

Relearn behavior they hadn't used for years. What kind of behavior is that? I think Archie Bunker said it best: "Stifle yourself, Edith!" We can also call it "becoming feminine."

Women who are unwilling to become feminine, or at least to act feminine, tend to be ignored or worse by the large majority of men. Such women are considered not *nice.* And we're certainly not candidates for romance until we mend our ways. The Annie Oakley Complex arises out of our deep fear that it is after all impossible to be autonomous—to be ourselves—and also find love with men. We're not afraid of independence, but we look with trepidation at the prospect of living as a cultural blasphemy and a pariah in the world of love.

Can You Be Autonomous and Also Feminine?

The answer to this question is beginning to look pretty obvious: No, you cannot be autonomous and also feminine. Unfortunately, the fact that this trick can't be pulled off doesn't prevent many autonomous women from hoping that there *must* be a way, if only we could find it. And little wonder we keep hoping, if the price for not finding the way is social and sexual ostracism or even invisibility.

This existential lesson in femininity is available to all women. It is graphically illustrated by the experience of the central character in Doris Lessing's *The Summer Before the Dark,* who attends a conference where male colleagues predominate:

> Soon she discovered that if she wanted to be alone, she should sit badly, in a huddled or discouraged posture, and allow her legs to angle themselves unbecomingly. If she did this men did not see her. She could swear they did not. Sitting neatly, alertly, with her legs sleekly disposed, she made a signal. Sagging and slumped, it was only when all the seats in the coffee-room were taken that someone came to sit near her. At which time it was enough to let her face droop to gain her privacy again, and very soon. . . . It gave her a dislocated feeling, as if something had slipped out of alignment. For she was conscious, very conscious, as alert to it as if this was the most important fact of her life, that the person who

sat there watching, shunned or ignored by men who otherwise would have been attracted to her, was not in the slightest degree different from the person who could bring it all on again towards her by adjusting the picture of herself: lips, a set of facial muscles, eye movements, angle of back and shoulders.[4]

You can choose to adjust the picture of yourself to please men, or you can choose to be yourself. You can't do both at the same time. We should know this truth, but most of us refuse to believe it. Meanwhile, we suffer from its reality. A therapist friend to whom I posed this question was true to form. "I have no difficulty with that," she said, "I think you can be both." When I pointed out that her difficulty could be surmounted only by excessive redefining of either term, she went to her dictionary.

Flip, flip, flip. "*Feminine*," she read aloud. "Of or pertaining to the female sex." So far, so good, went her tone. "Typical of or appropriate to women and girls, as in *feminine* gentleness." A mild frown appeared on her face. "Lacking manly qualities, effeminate." She threw up her hands and exclaimed, "Okay, you're right. I agree."

"That's a socially accurate dictionary you've got there," I said. "What else does it have to offer on this subject?"[5]

She scanned. "Well, here are the highlights: *Female* denotes sex strictly without further implications, whereas *feminine* characterizes the qualities that are regarded as belonging particularly to women—as in *female* voice and *feminine* modesty. *Effeminate* is applied only to men and describes attributes that are regarded as unseemly in man, though appropriate to a woman; *womanly* refers to things that are admirable in a woman, as in *womanly* pity; whereas *womanish* refers to those that are not, as in *womanish* tears."

That dictionary definition of our culture's fundamental contradiction between being autonomous and feminine codifies what was demonstrated by the landmark study, "Sex-Role Stereotypes and Clinical Judgments of Mental Health."[6] In it, Inge K. Broverman and her associates examine the definitions of mental health used by practicing mental health professionals such as psychologists, psychiatrists, and social workers. The study demonstrates that those behaviors and characteristics judged healthy for an adult, sex unspecified, resemble closely those judged healthy for men and differ significantly from those judged healthy for women. A healthy adult is thus the same as a healthy man; a healthy woman demonstrates her health by being "more submissive, less independent, less adventurous, more easily influenced, less aggressive, less competitive, more excitable in minor crises, having [her] feelings more easily hurt, being more emotional, more conceited about [her] appearance, less objective, and disliking math and science" more than a healthy man. No wonder men like to say, *"Vive la différence!" La différence* artificially makes them seem more of everything they want to be. A man expressed it perfectly at the end of a lengthy discussion in which another woman and I had argued that the concepts of masculine and feminine were damaging to both sexes and that *Vive la différence!* should be done away with. He said, "It feels like you just took away Christmas."

For our purposes the syllogism unearthed by the Broverman study goes like this: A healthy woman is a *feminine* woman; a woman who tries to be a healthy *person* is not feminine; therefore, an autonomous woman is neither feminine (nor healthy). By definition.

Most of us are like my therapist friend: we prefer to try to believe that things can't be this bad. But everything from daily experience to dictionaries to mental health definitions to popular songs shows us otherwise. Researchers in one major study found three major clusters of adjectives connected to people's idea of *woman.*[7] The first two clusters exemplified roles with high dependence on men, either as a sexually pure and maternal figure (housewife) or as a tempting sex object (bunny). The third cluster combined all the roles implying relative independence from men.

A number of things are interesting about these findings. First of all, *woman* comes in two models: females who show high dependence on men, and females who don't. This in and of itself is a telling division of humans into two groups. Note further how "high dependence" manifests itself (in terms of females servicing males) and how the servicing is of two opposing kinds (sexual or nonsexual). The roles of housewife and bunny were seen by both sexes as incompatible. So even within the ranks of those who service men, there is already a schism set up, which is a role with potential strife between women. Then there's the larger schism, the one between women who cater to men and women who don't. Men (but not women) viewed women in this third cluster, the kind of woman who is relatively independent from men, as *unfeminine.* Career women were seen as "a breed apart," as women who "have renounced their femininity" by choosing activities that "carry them beyond the traditional roles which serve men."

I greatly fear that this study puts the matter in a nutshell. To be feminine, as Doris Lessing so excellently puts it, is to adjust the picture of yourself in accordance with men's needs and demands. To be autonomous, as Isak Dinesen equally excellently puts it, is to desire and strive to be a person with a direct relationship to life.[8] These two states of mind and being are mutually exclusive.

The choice to pursue a direct relationship with life instead of an indirect one adjusted to the approval of men carries a terrible penalty. Those of us who make this choice may learn to live with the wrath of men; but too many of us carry deep in our hearts the corroding suspicion, nurtured not only by men but by almost our entire culture, that perhaps after all we really *are* as we're told: a cultural blasphemy, unnatural or even execrable and to be shunned as such. Every woman has to make her own peace with this situation. Most of us, to a greater rather than lesser degree, try to resolve it by redefining it.

A professor friend of mine told me a story that illustrates this perfectly. She gave her students the following question on an exam: "Can you be autonomous and also feminine? Discuss."

I phoned and asked how the answers to her exam question had

turned out. In a resigned voice she answered, "Most of them did very badly on that one."

"How so?" I inquired.

"Well, most of them argued that you could be both autonomous and feminine."

A feat of logic worthy of the best in the subtle art of sex-role thinking. "And what method did they employ to arrive at this comforting conclusion?"

"Oh, they did it by not defining 'feminine.' They just took it to mean 'being a woman,' as in 'being female.'" My friend sighed audibly into the phone. "Even though they'd been in the course and had heard the definition."

Some of the exam discussion was about Ibsen's play *A Doll's House,* which they had studied intensively. "You know what they did?" my friend asked incredulously. "They argued that Nora was autonomous all along!"

"But how did they account for her extremely husband-deferring feminine behavior before she left her Doll's House?"

"They said she was putting on an act," came the reply.

The students got one thing absolutely correct. There is only one way to resolve the ugly contradiction between autonomy and femininity, and that is to say that *one of them is an act.* This is precisely what Dowling says. Her problem is that she, so to speak, is barking up the wrong act with her "Cinderella Complex." The act that women put on in response to the necessities of our culture is not to hide our "fear of independence" in order to put on "a sophisticated brand of pseudo independence."[9] The act is to hide our autonomy because of men's fear of emasculation. As the author of that book on how men feel about women's increasing autonomy said, it is the combination of competence and sexuality in women that men seem to find so terrifically threatening.

The response to such a woman by the 90 percent to 95 percent of men who are thus threatened is portrayed in another book about men. Man meets autonomous woman at cocktail party and engages her in conversation (how familiar the scenario):

Nearly all begin by acknowledging with mock surprise and respect how unusual it is to find beauty and brains together. It can be as crude as, "I thought all lady lawyers were twenty pounds overweight and wore oxfords," or as subtle as a slightly raised eyebrow and a half-amused, half-appreciative smile when the woman's answer to the question, "What do you do?" puts her on the same general level of worldliness and power as the man. . . . Then, some men will draw the woman out about her work or schooling, maintaining a detached, amused attitude and making a running series of references to sex, as if to say, "You come on like a serious professional (lawyer, businesswoman, editor, etc.) and you've got all the credentials, but you and I know that all that is not the real you—a woman whose real concern is men and sex with men. You don't scare me and I'm not going to let you get away with your act."[10]

Putting on the Feminine Act

The point is, of course, that we *do* scare men like them. Like hell. And the point is also that we allow *them* to get away with *their* act. We do this by putting on the feminine act. It reassures men by denying our autonomy and our strength while we dangle a bit of passive sexuality at them. Show me the woman who doesn't know all about that one. Most of us have been practicing the feminine act since we were about twelve years old.

A telling study of masculinity and femininity from a childhood perspective outlines the stages of how we learn that we're supposed to defer to males.[11] The stages are: Assertion (from age six to ten), in which girls resent boys; Ambivalence (from age ten to fourteen), in which girls begin to swerve toward support of boys; and Accommodation (age fourteen and on), in which girls accept "the need of underpinning males." If we accommodate, this is how we act:

- Scene 1. "When a girl asks me what marks I got last semester I answer 'Not so good—only one A.' When a boy asks the same question, I say very brightly with a note of surprise, 'Imagine, I got an A!'"
- Scene 2. "I allow him to explain things to me in great detail

and to treat me as a child in financial matters. One of the nicest techniques is to spell long words incorrectly once in a while. My boyfriend seems to get a great kick out of it and writes back, 'Honey, you certainly don't know how to spell.'"

- Scene 3. "When my date said that he considers Ravel's *Bolero* the greatest piece of music ever written, I changed the subject because I knew I would talk down to him."
- Scene 4. "Once I went sailing with a man who so obviously enjoyed the role of a protector that I told him I didn't know how to sail. As it turned out he didn't either. We got into a tough spot and I was torn between a desire to get a hold of the boat and a fear to reveal that I had lied to him."
- Scene 5. "On dates I always go through the 'I-don't-care-anything-you-want-to-do' routine. It gets monotonous but boys fear girls who make decisions. They think such girls would make nagging wives."
- Scene 6. "Tomorrow morning watch your husband when he looks in the mirror. He sees an eighteen-year-old youth, with firm stomach muscles and a full head of hair. No matter what his age, he doesn't see his pouch or receding hairline. He sees what he wants to see, and wants you to see that eighteen-year-old, too."[12]

Real femininity in action is Mae West's quip in action. It lets every man you meet protect you, and without threatening him by asking, "What from?" Thus, for example, one may observe almost anywhere the daily ritual in which women allow men to guide us through physical situations that we can manage perfectly well without male assistance, or we'd be dead. Still, there it is, the ubiquitous masculine arm described in *Body Politics,* "reaching from behind, steering [us] around corners, through doorways, into elevators, onto escalators . . . crossing streets. It is not necessarily heavy and pushy or physical in an ugly way; it is light and gentle but firm, in the way of the most confident equestrians with the best-trained horses."[13]

Why do women perpetuate this charade? Because in playing it

out we not only reconfirm our supposed appropriateness in the world, we also reap more tangible rewards from the opposite sex: rewards that range all the way from sexual approval to jobs. That's the carrot, and the pickings seem easy since even otherwise sensible men readily succumb to the most blatant ego massage administered by a women who is doing the feminine number on them. But behind the carrot is the stick: the penalties for not performing the act are harsh. They range all the way from being rendered invisible, to becoming the focus of men's overt and covert hostility, to loss of livelihood and the status of a healthy person. In short, I'm saying that most women in our culture put on the feminine act, at least to some degree, because we have to. The panoply of attributes exhibited in this act—the flattering manner, the downward glance, the perennial smile, the corroborating laugh, the rising inflection, the cautious physical gestures, and so on—have rightly been called accommodation attitudes.

How political the seemingly personal or "natural" is becomes apparent when we discover that these traits, typical of the feminine stereotype, are also found among subordinate men with their superiors in power, as they have been found in the Indians under British rule, in the Algerians under the French, and in black Americans of both sexes.[14] Feminine behavior thus takes its place with the strategy used by powerless groups everywhere when they try to minimize the visibility of their success, lest the powerful notice it and take action against them. Sociologists call it "assuming a mask of inferiority."[15]

It is understandable that so many women yield to the temptation of putting on the feminine act. Understandable—but not acceptable. Because the price for women ultimately is far too high, and because the feminine act is fundamentally undermining to any honest relationship between the sexes. To dress up the sexual politics of the masculine protection racket and the complementary feminine accommodation act by calling it chivalry does not alter the truth—which has been concisely stated by Isak Dinesen:

It is often said that chivalry will disappear from the world if women start to *live* by their own efforts. To this I can only say that . . . [a] chivalry in which one first binds fast the legs of the object of one's homage in order to serve her, seems to me of scant value, and that it would be more chivalrous to cut the bonds.[16]

5. The Dragon

There exists a pithy cautionary tale about love and the autonomous woman. It comes in the form of a feminist cartoon. The setting is the land of dragons, damsels in distress, and knights in shining armor. A courtly damsel and her lady-in-waiting are gazing upward at the head of a huge dragon into whose gullet a knight is disappearing. The dragon looks pleased, the damsel looks relieved. Caption: "Thank goodness! I was scared to death he'd slay that dragon and I'd have to marry him."[1]

The Code of Chivalry awarded to her knightly savior the damsel who was saved from distress. We autonomous women go the Code one better: we bestow ourselves in ardent gratitude upon the slayer of our dragon.

What is the Dragon? It is the phantom created by our Annie Oakley Complex as it manifests in those of us who choose to maintain a direct relationship to life instead of adjusting the picture of ourselves to please men and our culture in general. We start each day with our mental, "Damn the torpedoes, full speed ahead!" and often succeed in going where we want to go. But we go there with a voice that whispers in our ear such words as "misconduct" and "reproachable." I call that voice the hot breath of the Dragon, and I knew it well before I had a name for it.

The great quest facing the autonomous woman is to find and slay her own Dragon. We start that quest in this chapter, and try to ascertain the nature of the Dragon by studying two creations it breathes life into: (1) in the world of work, to the autonomous woman as token woman; and (2) in the world of love, to the autonomous woman as Reverse Sleeping Beauty.

Can the Autonomous Woman Find Love?

Let's look first at the token woman. How might we expect a terrifically threatened (that is, normal) working male to react when he comes face to face with a female colleague who combines competence and sexuality? A man's most fearsome vision of such a woman is emblazoned on the cover of *MBA*, a magazine distributed to business school students and faculty. The issue is devoted to "Women in Business!" On the cover is a woman drawn in Varoom! comic style, a sultry blonde with blue eyes, bright red lips, and a massive cleavage. Above the cleavage her head is thrown back snottily as she says, "You're fired!"[2] The terrifically threatened man's reaction, as might be expected, is to lessen the threat by invalidating either a woman's competence or her sexuality. If she is manifestly competent, her sexuality is either denied outright (as in, "She's great on the committee, but I'll bet she hasn't been propositioned in ten years") or transformed, as Anthony Astrachan reports in *How Men Feel*. If she is manifestly sexual, her competence is invalidated, as Rosabeth Moss Kanter's landmark study *Men and Women of the Corporation* demonstrates.

The transformations are similar in both Astrachan's and Kanter's findings. The woman who has made it far enough to be a token woman and thus especially threatening to her male colleagues is transformed by being encapsulated in one of four stereotypical roles, each defined in terms of her perceived sexuality as it relates to men. The four roles are: mother, pet (kid sister), seductress, and iron maiden. They work like this: "Mother" is expected to listen to the men's private troubles and to comfort them. She is often expected to do laundry, sew on buttons, and so on. As a "good mother" she is also expected to keep her place in the background, and to be nurturing and noncritical. "Pet" gets adopted by the group as a cute, amusing little thing and symbolically taken along on group events as mascot—a cheerleader for shows of male prowess. She is expected to admire the masculine displays but not to enter into them, instead cheering from the sidelines. Shows of competence on her part get treated as special and complimented just because they are unexpected—a kind of look-what-she-did-and-she's-only-a-woman attitude. "Seductress" is rewarded for her femaleness and is sure of getting attention from the group. However, she is also the source of considerable tension. And, as Kanter tersely puts it, "Needless to say, her perceived sexuality blots out all other characteristics." "Iron maiden" is the woman who resists overtures that would trap her into one of the other three roles. She is "regarded with suspicion, undue and exaggerated shows of politeness (by inserting references to women into conversations, by elaborate rituals of *not* opening doors) and with distance."[3]

Transforming a female peer into such stereotypes produces reassuring results for a threatened male. Her uncomfortable competence is harnessed by being enclosed in a traditional male-centered role; meanwhile, her sexuality is nullified, since the roles of mother/wife/daughter and tempting sex object are seen as incompatible. Conversely, a threatening peer's competence is nullified in the act of validating her sexuality by placing her in the role of seductress. "Iron maiden" is in a class by herself. In the single step of refusing all the ascribed traditional roles that serve men either sexually or nonsexually, she wipes out her sexuality, renders her competence suspect, and puts herself beyond the pale in the eyes of her male peers. This is the role in which the autonomous woman is most liable to end up.

So repugnant a scenario of what lies ahead for the woman who wants to achieve something in the world of work goes a long way toward explaining women's supposed "will to fail." The term is actually a complete distortion of the original work by Matina Horner, now president of Radcliffe College, on what she called women's "motive to avoid success." Horner's work was embraced enthusiastically by media people like the author of *The Cinderella Complex*. "Look," they said, "one of them has said it herself. Women's failure to achieve equal status and success is their own fault."[4] Dowling, who claimed to use Horner's work as the mainstay of her argument that "women actually *make* themselves unsuccessful" because of our "deep wish to be taken care of"[5] perpetrated exactly the kind of distortion Horner felt called upon to counter directly:

> The presence of a "will to fail" would imply that women actively seek out failure because they anticipate or expect positive consequences from failing. Quite the contrary, I have argued that it is precisely those women who most want to achieve and who are most capable of achieving who experience the detrimental effects of a "fear of success." Their positive achievement-directed tendencies are inhibited by the presence of the motive to avoid success because of the arousal of anxiety about the negative consequences they expect will follow success.[6]

If the prospect of "mother," "pet," "seductress," or "iron maiden" doesn't give one a motive to avoid success, then studying the women who have "measured up" on what the business world likes to call the "fast track" should do the job. Six such women, culled as representatives of the female graduates of the Harvard Business School Class of 1975 and interviewed ten years later, are the central figures in a curiously repellent book called *Women Like Us.*[7]

The title is a stupendous misnomer. "Like us other women" is precisely what these women are *not*—as they undoubtedly would be the first to insist. Their most prominent feature is indeed their complete *lack* of a connection to other women. Their motivation for being interviewed appears to be merely self-serving—"It would be nice for my ego to know that I was one of the six selected"—as is their motivation for not doing so—"It doesn't do anything for one's career to talk about these things." The motivation for their choice to go where women haven't gone before is likewise conspicuously lacking in affiliation:

> "Why do you do it anyway?"
>
> "Oh, ego, I suppose. Why does anyone do it? To see if you can really do it, to see if you are as good as you think you are."

The goal of these women is, simply, "Power."[8]

Like the man in chapter 2 who wanted to win because "I can strut my stuff," these women are playing to win. Like him, they buy into the performance ethic that says you are worthwhile *because* you perform well, regardless of what you perform at. We've seen that men who successfully strut their stuff get to collect masculinity points. This system of reward would seem to pose a bit of a problem for the woman who chooses to strut her stuff on the "fast track." Her reward is etched chillingly in this image from Marge Piercy's poem, "The Token Woman":

The token woman stands in the Square of the Immaculate
Exception blessing pigeons from a blue pedestal. . . .
The token woman is placed like a scarecrow
in the long-haired corn: her muscles are wooden.
Why does she ride into battle on a clothes horse?[9]

Why? Because her clothes, those stylized caricatures of their masculine counterparts, are her suit of armor and the badge of her exceptional status. They announce to the male world in which she moves that, for all her strutting, she is content to play the game of the difference that makes no difference. In that world they call it "liberation"–as in, "Yes, this is what liberation is all about. We are striving for a sex-blind corporation."[10] There's just one little catch. "Sex-blind" does not mean a corporation that takes no cognizance of gender. It means a corporation that is blind to the female sex in the confident belief that all women who play the game of "liberation" will first of all try to become men. The fact that women obviously *cannot* become men, no matter how assiduously they emulate them, accounts for the pertinence of Piercy's sterile imagery. For the first rule of the game of the difference that makes no difference must be that the female player cut her connection to women, clearly her major handicap in such a game. Thus caught between political expediency and biological necessity, she becomes all that she *can* become: a eunuch. The safe, because neutered, guardian of the inner sanctum.

Seeing venturesome women turned into "mothers," "pets,"

"seductresses," "iron maidens," and especially into the scarecrows of the "fast track" is a profound lesson to the rest of us. It works the way the bike lesson in the children's book of that name works: Papa Bear is teaching Junior Bear to ride a bike. Each lesson comes to a bad end as Papa Bear does the opposite of what he's trying to demonstrate. Nevertheless, the lesson teaches by example. At the culmination of each miscarriage Papa Bear warns Junior Bear, "This is what you should *not* do. Now, let this be a lesson to you."[11]

The Real Annie Oakley

The question is, where is the positive lesson that will help us slay our dragon as we seek autonomy? Our predicament was neatly posed by one of Matina Horner's children "on the day Tia, not yet three, learned that a female friend of the family was a physician and after a lengthy silence inquired, 'is [she] still a girl?' 'Well, then, is she still Eric's mommy?' and before going on to other things concluded, 'She must be all mixed up.'"[12] To be an autonomous woman is to live on the horns of the dilemma created by men's fear of a woman who is both competent and sexual, and that is indeed to be all mixed up. Which is why those of us who most want to achieve and who are most capable of doing so are prone to develop the Annie Oakley Complex.

But wait . . . a closer look reveals that there are *two* Annie Oakleys. There's the Annie of the boisterous musical *Annie Get Your Gun* and there's the Annie Oakley on whose life that musical purports to be based.[13] Never was fiction more opposed to reality than in this complete falsification of her life. The artificial contrast created between fiction and fact is useful, however, because it tells us much about the Annie Oakley Complex and even more about romantic love.

Fiction: According to the musical, Annie is a rough country bumpkin whose skill with guns is so phenomenal that she can outshoot any man. She's discovered by Buffalo Bill, who makes her a star of his Wild West Show. The ace shooter of that show is

Frank Butler, with whom Annie falls in love on sight. Hopelessly, as it turns out, because he despises her for not being the kind of woman he would want to marry–namely, "soft and pink as a nursery," "a doll I can carry," and so on. They become a shooting team, but not for long, because Butler is so disturbed by Annie's superior prowess that he leaves to join rival Pawnee Bill's show. Annie goes on to become a solo sensation with the Buffalo Bill Show in Europe. On her triumphant return a contest is arranged between her and Butler to determine once and for all who is the champion. Realizing that "You Can't Get a Man with a Gun," Annie deliberately loses. Whereupon Butler, now able to see her as a woman, joins her in the romantic union that is the musical's rousing finale.

Fact: The true story of Annie Oakley is that she actually *did* "get" her man with a gun. She was fifteen in 1875 when she first met Frank Butler, then twenty-five and a ranking sharpshooter of the time. They met in order to compete against each other in a specially arranged match. Here is Butler's own account of this match and its outcome:

> I was shooting with a show and meeting all comers on the outside with my shotgun. . . . On reaching Cincinnati we put up at a hotel where farmers stopped. Some of the guests heard we could shoot and soon I was tackled by one who wanted to know what I could do. I told him I could beat anything then living, save Carver and Bogardus. He said he had an unknown who would shoot me . . . ten days from that time for $100 a side. I laughed and took the bet, barring only the two men mentioned. . . . From the day this match was made until I went I had heard nothing more. . . . I almost dropped dead when a little slim girl in short dresses stepped out to the mark with me. . . . I never shot better in my life. Never were the birds so hard for two shooters as they flew from us, but never did a person make more impossible shots than did that little girl. She killed twenty-three and I killed twenty-one. It was her first big match–my first defeat.
>
> The next day I came back to see the little girl who had beaten me, and it was not long until we were married.

Although Butler is said to have quipped that he married Annie because, "It was the only way I could get my money back," they came as close to living happily ever after as real life allows. Their marriage was often described as idyllic during the fifty years they worked and traveled together, Annie as a famous shot and Frank as her manager. She did join the Buffalo Bill Show, in 1885, but Frank never performed there during the more than seventeen years when she was the show's sensation in America and Europe, earning a reputed weekly salary of $1,000. Frank's devotion to Annie is apparent in the many poems he wrote to her, as it is in the many interviews printed in the press. They had no children but gave a lot of money to the children of relatives; they also made large donations to charities caring for poor children. In the spring of 1926 they moved back to Ohio. This was where Will Rogers visited them. He told his public:

> I went out to see Annie Oakley the other day as I was playing in Dayton, Ohio. She lives there with her husband, Frank Butler, and her sister. Her hair is snow white. She is bedridden from an auto accident a few years ago. I have talked with Buffalo Bill cowboys who were with the show for years, and they worshipped her. . . . I want you to write to her, all of you who remember her, and those that can go see her. Her address is 706 Lexington Avenue, Dayton, Ohio. She will be a lesson to you. She is a greater character than she was a rifle shot.

Rogers might well have said the same of Frank Butler. These two remarkable people, who died within eighteen days of each other in 1926, are a far greater lesson in love than Tristan and Iseult. Unfortunately, rather than learning from their example, we have instead seen fit to bury them in history while character-assassinating them in the legends of Americana.

Why was the true love story of Annie Oakley and Frank Butler discarded as the basis for the musical? Because that story is not romantic. The true story does not contain the proper elements of a script that defines the situation, names the actors, and plots their behavior so that something romantic happens. *Annie Get Your Gun,* on the other hand, contains all of these elements. It's practically a textbook case of how autonomous people, be they female or male, must adjust the picture of themselves in order for romance to blossom. In fact, *all three* major elements of the true story between Annie and Frank had to be changed in order to create "the thing that's known as romance," as the love song of the musical has it.

Thus the extraordinary whole human being who was Annie Oakley is bolted to the commonplace that is the feminine stereotype: a "real" woman who "learns her lesson" when she realizes that "You Can't Get a Man with a Gun" and assumes a mask of inferiority by deliberately lying about her competence. The equally extraordinary human being who was Frank Butler is likewise bolted to the commonplace that is the masculine stereotype: a strutting "real" man, whose "masculine pride" requires him at all times to maintain the exhausting fiction that "Anything You Can Do I Can Do Better." And the mutually enhancing partnership of equals that was their love relationship is degraded into the sly politics of the ego that we call romance.

How does the Annie Oakley Complex work? The contrast between the Annie of fact and the Annie of fiction says it all. Here we have the real-life Annie, a many-sided woman who was described by the contemporary press in glowing terms: the "brilliant conversationalist" who also was "blithesome" and "vivacious"; the toast of European royalty who yet delighted people with her "unassuming manners and rare modesty"; the person of slight physical stature with "the low sweet voice" who also was "frank and genial" and possessed an "unusual force of character." In short, a full-fledged woman who never adjusted the picture of herself and nevertheless found love with a man who actively treasured her unstifled self until the day he died.

This woman's fictional counterpart is Annie, the likeable but monotonously energetic bumpkin who commits *faux pas* after grammatical blunder because she "ain't had any larnin'"; who denigrates her phenomenal prowess by attributing it to the fact that, "My mother was frightened by a shotgun, they say," before denouncing it for making her life a failure, since, "A man never trifles with gals who carry rifles"; and who finally betrays it in order to win her man by bowing to his dictum that, "Sooner or later I'm greater than you." In short, she is the gauche misfit who "proves herself" by diminishing that self; who affirms that the great quest of a woman's life is not to use her given talents to have a direct relationship with life but to stifle and dishonor those talents in order to find fulfillment with Mr. Right. The romantic lesson she learns is to graduate from the cheap but straightforward skirmish of "Anything You Can Do I Can Do Better" to the careful deceit of conquest and surrender. Her diploma of victory is Frank's "love" song:

. . . she's broken my resistance . . .
she's got me where she wants me
And I can't escape nohow.

The Curse of Unfemininity

Suppose you don't give in to your Annie Oakley Complex. Suppose, in fresh romantic encounter after encounter, you refuse to adjust the picture of yourself in good feminine fashion and instead stay true to yourself, your sexuality, and your competence. The most probable result of such behavior, since there unhappily are few Frank Butlers around, is that you will abort those encounters before they get very far. Those of us who choose to behave like the real Annie Oakley instead of like the fictional one know this well from personal experience. The reality we face is perfectly expressed in a *New Yorker* cartoon in which two men of comfortable age and substance are sitting in the smoking room of what appears to be an exclusive club for just such men. Over cigars and brandy one man says to the other, "She turned out to be all I ever wanted in a woman—and more, unfortunately."[14]

Back in 1946 sociologist Mirra Komarovsky wrote up the prescription of how to become the kind of woman this man wanted—the kind who will never be guilty of going too far:

She is the girl who is intelligent enough to do well in school but not so brilliant as to "get all A's"; informed and alert but not consumed by an intellectual passion; capable but not talented in areas relatively new to

> women; able to stand on her own feet and to earn a living but not so good a living as to compete with men; capable of doing some job well (in case she does not marry or, otherwise, has to work) but not so identified with a profession as to need it for her happiness.[15]

Today, a prominent "with-it" example of this kind of girl is the "Cosmo Girl." We see her also in "Charlie," Revlon's signature woman for its perfume of that name. In the early 1980s Charlie had a brief life as an autonomous woman. As portrayed by actress Shelley Hack she was single, employed, independent, confident, unescorted, and sexy. Along comes 1984. Enter the "new Charlie":

> Revlon replaced Hack this year with a softer, rounder model. The pants are gone; in their place is a ruffled strapless evening gown. *And she's with a man,* a handsome, wholesome-looking young professional–a banker, a lawyer? The romantic scene is set as Charlie and her date walk home from a party. "Would you cancel your trip to the coast if I proposed?" he asks, and Charlie ignores him. But he persists. "Even my mother thinks it's time for you to settle down." Sweetly smiling, Charlie finally looks him straight in the eye and says, "Your mother is right."[16]

That's the "new Charlie." The autonomous woman is the woman who smiles and looks him straight in the eye and says, "Stop maligning your mother." Who goes on that trip to the coast without romance and probably with the Dragon's breath wafting down her neck.

It was Susan Brownmiller's thorough investigation, *femininity,* that first put me on the track of the Dragon. For years I had agreed with her contention that femininity in all respects is a matter of containment, and had therefore long since chosen against it. I felt that the price exacted by femininity was too high, despite the many inducements offered by our culture. The precise nature of the price I had been paying instead by making this choice was still unclear to me, even in the wake of my Ideal Romance. I did see that there was a connection between the two, so I pored over *femininity.* Certain passages stood out like road signs: This Way to the Dragon. Finally, there it was:

> There is no getting around the fact that ambition is not a feminine trait.

More strongly expressed, a lack of ambition—or a professed lack of ambition, or a sacrificial willingness to set personal ambition aside—is virtuous proof of the nurturant feminine nature which, if absent, strikes at the guilty heart of femaleness itself.[17]

At last I was face to face with the Dragon. It is "the guilty heart of femaleness itself."

At the core of this guilty heart lies the truth that refusing to let other people have their way feels bad. Especially if you're a woman and most especially if the other people are men. Even otherwise autonomous women know that twinge of guilt when faced with refusing anything from a man's arm to his proposal of marriage. The guilt comes, I think, from the unexamined suspicion that what we like to call healthy assertiveness or being true to oneself is merely a rationalization hiding the dark secret that we really are that cultural blasphemy, the unfeminine woman. Feminine-baiting is a time-honored technique for keeping women guilty and down. We get it in all-out assaults like the pronouncement by one of the male pillars of twentieth-century psychology that the educated woman is "the very apotheosis of selfishness."[18] And in the pronouncement by one of the female pillars that "Woman's intellectuality is to a large extent paid for by the loss of valuable feminine qualities. . . . All observations point to the fact that the intellectual woman is masculinized; in her, warm intuitive knowledge has yielded to cold unproductive thinking."[19] And we get it in the commentary by our fathers and our husbands or lovers, which effectively tells us that there is something wrong with us, that we're guilty of the sin of being ourselves. The three women who follow are cases in point.

There's Rachel, the pretty college "sunshine girl," who felt the need one fine day to "choose between their 'me' and my 'me'":

She hoped to leave behind the person she had been, with her lover and with her family, the passive, dependent, scared piece of clay, the good little girl, the performer, playing happy.

In thus trying to leave behind what she called "the feminine game," Rachel decided she must first create her new physical "me:"

She let the hair on her legs grow for the first time in eight years. She tied her long blond hair up under a cap and walked across the campus camouflaged, without makeup, in loose-fitting shirts and green pants. She wanted to know if anyone would look at her if she weren't pretty. She wanted to know if she would feel different if she weren't feminine.

Finally, she decided to confront her family. For this, she did "the most radical thing" she could think of; she cut off almost all of her hair. When she got off the plane "with my no hair and my green pants," her mother looked aghast. Her father put the matter in a nutshell. He asked, "What have you done to my girl?"[20] And the former housewife in her mid-forties, who recently became a management consultant:

My husband would always say to me, "If you would only do things in a less direct manner." And of course that not only hit me in terms of my feminism, it also hit me in terms of my roots, because Germans tend to be very direct. And I am not *sneaky.* I can't be. So I resented that terribly. What he was really saying was, "It's harder for me to fend you off if you're direct, it's easier if you're indirect." But it took me years to understand that.

"Did I try to be more indirect? No way. But I still felt guilty because I knew I couldn't be indirect."

And finally the successful playwright in her mid-fifties:

Until a few years ago I had a very ambivalent feeling about success and doing the things that matter to me. The ambivalence comes right from my childhood. When my father sees a strong woman's face, his next comment usually is something like, "She must be hard to be married to." The message is: You can't be a serious woman wanting to do serious work and also be loved–by a man. And I think that's largely true. It's changing, perhaps. I hope so. I'm looking to the next generation with an eager eye, hoping to see something different.

The guilty heart of femaleness itself beats especially strongly in our breast if we are autonomous women contemplating men and love, for here is the acid test that will reveal our selfish unfemininity. This anxiety is hardly surprising, given our culture's test (for women only) of love. How do you show a man that you *really* love him? There are variations, but even in today's world of loosening stereotypes this scene from the Harlequin romance *Rising Star* reverberates in our lives. The heroine is a professional horse jumper:

> "I love you Nick. I always will."
> "Enough to give up jumping for?" he insisted.
> "If you want me to." Her reply was without any pause. "It isn't important now."[21]

Most of us rightly scorn this appalling way of proving love, even at the risk of increasing feminine guilt. At full blast, feminine guilt makes being without a man seem the living proof of our inability to give. If at this critical point we don't see the Dragon for what it is, we're terribly at risk for what this thirty-year-old single woman calls "my crisis":

> I saw it as a matter of being true to myself. I couldn't be two selves. . . . So I didn't cover or underplay my background, my ambitions; I didn't "play it smart."
>
> Now I had a sense that all this was catching up with me. I was being punished, and God, it hurt. . . . And I thought of all the relationships I'd had with men that hadn't worked out—"worked out" now meant "ended in marriage" which was all that counted at the moment. Obviously, this was every relationship I'd ever had, since I was still single. All those relationships contained some kind of problem that reflected a shortcoming on my part, I fantasized, and I began to believe I had this dreadful flaw which must be perfectly obvious to everyone else but was hidden to me. . . . I saw myself as not only inadequate but incomplete, lacking something, not whole. . . . I could only save myself by pouring everything I had into an effort to end my aloneness: I had to find a man, a man I could marry.[22]

The Magic Button

What we have here is a well-developed case of a woman with her Magic Button—the one labeled, "Free me from the curse of unfemininity"—waiting to be pushed. A woman who has spent years scaring men by not putting on the feminine act is almost surely a woman with a deep schism. The man who pushes her Magic Button by seeming to heal that schism is the man who will get somewhere with her. Consequently, almost any man who shows an interest in her and says the magic words, "I find you very intelligent and I also find you very attractive, and I don't find your being intelligent a turn-off, on the contrary," evokes her awe and gratitude. One out of ten thousand, she rejoices, here's a man who finds me attractive and also accepts all the other things I am. At last I can be myself and also be loved. My Prince! He has pushed the Magic Button and the romantic ideal goes into overdrive. Sparkledust descends upon her eyes, and she bestows herself in quick order. If he decides to be her Prince, she will respond by becoming the Reverse Sleeping Beauty.

Now the autonomous woman's special vulnerability to making a fool of herself in love is entirely predictable. It's merely a special case of the general sociological proposition that social approval has its greatest impact when one has gone for a long time without receiving expressions of love or esteem, and particularly when one has recently been disapproved of. Or, in the words of social psychologist Zick Rubin, "Approval that follows disapproval comes like food to the hungry pigeon."[23]

This point is of central importance to the autonomous woman in love, so let's restate the "hungry pigeon" principle and see how it applies to her. Principle: Approval that follows disapproval satisfies a need that has been accumulating over a period of time and is therefore a very powerful social reward.

Autonomous women live in an atmosphere saturated with disapproval. It comes especially from men and is exemplified by this man's comment: "I may be a little frightened of a man who is superior to me in some field of knowledge, but if a girl knows more than I do, I resent her."[24] According to Webster's, to resent is to feel or show displeasure and indignation, from a sense of being injured or offended. He resents women like us because we offend him. To offend is to transgress the moral or divine law; to sin; to commit a crime or fault. In short, the fault is ours. We (and not he) have transgressed a higher law, and he can therefore righteously disapprove of us. Ordinary garden variety disapproval is hard enough to take; disapproval carried on the wings of divine law cuts deep.

Even disapproval so silly that it's humorous can undermine. Here's a small example. While doing research for a magazine article on hypnotic regression into past lives, I attended a seminar in Arizona. There were fifty or sixty of us there, all trying various esoteric experiments. In the breaks between sessions I was a quiet observer rather than a participant, because I was taking mental notes for my article. One man, who clearly fancied himself as uncommonly attractive and interesting, was usually the center of attention at these breaks. The time came when he was holding forth on the subject of palmistry and asked for a palm to read. When no one moved, I proffered mine. He took my hand, commenting with romantic flair on its piquant mixture of softness and firmness, and smiled deeply at me. Then his gaze dropped to my palm, and his smile stiffened markedly. "You're so independent you didn't even need your parents to get born!" he exclaimed and stared at me, quite unamorously, as though seeing me through the wrong end of a pair of binoculars. I looked at him in mild astonishment and then grinned to myself. He looked so betrayed. I realized that he must have taken my quiet and attentive behavior for that of a good feminine woman; instead, I turned out to be a hardworking writer with an indecent surfeit of independence. Incidents like that are funny, but they leave a regrettable aftertaste.

Now for the approval that comes like food to the hungry pigeon. Social psychologist Elaine Hatfield Walster's experiment with women college students provides a dramatic demonstration of this principle:

> As the laboratory drama opened, the subject arrived at an empty reception room, where a sign asked her to wait for the experimenter. A few minutes later a smooth, well-dressed graduate student . . . came on stage and explained that he was waiting for another experimenter.

The graduate student, chosen for his matinee-idol looks, then began a casual conversation with each woman, feeding her a massive dose of approval that ended with his request for a date. Of the thirty-seven subjects in the experiment, thirty-two accepted his invitation.

In the next act of the drama Dr. Walster arrived, escorted the happily deluded subject to another room, and explained that the purpose of the study was to compare various personality tests.

When the supposed reports on the personality tests were given to the subjects, half of the women got the reassuring news that they possessed, among other things, sensitivity to peers, personal integrity, originality, and freedom of outlook. The other half received far less approving reports about "superficial appearances of maturity," "basic insecurity drives," "lack of flexibility," and "antisocial motives." After the evaluations had had their effect, the women were asked to rate the graduate student whose date they had accepted. Result: "Those who received the negative evaluation indicated that they liked him considerably more than did those who received the positive evaluation. In other words, the girls who had the greatest need for approval were most attracted to the person who provided it." (After the experiment Dr. Walster explained the nature of the evaluations and the reasons for the deceptions, so that no young woman felt bad when she left.)[25]

Now think of all the social gatherings where you've met a man who, after an initial conversation where you did not adjust the picture of yourself and act feminine, exited with the classic masculine line for such occasions: "Excuse me, I'm going to get a refill." Then imagine this scenario:

You are at a cocktail party and have a conversation with a person you have never met before. Later that evening, while standing behind a potted palm, you overhear him talking about you. In fact, you encounter the same person at several consecutive parties and manage to overhear his comments on you each time. There are at least four interesting possibilities.

1. He is always saying positive things about you.
2. He is always saying negative things about you.
3. At the first one or two parties he seems down on you, but at subsequent parties his comments become more and more positive.
4. At the first one or two parties he seems quite favorably impressed by you, but at subsequent parties his comments become more and more negative.[26]

In which of these cases do you think you'd like the man the most? The hungry pigeon principle suggests that it would be in Case 3, where the man initially disapproved of you but gradually came to be approving. Case 3 is the perfect scenario for the drama, "Autonomous Woman with Magic Button Meets Mr. Right—At Last!" Its denouement is also as predicted: a likely metamorphosis to Reverse Sleeping Beauty.

Reverse Sleeping Beauties

How can an autonomous woman achieve the impossible? How can she at last enter the portals of the magic kingdom where reside "real" women? And more, how can she manage this feat and still persuade herself that she has not abandoned everything she previously stood for? Answer: She can fall madly in love—and the more madly, the better. This is why I say that when Prince Charming kisses us we don't wake up, like Sleeping Beauty. We fall asleep—to what we are, to what he is, to reality. The relief is *enormous.* Because as Reverse Sleeping Beauties we no longer hear the discordant inner voice that says, "Hey, wait just a minute!" Instead, we hear a chorus of approving voices that sigh, "How romantic!" As, of course, it is. The way is now clear for us to become prodigies at the romantic skill of reinterpretation—which we normally would call rationalizing.

Romantic love is a marvelous tool for rationalizing. Here is a mode of behavior, strongly endorsed by our culture as the greatest interpersonal experience life can offer a woman, which licenses us to behave quite irrationally and irresponsibly. What's going on with you when people feel prompted to say, "How romantic!"? What are the signifying features of being "madly in love"? (1) Something happened to you over which you had no control. (2) You're not supposed to have any control (that would spoil the magic). (3) You are in some essential way not yourself (that, too, is part of the magic). What are you supposed to do about it? (4) Where's the altar? Because (5) this "crazy feeling" is how you *know* you've found True Love. This woman's outpouring says it well:

Almost from the very first moment when Rick looked into my eyes—so deeply, he didn't merely look *at* me—I thought that word, "Ecstasy." After our first night together, I woke up with this strange and wonderful feeling like nothing describable or nothing I have ever felt before. Problems, troubles, inconveniences of living that would normally have occupied my thoughts became unimportant. . . . The landlord had given me notice and the bank loan had not gone through, and I could not bring myself to care! Whatever happened, it would be wonderful, somehow.[27]

Making major life decisions while under the spell of feeling that it will all be wonderful somehow is not seen as hazardous conduct but as reliable proof that you are at last among the elect who know the ecstasy of Love. Like Cinderella, you have been tested and found worthy. The proof is in the prize: the Prince.

Reverse Sleeping Beauties are recognizable by "the Look." Once you catch on to it, the Look is unmistakable. It's the kind of look you seem fat with, even if you are physically slender. It comes, I believe, from an acute case of smugness. One woman said:

I felt better than most other women. Because I had it all. I had what almost every woman wants and almost none of us gets. I wanted to be myself *and* I wanted a man who was not a complete jerk to love me and think I was great while being myself. . . . Where does the feeling of being better than instead of just more fortunate than come from? I think it was that in some sense I felt I had finally become everything a woman could become in our culture. To put it more horribly, I was finally a *real* woman. My success was authentic to me, but it wasn't enough. It needed the kicker—a man to tell me I was still all right.

When we become Reverse Sleeping Beauties, do we tell ourselves the truth and say we've done a classic reaction formation and become everything we deplored before the arrival of our Prince? Certainly not, that would definitely spoil the magic. Once again, the romantic skill of reinterpretation comes to our aid. It enables us to rationalize our unprecedented sex-stereotype behavior by calling it "exploring new laws of being." An ingenious move, since most autonomous women rightly feel like pioneers and therefore take readily to the notion that we are venturing into unknown territory.

To the Castle

We *are* moving into unknown territory. But, contrary to our fond expectations, it's not the territory of authentic love. Far from it. The destination for a Reverse Sleeping Beauty who goes the last mile into this territory is not a viable love relationship but instead a most unviable state of mind and being which I call the Castle.

The Castle is a mythic symbol borrowed from fairy tales. For, as we'll see in the next chapter, just as the castle is the final destination of the princess in a romantic fairy tale, so the Castle is the end of the line if a Reverse Sleeping Beauty follows that "crazy feeling" to the ending decreed by the Myth of Romantic Love. I've never seen the essence of the Castle described more perfectly than in these lines by John Donne from "The Sun Rising":

She is all states, and all princes, I,
Nothing else is.

There it stands delineated in a line and a half of poetry, the mythic Castle: isolated by its drawbridge from the ordinary life below, a universe sufficient unto itself with its own laws of being. And, we might add, a universe in which he is sovereign.

The sleep state necessary for entering the Castle, and even more necessary for staying in it, is an exceedingly dangerous one. I say this in great seriousness. The mind can perform the most exquisite tricks when we ask it to, and in the Castle the need to ask becomes increasingly powerful. To look back on that state is to feel a shocking kinship to Sybil, she of the seven distinct personalities. It is to know intimately her feeling when she would come to after having been someone else, and have no inkling of what acts she might have committed in the interim. For one of the most distinguishing features of the sleep state you enter as a Reverse Sleeping Beauty is that you don't know you're in it. You begin to recognize it only ex post facto when someone says, "Welcome back." Fortunately, those of us who have lived there and who have come back can describe life in the Castle to other women. Our message is twofold: You do not live happily in the Castle; therefore, it's a good thing that you also don't live there ever after. But both the life there and the exit are rough.

6. Life in the Castle

To live in the Castle is to live "in the cellar of [one's] soul."[1] Unfortunately, too few of us believe this truth until we've been there and have had the Myth of Romantic Love burnt out of our system. I'm hoping that my delineation will help other women to separate the truth from the fraudulence of romance in their lives, so that they may avoid having to go this route.

Transformation is the pivot on which turns the promise of the Myth of Romantic Love. The Ideal Romance spells it out: The hero will be magically remade by the heroine, but only if she transforms herself into the perfect wife-mother whose combination of womanly sensuality and mothering capacities makes his transformation possible. The key to the heroine's transformation is her romantic skill of reinterpretation.

The pivot on which turns the salvation of the woman who believes its promise is the fact that the Myth of Romantic Love is a lie. The magic never lasts. This is why the end of the romantic idealization that terminates the "honeymoon" after an average maximum of two to three years is known in the research literature as "disenchantment."[2] The Myth not only says that True Love lasts forever but that it, by definition, excludes conflict and disagreement. Since this is not true of any viable human relationship, the very basis on which we are exhorted to build True Love is fraudulent. The fraudulent promise of the safe fix generates not love but a deterioration in mental health. This deterioration manifests in the case of women at large as depression. In the autonomous woman who ends up in the Castle, it manifests as a classic case of psychosis.

Going Crazy in the Name of Love

A friend of mine is an anthropologist who specializes in epidemiology—the science that investigates the causes and control of epidemic diseases. Depression is now an epidemic disease among women in our society—and not among men. My friend suggested that I explore this issue as it relates to romantic love.

Epidemiologists tell us that overall, by a ratio of two to one, women suffer from depression more than men.[3] The primary psychodynamic patterns that are known to lead to depression include (1) submissiveness to a dominant other; (2) living for the sake of the dominant other or for obtaining approval and gratification from the dominant other; (3) dependency; and (4) living with romantic love as a dominant goal.[4]

Taken together, these patterns are virtually synonymous with being a "real" woman in our culture, so it's not surprising that they occur predominantly among women. And especially among women who feel exhorted by the Myth of Romantic Love to find True Love in the manner described at its most flagrant by the author of the best-seller *The Total Woman:* "It is only when a woman surrenders her life to her husband, reveres and worships him, and is willing to serve him, that she becomes really beautiful to him. She becomes a priceless jewel, the glory of femininity, his queen!"[5]

It is useful to remember, when one hears things like this statement about glorious feminine surrender, that the two to one ratio of depressive illness among women is largely accounted for by the higher rates for married women. In all other categories—single, divorced, and widowed—women actually have lower rates than men.

We must remember, says psychiatrist Silvano Arieti in his discussion of the sociocultural factors behind women's depression, that the dominant goal of many women is not the search for an authentic self but the pursuit of romantic love. He continues:

> Love is of course very important and has to be pursued by everybody, men and women, but when romantic love becomes the only concern or

aim in life and takes the place of any other aim including the pursuit of other types of love, then life becomes unduly restricted in rigid patterns for which it will be difficult to find alternatives later.[6]

Arieti concludes that our culture at large enters into a conspiracy with a woman's private conflicts between the search for autonomy and the pursuit of the dream of romantic love, and that the conspiracy on the part of the culture consists in diverting the woman from becoming aware of the masochism of such a pursuit.

I conclude that the mental state the autonomous woman as Reverse Sleeping Beauty develops in the Castle is a result of her determined, even compulsive, attempt to live out the exhortation to Total Woman. She becomes the extreme Arieti talks about: Romantic love becomes her only, or at least vastly primary, concern, and her life becomes unduly restricted in rigid patterns. And she does indeed develop a temporary inability to find alternatives.

The Love-Blot

Falling in love is the perfect basis for the True Love promised by the Myth of Romantic Love. First of all, this experience is built around projection and idealization, on image rather than reality. Try the riddle given by John Money in *Love and Love Sickness.*[7] Riddle: What do your beloved and a Rorschach ink-blot have in common? (The Rorschach test, named for the Swiss psychiatrist Hermann Rorschach, is a personality test in which the person being tested looks at a series of ink-blot designs of various shapes and tells what they suggest.) Answer: You project an image of your own onto both the ink-blot and your beloved. What you fall in love with is not your beloved as such, but with him as a Rorschach love-blot. Your friends say, "Whatever does she see in him?" because they see the person while you see your love-blot, which is your own idealized and idiosyncratic image of him.

Second, falling in love is not voluntary. As many researchers and personal experience testify, people do not seem to have control over whether or not they will become love-smitten. It's something that happens *to* you. You may agree to go along with it rather than try to abort it, but you cannot will it to happen.

Third, you also have no voluntary control over what kind of person will trigger your love-blot reaction. So you can no more decide to fall in love with a specific person than you can decide to fall in love in general.

Fourth, while you are "madly in love" you cannot tolerate or absorb criticism of your love-blot beloved. Cannot. Which is why few of us can tell a friend who's in love what *we* "see in him."

In sum, the process of falling in love is involuntary in its most significant aspects. Worse, the state of being in love is self-isolating (you see what others do not see) and self-reinforcing (you cannot take in what they do see). What we call our great love poetry is full of images that describe just this state. John Donne's poetry is typical. In "The Good Morrow" the past is cut away: "I wonder by my troth, what thou and I/ Did, till we loved?" and the world is cut away: "For love, all love of other sights controls/and makes one little room, an everywhere." In "The Legacy" life itself is cut away: "When I died last, and dear, I die/ As often as from thee I go." The lines that symbolize the Castle sum it up: Nothing else is.

The state the Myth calls True Love is a state in which virtually all possibilities of reality-testing are lost to the person who is under the influence. There is another name for such a state: psychosis. The clinical definition of a psychotic is a person who has lost contact with reality and is either occasionally or constantly incapable of rational behavior. What distinguishes a psychotic from a neurotic person is precisely the loss of touch with reality. This loss causes a person to "behave in bizarre and perhaps life-threatening ways."[8] The autonomous woman's behavior while she lives in the Castle is certainly bizarre, and especially so when compared to her behavior before she crosses the Castle's drawbridge. Ultimately, I think this behavior would be life-threatening. She is saved from this fate by the happy fact that the state of romantic love self-destructs before she does. She is very unlikely to lose her life, but she comes perilously close to losing her mind.

Someone Who Needs Me

What hooks the autonomous woman into the scenario of going crazy in the name of love? The fact that she is scrambling for an identity. She has rejected the socially prescribed identity for a "real" woman, opting instead for trying to live as a whole human being with a direct relationship to life. For all the reasons put forth in the previous chapter, chances are therefore high that she has also been living with the guilty heart of femininity itself. The extent to which she had not yet managed to slay that Dragon is the extent to which she now is scrambling.

What kind of identity will do the trick of removing her feminine guilt? Here we have a woman who in effect has been told by society and probably specifically by men as important in her life as her father: You're not a woman, you're not feminine, you have no maternal instincts, you're not a nurturing person. Such a message from a father carries great authority for a girl who is growing up. Before she gets old enough to see that he is not all men but just one man among millions, and to evaluate his message critically in light of this knowledge, she may very well take it in uncritically—Father says so, he's a man, he should know. The message in terms of love is: Men don't need you, you're not the kind of woman who attracts men.

How would such a message make her feel? One woman who lived in the Castle told me, "I felt that becoming lovers with a man was not my country." What is the most obvious ticket into the country that is not her country? A man who *really needs* her. And so that ticket becomes her transformation, which in this case amounts to what in psychiatry is called a reaction formation—the person acts out the opposite of what she or he really is. I think this is why so many autonomous women who went this route talked to me in terms of feeling schizophrenic—which literally means of split mind. These are not women who ever wanted to be a nurturer as a full-time occupation in a love relationship, but that's what they become in the Castle. Now they can show not only their fathers and/or society but also themselves. So they become the stereotype of the very kind of woman they haven't wanted to be before: the extreme of the caretaker—the good woman who dispenses passive, all-giving, all-benign mothering. Those of us who also are mothers probably didn't do that with our children, but we end up doing it with a man. Whatever mother guilt we have over not having "done enough" for our children because we wanted to pursue our own life as well as be mothers is thereby also largely assuaged.

In the realm of love our particular answer to the question, "Does someone have to feel needy to make me feel good?" is therefore, "Yes." This is the happy moment enshrined in the Ideal Romance as the pivotal point in which the heroine's transformation into "all woman" restores her identity. Remember the ideal heroine who exclaimed "'Rad . . . Rad' It was a threnody of joy. 'I'm glad I was able to give you so much"? Her hero's response at this moment is a superb statement of the Myth's love prescription for women: "'You're perfect. You give all the time, and it makes you so strong and sure and generous . . . all woman. My woman.'" Everyman's message to the autonomous woman is, "If you can't be part of this image, I don't want you." To which her response is liable to be like Avis's: "We try harder." At this juncture autonomous women try harder than more traditional women to be "perfect." I put my Avis theory to woman after woman, and all of them answered in the spirit of this woman: "You're correct. I did have the idea with him that this was *It*. I was finally Doing It Right. That's a quote, I used to say that to myself."

What this boils down to is that in matters of love the autonomous woman is doubly at risk. She's at risk for ending up with a "real" man because only such a man can give her the proper hit of femininity. But she will need a special kind of "real" man to give her that hit of "feeling good." Namely, a "real" man who *really needs* her. Enter the passive dependent man as romantic hero.

Here he is, in action: "I would say that within a week—less than that, within three days—my whole world had been transformed. It had a new center, and that center was Marilyn."[9] What kind of man will say, "You are the center of my world" three days after meeting someone? The romantic answer is, "A man who really loves me!" The sober answer is, "A man with a problem." What kind of world can be transformed by taking as its new center a Marilyn who three days earlier was a total stranger? A world without its own intrinsic center. Worse yet, a world waiting for someone else to make its center, and dependent on that someone to do so in order to have a center at all.

Dependency has been defined as the inability to experience wholeness or to function adequately without the certainty that one is being actively cared for by another. We all have dependency needs and feelings—like times of wanting to be babied, nurtured without effort on our own part—but for most of us these desires or feelings do not rule our lives. When they do rule our lives to the point of dictating the quality of our existence, we are dependent. The kind of man who will say, "You are the center of my world" three days after meeting someone is a man whose life is liable to be ruled and dictated by dependency needs. He is therefore liable to suffer from what diagnostically is called the passive dependent personality disorder.

Why do passive dependent men make such fitting romantic heroes? Passive dependent people, says psychiatrist M. Scott Peck, lack a sense of responsibility for themselves.[10] Consequently, they look passively to others as the source of their happiness and fulfillment. I say, where would such a man look? Especially since he's been trained as a man to delegate the emotional world to women, and since the "man's world" of competition is not exactly nurturing? One guess. He must find a woman. *His* woman, who will love and nurture him steadily and unconditionally without effort on his part.

Passive dependent people seek obsessively for love and when they think they've found it their dependency causes them to attach themselves fiercely to it. Romantic declarations serve this need as if made for it: "It's never been like this before," "I only have eyes for you," "You were meant for me," "This is bigger than both of us," etc. Because of their hunger to fill their sense of inner emptiness, passive dependent people not only attach themselves fiercely to people but will brook no delay in gratifying their need for them. How nice, therefore, that romance offers such a man the splendid opportunity to "sweep her off her feet." A moment's sober reflection should make one realize that rushing someone like that may be romantic but is not loving at all, because a person who cares for you rather than for his own dependency needs will want to make sure that a step as serious as committing yourself to another in the name of love is made by you in your own time and in balance with your own life.

A person who looks to his mate instead of to himself as the primary source of happiness and fulfillment is in a precarious position. What he needs is a mate who is as dependable as possible. Growth on her part, which by its very nature means change, is therefore a threat to him. This is why it is one of the hallmarks of passive dependent relationships that their role differentiation is rigid. In this, the mutual needs of the passive dependent man and the autonomous woman with feminine guilt suit each other perfectly. So he will probably put pressure on her to act out the complete feminine nurturer stereotype with him, and she will probably comply. In his need to be able to "count on her" he will also seek to increase rather than decrease mutual dependency. He will not cheer her acts of strength but will subtly undermine them. He *will* subtly welcome her lessened ability to cope with anything or anyone else, taking it as a stronger guarantee of her allegiance to their relationship. This is why every one of the many women I interviewed who got involved with this type of man felt far less capable in the world at the end of that relationship than she did at the beginning. Depending on another person to make one happy is, of course, a futile undertaking. One is bound to feel disappointed, and powerless into the bargain. This is why the end of the romance with a passive dependent man so often is precipitated by him in so angry and vengeful a manner. You, the former center of his world, have become the fix that failed. As a woman therapist I interviewed put it:

> You're the patsy for making him feel better about himself, you're the patsy for everything that goes wrong with him. So a split from that kind of man is set up to become nasty, because you also become the patsy for the fact that the relationship didn't last. And what hooked you in is what tossed you out: the patsy.

With Peck, we may sum up the passive dependent man as lover this way: His is the "addictive personality." He is addicted to people, sucking on them and gobbling them up. His love is not love but a form of anti-love that nourishes infantilism rather than growth. It works to trap and constrict rather than to liberate. Ultimately, it destroys rather than builds relationships, and it destroys rather than builds people.

The passive dependent man may be sick, but as a romantic hero he is not an aberration from the norm. If a book on men can say that the ideal relationship with a woman is seen by men as the "rest stop" of constant freedom from tension, complete relaxation, evenness, stasis, then it becomes apparent that the difference between a normal and a passive dependent romantic hero is one of degree rather than of kind.[11] Their common ground is that what they both call love is a form of addiction. "To serve as an addiction," says Dr. Stanton Peele in *Love and Addiction*, "something must be both reassuring and consuming; it must also be patterned, predictable, and isolated."[12] You can get this from heroin, you can get it from Valium; you can also get it from a woman who is a "rest stop." Addiction, in short, is not a chemical reaction, it is an experience. You are addicted not to the agent but to the experience provided by that agent. What most men and especially passive dependent men desire from their ideal woman lover is what an addict wants from a fix: something safe and reassuring that can be returned to again and again for the same experience. No wonder so many Reverse Sleeping Beauties feel some version of that insistent mental command to Be Serene. Since the average man is socialized to think of this kind of dependency as love, and since the average woman is socialized to defer to men, it follows that our society's norm is addiction rather than self-fulfillment in love.

What hooks the autonomous woman into such a relationship is the promise of an identity that proclaims in indisputable terms that she is after all a "real" woman. And not only that. She gets to prove that you *can* have it all: You *can* be yourself and still be loved by Mr. Right. Because here he is! Other men may be threatened by the combination of competence and sexuality in a woman, but not this man who says you are his ideal woman and who lavishes attention and sex upon you. I think it's fair to argue that a woman who generally is autonomous in life is a woman who generally is not an addict. Being autonomous is practically by definition the opposite of being dependent, since seeking a direct relationship to life is to seek precisely the sense of responsibility for oneself that passive dependent people lack. Yet such a woman is still prone to experience a regression in love relationships to ways of relating she has rejected in society and in other parts of her life. The dynamic symbolized by the Dragon has far more influence than she really wants to accept, and that fact is what she's struggling with in her scramble for an identity.

What we have in the union of a passive dependent man with a Reverse Sleeping Beauty is the union of an addict with an addict *pro tem.* The autonomous woman in such a union is a sterling example of Peele's statement that,

> For the nonaddicted partner, there may be motivations which temporarily cause him or her to agree to things he or she does not ultimately want in a relationship. . . . The person might then have a need for a clinging affair which does not really represent how he or she approaches life in calmer or more congenial circumstances.[13]

Fortunately, as he adds, such a union would by definition not be a permanent arrangement. But until it self-destructs, life in the

Castle will have an increasingly disastrous effect on the woman involved. She will come to experience the Castle increasingly schizophrenically as both paradise and tomb.

Meanwhile, he will behave like the prototype outlined here by the therapist who earlier described "the patsy":

> He would as much as possible isolate her—by cutting out other people, by denigrating the rest of the world in comparison with what "we" have, by talking about "new laws of being"—so she'll concentrate all her attention on him and behave as he wants. And he'll base all that on "loving and needing her" and he'll do it in the guise of an adult so that he's really fostering what *seems* like adult interdependence: the two of us need each other.
>
> But it isn't interdependence at all, because those are very possessive, absorbing, infantile needs—that's what you do with a small child who wants mommy all to himself to take care of him. And if she's needy enough to get sucked in she won't say, hey, these are neurotic needs, these are not healthy needs; this need for isolation, exclusivity, that's not the real world, that's not *my* real world.

Here is that prototype in high gear, at home in the Castle with Sheila Graham. It's interesting to note in passing that Graham was hooked by the inverse of what hooks an autonomous woman. Men celebrated her blonde beauty but tended to ignore her mind. Along comes F. Scott Fitzgerald and pushes *her* Magic Button: "This man appreciates my mind as well as my face." Of life with her "beloved infidel" Graham writes that she and Fitzgerald were "virtual recluses in Hollywood," spending almost all of their time together. When she would speak wistfully about going back to New York for a visit, he would lead here through "a gentle catechism:"

> "Why do you want to go to New York, Sheila?"
>
> "I'm not really sure why. To go to the Stork Club and places like that."
>
> "Why do you want to go to the Stork Club and '21' and places like that?"
>
> I thought. "To see the people, I guess."
>
> "But who are the people you see at such places? They're not real. I have been there. I have given all that up. What can you get from such people? What can you get from New York?"

"Oh . . . " I could not find the words. "New York excites me. It thrills me."

He shook his head. "Sheila, what you are looking for, you have found. You are looking for love, for someone to understand you. You have me. I love you and understand you. There's no need for you to go to New York."[14]

Glowcoma

Kenneth Burke once observed that a way of seeing is also a way of not seeing. As a graphic illustration, let me now tell you the following true story of my brush with glaucoma–or *glow*coma, as a friend who remembers The Look I wore when I lived in the Castle laughingly calls it.

Glaucoma is a disease of the eye. It is characterized by increased tension within, and consequent hardening of, the eyeball. It usually happens to both eyeballs at the same time and leads to gradual impairment of sight, often resulting in blindness. *Glow*coma I would call a disease of attention. It is characterized by what the American psychiatrist Harry Stack Sullivan called selective inattention. It leads to a gradual impairment of reality-testing, often resulting in a mental blindness which no longer can distinguish between reality and delusion. In my story the two diseases confirm the mind/body connection by meeting completely.

About two years into my five-year sojourn in the Castle I was told by an eye specialist at my first check-up with him that the pressure on my eyeballs was in the "high normal range." Which meant that it should be watched carefully, because if it got very much higher I would be in the glaucoma range. Needless to say, I was somewhat alarmed. The specialist recommended frequent check-ups and a treatment by drugs (for life) to lower the pressure if/when it got to the glaucoma stage. This was not very reassuring. For the next three years following that diagnosis my frequent check-ups confirmed that, though I was not yet at the drug treatment point, I was approaching it slowly.

Then the entire edifice of the Castle collapsed upon me without warning, and my body went into shock. It wouldn't stop shaking. When the shaking had kept me awake at night for a full week I went on tranquilizers for the only time in my life, so that I wouldn't have a complete physical breakdown. I fled, got myself together enough to return to Vancouver, and promptly went to my doctor for a complete physical examination. I had read that people who go through a period of enormous emotional stress run a risk of getting a serious disease, like cancer, eighteen months later. Although this was only six weeks later, I was taking no chances. When he was done I asked my doctor, "How am I doing?" He said, "You're doing excellently, and you're also twenty-five pounds lighter than you were last year."

Then I went to the eye specialist. I had evolved a theory about my glaucoma problem while I was away regaining some sanity from examining the rubble of my Castle. My theory was that for five years I had worked extremely hard *not* to see what was right in front of my eyes and that this had a lot to do with the fact that I was heading toward blindness. Therefore, now that I had spent six weeks scrutinizing the fantasies I had built up so as not to see reality, the pressure on my eyeballs ought to be down even though my body otherwise had gone through great stress. The specialist did his examination and announced that the pressure was down. He was surprised, I wasn't. When I told him my theory he looked dubious, but he couldn't deny the fact that the numbers were down. Nor, when asked, could he come up with a better theory to explain this surprising result.

For the following three years I continued my investigation into where I had been during that relationship broadening and intensifying it when I began to do the research for this book. During that time frequent eye examinations revealed that the pressure on my eyeballs was falling slowly but steadily. The day before I left Vancouver to write this manuscript in Wyoming, I went for a final check-up. The specialist announced that for the first time in the six years he had examined my eyes the pressure was "completely normal." I no longer needed to be checked frequently, I no longer had a problem. He still couldn't accept my theory, but he also couldn't deny his own figures; so he sent me off with a slightly confused smile and the comment, "I certainly am pleased that you can leave with such good news."

Glowcoma is developed by the prolonged use of selective inattention, which makes you skilled at screening out what you don't want to see; and by the use of the romantic skill of reinterpretation, which enables you to change what you can't ignore into something you can live with. For this mental sleight of hand to work, however, you must also ignore the fact that you're employing it. Woman after woman told me the same story. Here's one:

> If I had said to myself, "This man is an authoritarian," I would have had to leave. I'm not going to live with an authoritarian, it's probably the one thing I'll never live with—if I recognize it. So the trick is, you don't recognize it.

And another:

> I'm perfect, right? Unique, exquisite. Strange thing, though: everything I ever did before him was somehow wrong. I had a disastrous marriage which I stayed in for far too long, I had a disastrous love affair which should never have happened, my father was bad for me. . . . my mother I haven't understood, she was bad for me. You name it, everything I did before him was *bad* for me. And I started wondering, How could I have turned into this perfect flower in spite of this dreadful past where I made all these errors? You're right, the message was that he was going to rehabilitate me. Did I tell myself that? No. Who wants to be rehabilitated? So I told myself how lucky I was finally to be with a man who really understood and appreciated the true me that somehow hadn't had a chance to bloom before. I felt *grateful* to him, dammit.

And yet another:

> When you're reinterpreting you do not say to yourself, "This guy is a schmuck in this area, but I am going to reinterpret him into being quaint and charming and loveable in this area," or it wouldn't work. What I'm saying is, the reinterpretation only looks like reinterpretation in retrospect. When you're back on your feet, on the ground.

So what we're really talking about when we talk about glowcoma is rationalizing gut reactions. Gut reactions are our direct responses to the red flags which signal that something is rotten in the Castle. They are experienced in the form of squirms. A squirm says, "Oh, oh, I don't like this." Glowcoma is the process of getting better and better at going along with behavior your gut reactions tell you is not okay. You do it by reinterpreting your squirms, because in your mind the Castle has a "No Exit" sign over its drawbridge. What locks you into the Castle is your belief that to leave would be to destroy love, and you can't destroy love because then you'll be the way your father and/or society said you were. So you stay, and your glowcoma makes you increasingly incapable of seeing that your vision of True Love is not only myopic but also delusionary.

How do you maintain a delusion in the midst of reality? Ultimately, you can't. But you can give it a darn good try, and most of us Reverse Sleeping Beauties do. Thus, like Alice's wonderland, life in the Castle will get "curiouser and curiouser!" What glowcoma teaches you is that Alice was wrong and the Queen was right:

> "There's no use trying," she said: "one *can't* believe impossible things."
> "I daresay you haven't had much practice," said the Queen. "When I was your age, I always did it for half-an-hour a day. Why, sometimes I've believed as many as six impossible things before breakfast."[15]

The most curious thing about glowcoma is that you don't notice that life is getting curiouser and curiouser. Why don't you? The best explanation I've come across is Gregory Bateson's. He says that we are almost unaware of trends in our changes of state, be they of mind or body, because the mind can receive news only of a difference. A difference that is small enough doesn't register as news and is therefore not perceived. Because of this characteristic of mind, there is necessarily a difficulty for us in discriminating between a process of slow change and a static state. This truth of nature is a nontrivial matter for the woman who is living in the Castle, as it is for the frog in the following situation:

There is a quasi-scientific fable that if you can get a frog to sit quietly in a saucepan of cold water, and if you then raise the temperature of the water very slowly and smoothly so that there is no moment *marked* to be the moment at which the frog should jump, he will never jump. He will get boiled.[16]

Deus ex Machina: The Road Out of the Castle

Fortunately for the autonomous woman who is living in the delusionary world of the Castle and has become increasingly incapable of getting out, rescue is guaranteed. If she has lost enough self-preservation to be incapable of leaving so unhealthy a relationship and so contaminating a lover, she will have the opportunity thrust upon her when, as Tennyson aptly put it in "Locksley Hall," "his passion shall have spent its novel force."

We know that the average maximum lifespan of the passion that is romantic love is two to three years. In other words, this state is inherently unstable; eventually, the "spark" goes out. It should be clear by now that addiction is also an inherently unstable state. Both states are "marked by a compulsion to deny all that you are and have been in favor of some new and ecstatic experience."[17] And, since he is the addict and you are only the addict *pro tem,* chances are that it is he rather than you who will feel the compulsion to seek some new and ecstatic experience. The moment when he acts on this compulsion is your *deus ex machina.*

Deus ex machina. Literally, god from a machine. It refers to the practice in ancient Greek and Roman plays, where a deity would be brought in by stage machine to intervene in the action at a crucial moment and save the day. Although it will feel like a disaster, your moment of *deus ex machina* will actually be the blessing that suddenly and improbably is introduced to restore you to yourself.

The immediate result will most likely be that you are abruptly turfed out of the Castle. Since this is a forced exit, sudden and seemingly inexplicable, chances are that you will land on your exit route in great pain and confusion, sorely feeling our conspicuous lack of coherent tradition for such exits. From the experiences reported to me as well as from my own, I have pinpointed three key stages on this exit route: loss, loss and change, and gain. These are the points where positive action on your part will be most called for, where clear perception is most necessary, and where your turmoil will be at its worst. So while you're making your exit, remember the following:

1. You are experiencing a major existential crisis and you must respect that fact. In some significant ways your crisis is greater even than the one for which we do have a coherent tradition and much respect—the bereavement that follows the death of a mate.
2. All is not lost. As Peele says in *Love and Addiction,* a partial, temporary addiction can be a constructive, though costly, stage in a person's development. The cost is great, this you already know. The benefits can be equally great, if not greater: This is your chance at last to slay your Dragon.

In the drama now unfolding you get to be the hero, rather than the heroine whose function is to help the hero with his quest. Your quest is to restore your own identity, yourself. If you are successful in this quest, you will never again be at risk for the kind of man who hooked you into the Castle, and you will know the Myth of Romantic Love for what it really is because you've been where it takes you. If that isn't liberation, what is? So onward!

Stage One: Loss

Your first reaction is most likely to be outrage. Outrage that someone who professed to love you could suddenly turn around and treat you so entirely without empathy. There must be some mistake, you repeat to yourself, people just don't behave in so inhumane a manner—not even to a dog. All people don't, but addicts *do.* In fact this kind of behavior, according to Peele, is exactly what conclusively establishes that you've been involved with an addict and are being ejected from an addictive relationship. Addicts tend to be "incapable of respecting, or even conceiving of, the other in his or her own terms."[18] If the other no longer satisfies the addict's needs, he or she *ceases to exist.* Your proper role from such a lover's viewpoint is therefore to fade away into the darkness without getting an explanation and without making a fuss.

That is indeed outrageous. I was reading a Margery Allingham mystery while I was in this situation and came across an observation which I found profoundly true of my feelings at the time. I pass it along because I also found it very calming: "Outrage, combining as it does shock, anger, reproach, and helplessness, is perhaps the most unmanageable, the most demoralizing, of all the emotions."[19]

At this juncture you need a quick course in anger management. The first piece of good advice comes from psychologist Dorothy Tennov: The best cure you can administer to yourself is to remove all contact and all possibility of contact between yourself and this man (except by intermediaries, such as lawyers). The next advice comes from me: Get yourself a copy of one of the only good books written on the subject—*Anger: The Misunderstood Emotion* by Carol Tavris—and use it.[20] In an interview with me about the anger you're probably feeling, Tavris explained that it has "a natural life, like grief." She continued,

> Most societies have social rituals to help the grieving person get through it. They go something like this: All right, you get one intense month of grief, you get six months of sort of listlessness around the house, you get one year to get over the whole thing; we will not let you dangle around there, being grief-stricken your entire life.
>
> Most Western societies don't have those rituals for the kind of anger we're talking about. Therefore: no social support, no help for dealing with this, no rules for getting over it. And that's too bad. Because without those kinds of rules of containment, without knowing how you're supposed to express it or when or to whom or for what purpose, people can flail around in these negative emotions for a long time. They just get stuck in a spiral of recrimination.

If you find yourself taking a few turns on that spiral of recrimination, remind yourself of what Tavris says in her book: You're wrong if you think that talking out anger gets rid of it. On the contrary, the research suggests that talking out an emotion doesn't reduce it, it *rehearses it.* Ventilating anger makes you angrier, solidifies an angry attitude, and establishes a hostile habit. You know this is true when you see even your most well-meaning friends' eyes glaze over as you repeat yet another outrage perpetrated upon you; and if you pay attention at those times you can feel your own emotions hit a familiar overdrive where you bore even yourself and yet find it hard to stop.

What you are doing is wasting perfectly good anger. I agree with Tavris that anger is a moral emotion. It erupts out of one's ideas of justice, human rights, fair play, out of one's sense that people–oneself included–should be treated with some concern for their welfare. Anger, in short, is the "assertion of an ought"–it announces to you that someone is not behaving as you think she or he *ought.*[21]

So there you are, and we can probably all agree that He is not behaving as he ought. It's his right not to want you, but it's not his right to behave like a cad about it. *Now* what? Now take some time out to think. Use your anger to pinpoint exactly how and where you think he's behaving like a cad. If you find this behavior finally not worthy of being raised to the level of argument or any other serious response, and if it cannot harm you, then dismiss it and get on with your life. If his behavior is imposing large indignities on your life or if it can harm you financially, professionally, physically, and so on, now is the time to make calm and concerted moves to checkmate him. This is an example of what Tavris calls the moral use of anger. "It's an act of courage to do this," she told me. "And it's the most desirable anger strategy–ironically whether it works or not. Because you know you've tried to do something about a situation that's intolerable to you, and that's a great step for self-esteem."

Stage Two: Loss and Change

The next juncture will be a serious threat to whatever self-esteem you've mustered by anger management. For when your anger has subsided enough that you no longer see red you will seek some understanding, and your first important insight will hit like an all-out assault on your sense of reality.

This is where your existential crisis, in my opinion, is more profound than the one which follows the death, even the sudden death, of a mate. After a death you have to find out: Where do I go from here? You've lost love, and you have to reconstruct your future. That's painful. After the kind of relationship and exit we've been talking about you've also lost love and you also have to find out where to go from here. But over and above that you have to make your peace with the far more difficult question: Where have I been and how did I get there? To ask that question is to look into the cellar of one's soul and find it existentially untrustworthy, and that goes beyond pain and into the annihilation of meaning that produces primordial terror.

Let me put it this way. Suppose you've been close to somebody—married or living with the person—and then he suddenly says, "Go away, I don't want you" in the outrageous manner we've been discussing. You will be forced to wake up to the fact that this is not a nice person, this person is treating you terribly and no caring person would do that—and yet this is the love of your life. What do you do with that? You can rev up your anger and say, This man is a turd, who's sorry to lose him? But if you say that, which will feel like a relief, you then have to face the fact that, for however long, a turd was the love of your life. Then the relief will turn into the realization that you've been living in never-never land, all the while thinking this was Really Living. In one fell swoop that realization will shatter your past, present, and future. Because you will have examined your sense of reality and found it so wanting that you are left with the terrible question: How can I ever trust myself again?

This is the point when you either run for cover (probably into some new lover's arms, a very unwise move) or decide to do the serious work of regaining your trust in yourself. You are now in what Peter Marris in his wise and kind book *Loss and Change* calls a crisis of discontinuity: all your familiar assumptions about life and love appear discredited and from this loss rises despair—but also innovation.[22] The innovation that will move you out of this crisis is to reestablish the continuity of meaning in your life. How do you do this? You do it by reinterpreting those familiar assumptions in light of what has happened to you (at last you get to use reinterpretation for a *healthy* purpose) and weaving them into the new context that now is your life. Some assumptions, like the ones you had about romantic love, will have to be either discarded or radically changed; some will look irrelevant and can be put on hold; some will feel like a red thread of incontestable personal truth running through your life, and they're the ones you gather to you so that you'll have a place to stand from which to repair the lacerated fabric of meaning that now makes life look unmanageable.

I didn't know Marris's book when I reached this point in my exit route. I wish I had. As it is, I can confirm the usefulness of his ideas because I spontaneously did what he suggests, and it worked. At the time if felt like a spiritual tonic. I found myself looking all the way back to my childhood, remembering and underscoring things along the way, often things I hadn't thought about for years. What I see in retrospect is that I was drawing some very fundamental lines for myself concerning the following: Who am I, why am I what I am, what do I choose to continue being? What are the values that matter to me, where do they come from, who are the people I want in my world, what *is* my world, what kind of lover (if any) do I want in that world, and what aspects of all this are essential to me that I'll probably never want to change? In answering these questions I grounded myself in the things that are truly sustaining to me. I began to feel that I was coming back to myself and to my world after a strange and still to be examined detour.

The central theme of *Loss and Change* is that loss disrupts our ability to find meaning in experience, and that grief represents the struggle to retrieve this sense of meaning when circumstances have bewildered or betrayed it. Grief is usually associated with death; Marris's argument is that grief will be evoked not only by death but by any profoundly disruptive loss of meaning. He gives the examples of eviction from a home, dismissal from a job, and rejection from a relationship whose meaning was important. In all cases the severity of grief depends on the degree of disruption. When the loss that brought about the grief is irretrievable, the first step is to accept that loss as something you have to understand and not just as something that happened *to* you. And one of the main things you have to understand is this:

> Although it seems natural to grieve for the loss of someone or something you love, love does not explain grief. The intensity of grief does not vary with the intensity of love, but is often greater when the feeling for the [lost] person was mixed. . . . We have words for many moods relating to the absence of what we love—sadness, nostalgia, pining—which do not describe grief. The fundamental crisis of bereavement arises, not from the loss of others, but the loss of self.[23]

Why does falling into the arms of a new lover not make good this loss of self? Because the attachments that make life meaningful are characteristically specific. So to graft one of those major attachments onto a new person is really to cover up rather than to restore the loss of self. The sense of continuity of meaning on which a person's identity rests is restored through a process of reformulation, not substitution. This reformulation is the all-important function of grief, which detaches the familiar meanings of life from the relationship in which they were embodied and reestablishes them independently of it. If your characteristic response to a crisis of discontinuity is to leap at the nearest likely substitution you may successfully cover up the loss of others, but the most probable result is that your loss of self will thereby become irretrievable and you will suffer lasting emotional damage. In short, the road back to the mental health you lost in the Castle is the working through of the grief that is the gift of your *deus ex machina*.

What can you expect in the working through of grief? Before I outline some main features of the process, let's just get one thing out of the way: the guilt you may feel for being "selfish" while you concentrate your energies on this process. If you get immobilized by reproaches of self-centeredness during this time, be reminded that the job at hand is to retrieve and reconstitute your own identity. So if you or someone else suggests that you should be "getting on with your life," know that this is precisely and in the most meaningful way what you are doing. At this juncture it is the *only* deeply meaningful activity in which you can be engaged. That doesn't mean you must think about yourself all the time (which can get awfully boring); it means that the working through of grief is your central activity for the present.

Marris summarizes the typical signs of grief as: (1) physical distress and worse health; (2) an inability to surrender the past—expressed, for example, by brooding over memories, clinging to possessions, being unable to comprehend the loss, and feelings of unreality; (3) withdrawal into apathy; and (4) hostility against others, against fate, or turned in upon oneself. Grief, he says, is a mental wound that heals slowly and leaves scars. First, there will be a state of shock; when the numbness of the shock has worn off there will be acute pain; then the attacks of sharp distress will gradually become less frequent and the despair duller, until at last they hit only on rare occasions. If the loss is severe the acute phase normally lasts for several weeks and abates slowly and intermittently for up to a year or more. Marris concludes from his interviews that you can expect the process of recovery from grief to take two years.

If this process fails or is aborted, what can you expect? The prognosis is not encouraging. You can expect your life to become "mummified in a phantasy of the past" or empty and meaningless behind your facade of keeping busy or obsessed by the unresolved conflict that comes from your permanent crisis of discontinuity.[24]

Can you get help? Certainly. You need a supportive structure within which you can articulate and contain your crisis as you work it through. That supportive structure has three mainstays: work, counseling, and friends. "The best remedy for a bruised heart is not, as so many people seem to think, repose upon a manly bosom," notes Dorothy Sayers in one of her mysteries. "Much more efficacious are honest work, physical activity, and the sudden acquisition of wealth."[25] Work is likely to be your overriding mainstay during this time. The reality that the attachments that made life meaningful cannot readily be transferred has a flip side which here comes to your aid: Work is the place where you can be your old self again because work is the one set of relationships you have whose meaning is not affected by the loss of your lover—unless you are unfortunate enough to have been working with him. The vagaries of love being what they are, one is probably prudent to keep work and love reasonably separate in one's life. The woman who is turfed out of the Castle that also contains her place of work is truly bereft.

Counseling by some outside person is useful at this time because a stranger who understands grief in general, and who stands in some kind of acknowledged therapeutic role, can probably give more support than friends to the working out of grief itself. Because this kind of support is, in a sense, impersonal, it leaves the personal resolution of the crisis where it should be left—with you—while offering the much-needed reassurance that your crisis is natural and that you will find a resolution in time.[26] I strongly recommend finding a person who can zap you with the truth while you are trying to answer that necessary question, "Where have I been?" I also strongly recommend that this person be a woman and a feminist.

Friends. I include in this category your family members if you are fortunate enough to count them as friends; they are of particular value here because with them you can more easily look to your roots for support in reconstructing your sense of meaning in life. What does a woman who is working through her grief need from friends? She needs a sense of practical and unassuming support.

She needs to know that her friends understand the nature of her cirsis, that they are ready to offer companionship and useful help whenever they can, and that they respect the ultimate privacy of grief.

There are things friends can do for you during this time, there are things they can't and shouldn't do. Learn to recognize which things are which, and who among your friends is doing them. And stay away from women who say they "share your problem" but are really stuck in a spiral of recrimination.

The best procedure, in my experience, is to surround yourself with people whose values you respect and who have *heart*. This last point is very important, because being around such people will come as food to the hungry pigeon we heard about earlier. Life with an addict is above all sterile, rigid, and untrustworthy. Therefore, people who have warm and encompassing natures and who celebrate life in all its variety are just what you need around you at this point. To me, they felt like spring rain in the desert. I soaked them up and felt more myself again.

Stage Three: Gain

The last stage is where you lay to rest your ghosts and anchor down the insights you've gained. With regard to the man who was your cohabitant in the Castle, I suggest that you henceforth think of him as a catalyst. I've seen too many women get caught in the trap of thinking that because they are learning great lessons in their exit from the Castle, he must somehow be a Great Teacher. That is nonsense. He is not venerable at this point, he is passé. Technically, a catalyst is a substance that either speeds up or slows down a chemical reaction, but which itself undergoes no permanent chemical change thereby. He may or may not have changed since your exit from the Castle. The question is really not your concern. Thinking of him as a teacher amounts to continuing the relationship by other means: being preoccupied by thoughts about what he is doing, how he is feeling, what he is learning, and so on, all of which is irrelevant. The meaning to be restored is yours, not his. If he is getting on with his end, fine; if he isn't, fine.

Thinking of him as a catalyst keeps your attention where it belongs–on you and your life.

What insights can you anchor down? That you have a tendency to get hooked into relationships of unhealthy dependency. That feeling more comfortable in a nurturing role with possible lovers attracts you to men with infantile needs, and them to you. So they get to be infants and you get to be caretaker, and that's the insight you anchor down because you don't want to hook into that scenario again. Here's another story from my annals of life in the Castle that bears on this point. I was heading for the door in my friend's house, on my way to the plane that would fly me out of Vancouver just after my Ideal Romance had come tumbling down, when the phone rang. I answered it, and without preamble my father's voice said, "I have just one question for you. When are you going to bring home an adult?" I started to chuckle. He continued. "The first one was an adolescent, but at least he had the excuse of actually being an adolescent. The next one was also an adolescent, only he was thirty years old. The last one–approaching middle age and infantile. So I want you to go out that door with your chin up and start looking for an adult."

"At the airport?" I asked.

"At the airport."

"I don't think I know how to recognize an adult."

"That has become manifestly evident, but they're out there. Learn to recognize them, and no time like the present."

It was so absurd that I agreed to do it. I left for the airport feeling fortified and still chuckling. I had nearly an hour to wait after checking in. "Okay," I said to myself. "Anything that's male and looks older than fifteen I'm studying." My first realization was that my father was correct: I didn't know what to look for. Then I began to realize that most of the men looked to me as if they had a "Feed Me" sign hanging around their neck. Feed me with attention. So I began to study the men who did not have those signs. They were an interesting lot, though not in great numbers. They looked self-contained without looking self-absorbed. They looked quiet without looking needy or softly demanding. They didn't push on all the air around them but seemed to move through space with their own grace. And they looked interested in the life around them for itself and not for how it related to them. I labeled them "adults" and boarded the plane, where my exercise happily continued when I found myself seated next to one of them. It was a midnight, transcontinental flight, which we spent in a long and satisfying conversation. When I left the plane at dawn I had an invitation to visit him in India, where he was a schoolteacher, and the invigorating knowledge that I had recognized my very first adult. I have never since had reason to change my general criteria of classification.

What can we say about your relationship in the Castle that will lay it to rest? I think Peele provides an adequate epitaph: "The couple's closeness was an artificial creation, based on their having been available to each other at a time when they shared a special need."[27] Must you see the specter of addiction in any signs of intensity in future encounters with lovers? On the contrary. Addictive passions are not vivid or intense. As you should know by now, they are passive, shallow, and banal. They are also common. This being so, the following question becomes legitimate: If the difference between a psychiatric disorder in action and the Myth of Romantic Love's ideal of True Love between man and woman is so difficult to distinguish, just who is sick?

As for yourself, take heart. The future looks bright. One woman put it well when she laughed and said, "*Now* when people talk about romance and True Love, I can say, yeah, I've been there. And that's something to be able to say in our society, it's a great thing to be able to say. Especially if you don't want to go back."

And you won't go back. Alice Koller saw it clearly in *An Unknown Woman*, the journal of her quest to reshape her own life:

> Oh, god, what I put up with for the sake of what I called "loving." My hands veil my eyes. Then quickly I look up again. No need to shudder about it. I can't be that way again. Can't. That doesn't mean I vow not to be. It means that I, what I am so far, am not like that any longer.[28]

The need that got you into the Castle is very grave. But it's also very instructive. As one woman told me with a shiver, "It's really dreadful. It makes you feel: this is the being I always wanted to have; you are giving it to me, please don't take it away. One of the great things I've learned is that he can indeed take the whole damned thing away, and I can still feel *fine*."

At the end of your *deus ex machina,* if you have started on your quest, you can look forward to seeing romantic love with knowing eyes. To taking it or leaving it, but never to let it take you to the Castle again. You can move into love with reasonable assurance that this time it will be with an adult. And you can do all this with the confidence that comes from having "been there" in the worst way—*and* survived. By dint of your own courage and effort. You will be able to say with my friend the actress in chapter one, who wrote this note to me when she reached this point, "I have met my Waterloo. (signed) Wellington!"

II EXIT THE CASTLE–
To Authentic Passion

7. Love: Theory

In Part I we reexamined the myths that make up our customary vision of love. Such a reexamination is necessary if we want to experience love in new ways. Because, unless we can look at the Myth of Romantic Love with knowing eyes instead of as the only path to love, it will continue to rule our love lives in the manner I call Maslow's Hammer: We sigh, "This must be love!" Psychologist Abraham Maslow says, "If the only tool you have is a hammer, you tend to treat everything as if it were a nail." If a person cannot conceive of a new way to love, then he or she surely will remain stuck in the old one. I also think that if our visions and beliefs about love change, so will our experiences of it.

In Part II, we'll explore some alternate models of love and of passion, and so become astronomers. They view the heavens, observe planetary motion, and from that motion predict the existence of a new planet. Eventually, that planet is itself observed. We can view the interaction of "real" men and "real" women in the prescribed "attraction of opposites," which the Myth calls True Love, and try to predict how love might look if we got beyond those stereotypes and to the human core. And we can trust that when we have new models of love and passion to believe in, they will come alive in our experience.

Autonomy and Love

A person's concept of love does not exist in a vacuum. It follows from how that person conceives of his or her identity and its connection to the cosmos. The kind of love you are likely to experience is determined by two prime factors: your worldview (the way you think of "reality") and your self-view (the way you think of your "I" in relation to that reality). Since patriarchal ideology has given us several thousand years of corrupt notions of relationship—with each other, with the natural world, with the universe—we hardly have a language of self and connection that is *not* corrupt. If one is writing a book that attempts to rescue love from the clutches of patriarchy, one must therefore do likewise with the idea of autonomy.

I had read many books and thought many thoughts before it dawned on me that autonomy as I conceived of it is not how the word is defined in dictionaries. This should not have surprised me, but it did. I was appalled at what I actually found in the dictionaries, and it was obvious to me that the difference between "their" autonomy and "my" autonomy would have to be spelled out. So here we go, and I think you'll see that "their" autonomy is the perfect basis for love à la the Myth of Romantic Love, with its sexual politics of distance and control between "opposites," while autonomy as I conceived of it is necessary as the basis for the kind of love I am going to advocate.

The word autonomous comes from the Greek words for self (*autos*) and law (*nomos*). To me, this has always meant being self-governing: taking responsibility for oneself in the context of others and the cosmos. Taking the word "responsible" literally from its Latin root meaning "requiring an answer," I see an autonomous person as someone who seeks to know her or his particular individuality in responsible (self-correcting) connection to others and ultimately to the universe. To me, autonomy means the continuing exploration of one's self, while holding that self accountable to everything that is not oneself. In such a scheme, autonomy and relationship are inherently connected: You can't have one without the other.

In this conception of autonomy, I depart radically from traditional Western thinking. Instead of seeing autonomy in terms of connection, this tradition sees it in terms of separation. It starts, as I do, with the root meaning of being autonomous as being self-governing. But, as dictionaries show us, it then goes on to define self-governing as "conforming to its own laws only and not subject to higher ones," and as "functioning independently without control by others." Individualism is therefore seen, not as being an entity in one's own right, distinctly different from others, but rather as "the leading of one's life in one's own way without regard for others."[1] Here, being an individual stands in direct conflict with one's connection to others. Connection is seen, not in terms of caring, but in terms of control (either being controlled by others or controlling them) and the very notion of relationship becomes poisoned. In such a scheme autonomy and love are fundamentally opposed: each is a threat to the other.

When I first was struck by the realization that autonomy, as defined in our dictionaries, is a "bad word" to me, I had a small fortuitous opportunity to test my own idea of autonomy as a "good word" with a large and varied group of women. The ranch on which I live has an annual Christmas cookie-swap, where women from all over Jackson Hole gather. I went to a number of these women, one by one, and said: "If you will, I am going to say a word to you. Please tell me (1) whether you have a positive or negative reaction to it, and (2) what it means to you." To a woman, they said that "autonomous" was a positive word and that it meant the search for one's true self, but not in isolation from others or from the world. Most of them even quoted John Donne's line that "no man is an island." This little exercise prompted a general discussion at the party, where we agreed that we could take Donne fairly literally at "man" and that the island problem is one of the tragedies of becoming masculine in our culture.

Having said that, I add that one of my favorite explorations of autonomy is by a man. In *The Betrayal of the Self* psychoanalyst Arno Gruen argues that "being autonomous does not result from having *ideas* of one's own importance, nor from the necessity for independence."[2] To Gruen, the key to autonomy is *attitude,* and we will find autonomy if we allow our sympathy and love for others to flower. There is no method or technique that leads to a real self, he says, because individuals are unique and the paths leading to autonomy therefore diverse. Though friends and supporters are essential, each of us will have to find his or her own path, and the responsibility for the choice of a path must be our own.[3]

In my conception of autonomy, to seek such a path is to become more fully alive—to oneself, to others, to the universe. And it is to have the universe return the favor. My key to autonomy is my own version of Vincent van Gogh's affirmation to his brother that the best way to know oneself and God is to love many things.

In the matter of love between two people, this conception of autonomy means that if you don't include yourself in the equation of loving, you are not capable of love. But if you don't also include the other, you also are not capable of love. In this equation women traditionally err in the first part and men in the second. Women tend to deny the self, while men deny the other in the activity of loving. In popular parlance this translates into the often-heard claim that women love "too much" and men "too little" or not at all. In other words, to the extent that women and men do this, they both love poorly.

If autonomy is central to loving, we need to talk in terms of love as a relationship in which both people are subjects—both are empowered and mutually respectful. One person does not exist "for" the other but as a distinct entity in her or his own right, to be valued as such and not merely as a means to an end or an adjunct. Thus love becomes a process of mutual recognition, of recognizing as well as being recognized by the other as a separate person who is like us and yet distinct.[4] The delight of genuine love lies precisely in experiencing one's autonomous self in increasingly intimate connection to the beloved's different and equally important autonomous self.

The Paradox of Love

The problem for those of us who seek to experience love in the mode I have just described and advocated is that such a concept of love is inconsistent with our dominant worldview. A worldview is a model of reality built of our implicit and explicit assumptions about how the universe works. It tells us what is "real," what is "normal," what "makes sense," and what "sane" people believe and do. It also tells us what "real" love is. I put all these quotations marks here in order to indicate that there also are other ways of conceiving of reality, normalcy, and sanity and, of course, love.

Our Western dominant worldview would define the kind of love I am advocating as a paradox: contradictory, unbelievable, or absurd, and certainly inconsistent with common experience. Byron's observation that man's love is of man's life a thing apart is true not only of men in general in our culture but of our culture's view of reality. To "real" thinking, as to a "real" man, love *is* a thing apart—from what's important. The professor who exclaimed to a colleague who wanted to teach a class on love was speaking for our dominant worldview when he called love, and anyone who purported to teach it, "irrelevant!"[5]

The Mechanistic Worldview

What kind of mind would consider the study of human love irrelevant? The kind that says of something, "I have measured it, therefore I know it." And, conversely, "If I *can't* measure it, it isn't important (if it exists, which I doubt)." This is the kind of mind, as Kenneth Burke used to say, that thinks ultimate knowledge of reality will be achieved when we know the name and address of everything in the universe. Such a mind knows reality by means of abstraction, quantification, measurement, and control. To know something is to distance oneself from it; real knowledge, by definition, comes precisely from such an act of detachment. That's what "objectivity" means.

The idea that you must distance yourself from something in order to grasp its nature more carefully seems odd indeed, and it clearly does not bode well for intimacy and love. Nevertheless, this idea was central to the way of perceiving reality that was fashioned in seventeenth-century Western Europe by the Scientific Revolution. In the worldview of the Scientific Revolution, what is real is that which can be broken down into basic building blocks of matter, and the acid test of existence is quantifiability as measured by a detached observer.[6] This is still the dominant worldview in the West. So the kind of mind that would consider the study of human love irrelevant is the kind that now is dominant in the West.

A worldview with this method of deciding what is real and important thus leaves the human sciences with little or nothing worth saying about the deeper aspects of human experience, since these aspects do not readily lend themselves to quantification. Preeminent in the land of this scientific mutism is the experience of human love. In the human sciences love, if it isn't dismissed outright as not important, is all too often studied as mere appetite (which *can* be measured) or according to "complementary needs" hypotheses about the "attraction of opposites." Here we regularly find psychologists running around in circles among sex stereotypes in order to prove the obvious. "When do opposites attract?" asks a typical study. "When they are opposite in sex and sex-role attitudes."[7] Surprise. Worse yet, the results of this kind of investigation are then too often offered to the public in the form of "clinically proven programs" and "Intimacy Formulas" for sure-fire success in (romantic) love.[8] Of these approaches, outright dismissal is probably preferable.

If love fares poorly with the materialist worldview now dominant in the West, it does likewise with that worldview's dominant idea of personal identity. Which, as we know from the Broverman study of mental health and from our dictionaries, is the idea of the male "I" as defined in separation. According to this view healthy psychological growth from childhood to maturity is traced along a single line of progression from inequality to equality, where attachment is associated with inequality and development is linked to separation.[9] Thus, to become an adult with a fully certified sense of self, the normal male must emphasize separation over connection, difference over similarity, boundaries over union, self-sufficiency over dependency.[10] In fact, as has been noted by many, the devaluation of the need for the other in relationship becomes a touchstone of the adult male's sense of identity.

The high value placed by the materialist worldview on separation as central to the normal or healthy development of personal identity has rightly been challenged as providing instead a pathogenic potential for detachment and disengagement.[11] It also provides a pathogenic potential for love as we are discussing it here. That is, it makes such love difficult if not impossible. The normal male who has developed the proper sense of self along these lines will approach the kind of love we're talking about with trepidation, if not outright panic. Because such a person will experience intimacy as a threat to his sense of self. And he will experience feelings of emotional attunement, on which such love is built, as moments of existential crisis.

A man I once was involved with poignantly expressed what I think must have been this sense of existential panic. I had become confused and upset by what I saw as his pattern of response to me. I characterized it to him as erratic in the sense that sometimes behavior from me that felt like just "being me" would make him smile and open up and feel right there. But more often the same kind of spontaneous behavior from me would make him look scattered and hunted and not there; and then I would feel as though I had just done something wrong, only I couldn't figure out what. This was disconcerting and painful to me, as he could see. I remember his response to this day (though I didn't understand it at the time) because even then it felt somehow quintessential to what often seemed to happen in my involvements with men. After a thoughtful pause he said, "No wonder you feel that way. I feel something, hear something from you, some idea or emotional insight, or emotion, and I say, 'Yeah! Wow!' Then I think I have to give everything to you, or you're going to ask me for everything, and then I . . . withdraw." My question then was, what is "everything"? Now, I think the answer is: Thinking I have to give "everything" to you because I feel a strong connection to you means that emotional attunement with you feels dangerously close to losing myself in you—therefore, in the name of self-preservation, I withdraw.

From all of this I conclude, sadly, that the extent to which a person is influenced by our dominant worldview's perception of reality, and especially by its perception of individual identity, is the extent to which that person will be incapable of love.

Except, that is, of the kind promoted by the Myth of Romantic Love. Here, the person and the mode of loving are well-matched. Because, like our dominant worldview, this kind of love is based on abstractions and distance (the idealization of the beloved) rather than on mutuality and intimacy; on objectification and control (the game of conquest, surrender, and "protection") instead of connection and caring. This is why the major defenders of the Myth of Romantic Love and the sentimental promoters of the "Romantic Revival" are the men and women of the New Right, who correctly see the "attraction of opposites" as a match made in heaven according to the Book of Genesis. And why we so often see on these defenders of patriarchal love the rigid face of domination; of protector and protectee, locked into the dominance/submission complementarity bond with each party claiming de facto master status, each unable to make "live" contact with the other because he or she is experienced as an object to be "protected" or "handled" (depending on which sex is doing it) instead of as an open entity in his or her own right to be mutually engaged with.

But for men like the one I was involved with, who was of a sensitive and generally responsive disposition not cut out for domination, the fated response to the panic attacks brought on by the experience of intimacy seems to be spasmodic or permanent withdrawal.

When even the best of men feel apprehensive about intimacy and emotional attunement, when attachment directly threatens their sense of identity, it becomes clear that we sorely need a new model of the psyche; a model, as Jessica Benjamin proposes, in which the self truly seeks to know the outside world and longs for genuine contact with the other in relationship.[12] We need to endorse a way of being in the world where the sense of self is not lost but instead heightened through the pleasure of engagement.

I think this is what van Gogh meant when he said that the best way to know God is to love many things. It's also the best way to know oneself. And it is far more delightful than the way of disengagement—which, first among its conspicuous liabilities, is rooted in anxiety instead of *joie de vivre.*

A New Worldview

We need another way of perceiving reality and the self within it. We need a new and more holistic worldview in which love as intimate connection between two autonomous peers would not be considered inconsistent with reality, absurd, or irrelevant. Fortunately, such a worldview is emerging in our time. We've heard it expressed by the women at the cookie swap. This new worldview contradicts the claims made upon reality by the one we got with the Scientific Revolution and is, ironically, most clearly stated by modern physics. How can one not delight in a world where revolutionary shifts in dominant worldviews and people's consciousness can be traced simultaneously in cookie swaps and theoretical physics?

The voice of the cookie swap is the voice elucidated by Carol Gilligan's ground-breaking work on women's view of what is important in life. This voice describes a way of being in the world that is very different from our dominant one, and it offers new images of the self in relationship. What is women's worldview? Women tend to see the world as comprised of relationships rather than of people standing alone; they see a world that coheres through human connection, where human beings are members of a network of relationships on whose continuation we all depend. They see personal identity as defined in attachment and care rather than in detachment and individual achievement, and the act of self-assertion as an act of communication rather than of control. They see autonomy in terms of being faithful to self and others, and morality as an injunction to act responsively toward self and others and thus to sustain connection.[13] In short, women tend to agree with biologist Jonas Salk that the fundamental unifying principle in the cosmos seems to be relationship, and that in detachment lies not only an error in perception of reality but a danger to the survival of the world.

This worldview is radically different from the mechanistic one, which generally has ignored, belittled, or ridiculed it for being "unrealistic" and certainly not important. But it turns out to look quite realistic and very important to the worldview of modern physics, whose advent is forging revolutionary changes in our concepts of reality.[14]

When modern physicists started to probe nature at the level of atomic reality, they got one surprise after another. Out went the basic building blocks of matter so dear to the mind of the detached observer, because they do not exist at the atomic level. Atoms consists of particles, but particles are not made of any material stuff. "When we observe them," says physicist Fritjof Capra, "we never see any substance; what we observe are dynamic patterns continually changing into one another—a continuous dance of energy."[15] In modern physics, reports Nobel Prize physicist Werner Heisenberg, one of the original discoverers of the laws of atomic physics, "one has now divided the world not into different groups of objects but into different groups of connections. . . . What can be distinguished is the kind of connection which is primarily important in a certain phenomenon."[16]

Gone, too, is the detached observer. The old division between the observer and the observed cannot be made in the world of atomic physics. Here the world appears as a complicated web of relations between the various parts of the whole, and these relations include the observer in an essential way.[17] This fundamental truth about nature has prompted one eminent modern physicist to suggest replacing the word "observer" with the word "participator." Nothing is more important about atomic physics, says John Wheeler, than "that it destroys the concept of the world as 'sitting out there,' with the observer safely separated from it by a 20-centimeter slab of plate glass." The discoveries of modern physics mean that "the universe will never afterward be the same," he concludes, because they have shown that "in some strange sense, the universe is a participatory universe."[18]

I state it unequivocally. I love modern physics. Let me count the ways. . . . I love it for its elegance and for its breathtaking scope. I love it for its spirited quest to fathom the workings of the universe, and for the sheer aesthetic appeal of its description of the beauty of nature's underlying design. I love it for its sense of wonder, and for its sense of humor when it encounters nature at its seemingly most bizarre. I love it for its nerve, for its poetry, for its truth. And I love it for what it makes possible for love itself. Because I infinitely prefer to think of love as a continuous dance of energy, as a relationship of mutual self-renewal and self-transcendence in participation with a life-affirming universe.[19]

That inspires me. The grubby little world of "attraction of opposites" and clinically proven programs for meeting your "complementary needs" does not inspire me at all. And, I say, if love is not inspiring, we are not doing it justice. Such is my love affair with physics, and with love. I say goodbye to that grubby little world with a rephrasing of words by William James—who, I like to think, would have agreed with me: Genuine love lives by sympathies and admirations, not by the imposed dissimilarities of the "attraction of opposites." Under all misleading wrappings, foremost among which is sex-role complementarity, it pounces unerringly upon the human core.[20]

What Love Deserves from Us

And now, in the spirit of William James, on to what love deserves from us. We arrive at one of the most promising theories of love I've yet encountered. I use it as one of the bases for my own. It is Jessica Benjamin's intersubjectivity theory. She asks, How is a person's sense of self consolidated? How does one come to know, "I am me?" The answer is that one comes to know in the process of being recognized by an other; by being seen as someone distinct and unique and being responded to affirmatively as that.

A person comes to feel that "I am the doer who does, I am the author of my acts," by being with another person who recognizes her acts, her feelings, her intentions, her existence, her independence. Recognition is the essential response, the constant companion of assertion. The subject declares, "I am, I do," and then waits for the response, "You are, you have done." Recognition is, thus, reflexive; it includes not only the other's confirming response, but also how we find ourselves in that response.[21]

Recognition, as I understand it, is a very specific type of feedback. In the most profound sense, recognition has to be feedback that is *news* in the sense that it could make a difference to what you think you know about yourself. Therefore a mere echo or a mirror reflection or a predictable sex-role stereotype response will not be useful, but will instead tend to objectify you and lock you into whatever image is being reflected. And active flattery, in the sense of only feeding back what you most want to hear, is even worse, because it will isolate you in one very narrow loop of feedback. In the matter of exploring a sense of self, flattery and mirroring quite literally will get you nowhere. Recognition has to do with getting clarified in our sense of self, by being perceived and responded to from a perspective that is different from our own—similar enough to understand us, yet separate enough to offer by its possible incongruity a new truth.

In short, recognition has to do with being and feeling discovered to yourself. As in, "I am the doer who does, and sometimes I do stupid things . . ." (pause) "You are, and you just did a stupid thing"; but also as in (pause), "You are, and this wasn't one of your stupid things, because . . ." The experience of self-rediscovery in a moment of recognition produces the leap of delight that comes from feeling you've just been given a gift of new insight about yourself which confirms: "Ah, yes! I recognize that this, too, is who I am." Intimates who can give you such gifts are those with whom you share what a close friend wonderfully calls "areas of luminosity."

The essence of all love, as I conceive of it, is a mutual process informed by the actual and potential presence of such moments of recognition, where both persons feel cherished because of what is discovered. What this process requires is that each person be a subject. It requires that each must see the other as an agent, a doer, in his or her own right; as a distinct but interrelated being. Neither exists "for" the other or as an adjunct to the other, a means for "meeting my needs." Each is autonomous, as I take the meaning of that word. This means that each person is seen as a separate self, alike and yet his or her own, who is equally important as the author of his or her own self, and who is valued for just that.

The following story of psychiatrist M. Scott Peck illustrates the difficulty we so often seem to have in fully approaching the autonomy of those we are close to.

> Not too long ago in a couples group I heard one of the members state that the "purpose and function" of his wife was to keep their house neat and him well fed. I was aghast at what seemed to me his painfully blatant male chauvinism.

Struck by what seemed this man's "painfully blatant male chauvinism," Peck turned to the other members of the group. To his horror, he found that all the men and women were of a like mind:

> All of them defined the purpose and function of their husbands or wives in reference to themselves; all of them failed to perceive that their mates might have an existence basically separate from their own or any kind of destiny apart from their marriage. "Good grief," I exclaimed, "its no wonder that you are all having difficulties in your marriages, and you'll continue to have difficulties until you come to recognize that each of you has your own separate destiny to fulfill."

The members of the group reacted somewhat aggressively to Peck's outburst and demanded that he in turn define the purpose and function of *his* wife. "The purpose and function of Lily," he responded, "is to grow to be the most of which she is capable, not for my benefit but for her own and to the glory of God."[22]

Although I might prefer to say, "and to the affirmation of life," I couldn't agree more. The purpose and function of an individual is intrinsic to himself or herself, and love is the process of mutually furthering that purpose and function in each other—by recognizing it and cherishing it. *This* is the sense in which we truly can say, "This is bigger than both of us."

This vision of mutual recognition between equal subjects gives rise to a new logic. Benjamin calls it the logic of paradox: of sustaining the tension between contradictory forces. "Perhaps the most fateful paradox is the one posed by our simultaneous need for recognition and independence: that the other subject is outside our control and yet we need him." There's no way around this paradox of love, because the recognition we need must be authentic in order to make us feel known. And in order to be authentic, it must be spontaneous—literally, of free will, acting by its own impulse. Because if you don't get it freely but instead through demand, repression, manipulation, or knee-jerk conformity to a gender stereotype, you will lose the very essence of recognition: genuine contact with the other. That contact can be genuine only if the other is allowed to be an original self. To embrace this paradox of separateness and connection is our first step toward unraveling the bonds of love. "This means not to undo our ties to others but rather to disentangle them; to make of them not shackles but circuits of recognition."[23]

Making the bonds of love into circuits of recognition leads to what Milan Kundera calls "co-feeling"—the ability to share feelings and intentions without demanding control, to experience sameness without obliterating differences. Experiences of co-feeling are experiences of "being with" that arise out of a continually evolving awareness of difference, out of a sense of intimacy felt as occurring between "the *two* of us" as separate beings together. "The fact that self and other are not merged is precisely what makes experiences of merging have such high emotional impact. The externality of the other makes one feel one is truly being 'fed,' getting nourishment from the outside, rather than supplying everything for oneself."[24]

The leap of delight one feels in a moment of mutual recognition arises from the sense that inner experience can be joined. I know it as a feeling of simultaneous expansiveness and grounding. It comes from the spontaneously felt connection with a separate other where you both recognize that this *other* mind can share *my* feeling.[25] I'll give you two recent examples from my own life.

I recently went to New York on business. While there I visited a friend who is a composer of very unusual and captivating music that often is based on children's literature. When I arrived at his place he was just finishing work on a score based on the novel *Heidi* for performance at an upcoming children's concert. "Ah, *Heidi*," I said. And told him how as a child in Denmark I had first encountered that story, and how what above all had made an impression on me was the description of Heidi's arrival on the mountain where her grandfather lived. I, a child from one of the flattest countries on earth, had never seen a mountain. Nor had I seen the huge conifers described. "And the sound!" I exclaimed. "The sound of the wind in those trees high on the mountain when she first went to sleep in her grandfather's loft. That sound inspired in me an intense wish to go and hear it." My friend stopped as if in suspended animation and his face lit up, then he took me by the shoulders and led me to the table with the open score. There, as the sound that set the mood for the whole composition, was what I for many years had called to myself, simply, "the Heidi sound."

Story number two: While I was in New York I went to see the enormous exhibition of paintings by Georgia O'Keeffe. It was jammed with people, and I wandered hither and yon, looking at some of the famous paintings that I recognized. Then, in a big room with many paintings I did not know, my roving glance over the sea of people's heads suddenly was riveted by one small painting. The impact it made on me was so strong that I forgot about everything else in the room as I moved up to take it in. It was a small white painting with just one exquisite curving black line, called "Winter Road." It spoke to me in a way that felt palpable. When I returned to Wyoming I went to visit my mother, who is a devotee of O'Keeffe's work and who was unable to come to New York. "You were right," I said. "The exhibition is fabulous. And there's this *one* painting! It's so stunning and evocative that I can hardly tell you." And she said, "'Winter Road'?" Out of such luminous moments of recognition comes the essence of love as I understand it. This is why I tend to say that the core of love must be delight.

Such moments cannot be manufactured or manipulated into being. They occur only spontaneously, only if both people are acting freely as distinct and different selves. The experience of merging in such a moment of co-feeling does indeed have such high emotional impact *because* it occurs between the two of us as separate beings together. And when such moments occur between two autonomous, separate beings who have the potential together for the kind of love I am exploring in this part of the book, the experience of merging produces the dazzling and illuminating connection to the core of one's being that generates what I call aspiring passion.

Is Gender Necessary?

Is gender necessary? This question is posed by science fiction writer Ursula K. LeGuin in a discussion of why she wrote *The Left Hand of Darkness*.[26] I find it a very interesting question. Having come this far with me, you probably have more than a sneaking suspicion as to how I am going to answer it.

First off, I define the term "gender" to denote whether a person is male or female. I use it instead of "sex" because that term often refers to sexual activity, as in "having sex." I also prefer to use "gender role" rather than "sex role" for the same reason, though the latter is now so common that I use either, depending on context. In this chapter I'll stick with gender and gender roles.

In answering the question, I find it most useful to ask another one: "For what?" For love? Obviously not. People of either gender clearly love people of either gender, sometimes of both genders, erotically and not. For a happy life? The proposition is dubious, since gender roles plague our lives and especially our love lives. For becoming parents? Again, obviously not. People who, for whatever reasons, cannot have children together still become parents. For propogating the species? Yes, though we could do it far more parsimoniously than we do; but, yes.

After ruminating on this question, I am led to the conclusion that gender is necessary for only two things: to produce offspring, and to produce the culture we now know. That culture is based on the deep structure of gender opposition—which, as we have seen since the framing of Eve in Genesis, has recast the knowledge of difference as invidious comparison.[27] The structure of binary opposition, which our culture has built on the fact of two genders, became so deep as to be rendered invisible. Thus, for example, more than two thousand years after Genesis, we have the birth of the United States. Here, a nation proclaiming to be conceived in liberty and in its Declaration of Independence intending to create a government whose just powers derive from the consent of the governed, could still leave the female half of the governed constitutionally without such consent—and not seem to notice that this rather glaring omission ipso facto cancelled its intent. This kind of historical evidence can lead a person toward cynicism, but let's try to move in a more positive direction. My point here is this: The fact of gender in the human race does not *necessitate* the fact of a culture based on gender polarity. It merely makes it possible, and this dangerous possibility should be taken into account when we idealize *la différence.*

There are other ways of conceiving a culture than on the basis of gender polarity, and it would behoove us to start thinking of them. There are also other ways of structuring our private lives and those, too, we should try to imagine. Because our gender polarity is so entrenched, this kind of thinking requires a leap of imagination. I offer two here, one cultural and one private, in the mode of the Gedanken (thought) experiments made famous by modern physics, especially by "Einstein's elevator" and "Schrödinger's cat." Thought-experiments are performed in the mind, not in the laboratory, because they involve probing a deeper reality than can be produced in a lab. Therefore they begin, "Suppose we . . ."

Experiment I: A Genderless Society

I agree with LeGuin that supposition is one of the essential functions of science fiction, which lends itself very creatively to leaps of imagination that might produce profound changes in our habitual way of thinking—or, as she puts it, metaphors for what our language has no words for as yet, experiments in imagination. *The Left Hand of Darkness* is such an experiment. It asks, "Suppose we eliminated gender. What would be left?"

The novel takes place on a planet called Gethan, whose inhabitants are human—but with a significant difference. Instead of our continuous sexuality, the Gethenians have an estrus period called *kemmer* which lasts for one-fifth of every month, when it dominates them completely. The vigorous sexual activity of *kemmer* is expected and approved of by everybody. When they are not in *kemmer* Gethenians are sexually inactive and impotent. They are also androgynous in the sense of physically being neither male nor female. Into this imaginary culture that she has made "totally free of sex-roles because there is no, absolutely no, physiological sex-distinction," LeGuin sends a conventional young man from Earth. He reports back that in the first phase of *kemmer* the individual remains completely androgynous. The sexual impulse is tremendously strong in this phase, and controls the entire personality. When the individual finds a partner in *kemmer,* hormonal secretion is stimulated until either a male or female hormonal dominance is established. Then the partner, triggered by the change, takes on the other sexual role. The Gethenians have no predisposition to either sexual role in *kemmer;* they don't know whether they will become the male or female, and have no choice in the matter. The culmination phase of *kemmer* lasts from two to five days, during which sexual drive and capacity are at maximum. It ends fairly abruptly, and if conception has not taken place, the two people return to the latent phase and the cycle begins anew. If the person in the female role was impregnated, hormonal activity continues and for the gestation and lactation periods this person remains female.

When lactation is over the female once again becomes a perfect androgyne. No physiological habit is established, and the mother of several children may be the father of several more.

Why did LeGuin invent these peculiar people? Not just so the book could contain the sentence, "The king was pregnant," though she admits to being fond of it. She eliminated gender, she says, in order to find out what would be left. "Whatever was left would be, presumably, simply human. It would define the area that is shared by men and women alike."

What were the results of LeGuin's experiment? She herself says that they are inconclusive, as they would have to be. What she proposes as the three major results are therefore not definitive, but they are suggestive: First, the absence of war. Second, the absence of exploitation—of women, of the weak, of the earth. Third, the absence of sexuality as a continuous social factor. Except for the last result, they are debatable as stated, even as they are provocative to ponder. The most her experiment says, she suggests, is something like this: "If we were socially ambisexual, if men and women were completely and genuinely equal in their social roles, equal legally and economically, equal in freedom, in responsibility, and in self-esteem, then society would be a very different thing." That seems undebatable. Equally undebatable is her conclusion that, without gender polarity, we might have a world in which the dualism of value (superior/inferior, ruler/ruled, owner/owned, user/used, and so on) that now divides us against ourselves might give way to a more promising modality of integration and integrity.

I like to think of her experiment when I view everyday life. As I read newspapers, I ask, "How would this news look if we did not have gender polarity? Would it even exist to be reported on?" On the rare occasions when I watch television mainstays like "Dallas" or "Falcon Crest" or "Knotts Landing," I ask—well, I don't even have to ask. Gender polarity at its ugliest and silliest is so rampant that without it, what would we have? No "Dallas" or "Falcon Crest" or "Knotts Landing," and not much else that's now on TV.

Experiment 2: A Love Story

The second thought-experiment invites us to imagine love in its purest sense. It is a love story that shows that cherishing the purpose and function of a beloved can rise above even gender fixity. Few of us get to experience this kind of love story precisely, because few of us get to live a life like the one lived by Jan Morris, who lived and loved as both a man and a woman—and with the same person as his and then her continuing mate. What happened to Morris is indeed "one of the most fascinating experiences that ever befell a human being."[28] I think it is also one of the most beautiful experiences of love.

James Morris, the acclaimed English writer and foreign correspondent, was a handsome and accomplished man who led what on the surface looked like a normal successful life: He had a successful stint in the army, pursued a successful career, married, and became the father of five children with his wife. Yet throughout it all he experienced his male body as an entombment that yearly grew more terrible to him. This torment prompted him at the age of thirty-five to begin a ten-year hormone treatment which culminated in his emergence as Jan Morris. His conundrum, as he described it, was not simply a matter of penis or vagina, testicle or womb, "for it concerned not only my apparatus, but my *self*."

By the time in his twenties that he met Elizabeth, James Morris's life was blighted by "a detachment so involuntary that I often felt that I *really* wasn't there, but was viewing it all from some silent chamber of my own. If I could not be myself, my subconscious seemed to be saying, then I would not be." This elusive quality is wistfully evident in photographs of him at the time, and quite absent in photos of Jan Morris. "Love rescued me from that remote and eerie capsule, as it rescued me from self-destruction."

We hear nothing directly from Elizabeth in Morris's account of his/her quest for peaceful selfhood. But we can glean enough to piece together a love story of two people who, in the words of Heraclitus, were magnificently capable of listening to the essence of things. Of this love, "on a plane so mysterious and a texture so rich" that it acted like "a key to the catch of my conundrum," Morris writes,

> It was a marriage that had no right to work, yet it worked like a dream, living testimony, one might say, to the power of mind over matter—or of love in its purest sense over everything else. People often express themselves baffled by its nature, but it has never seemed strange to me: all the ambivalances of the relationship seem to me petty beside the divine emotion that inspired it.

As might be expected, the normal gender polarity could not easily function under the particular circumstances of their relationship. "It was a friendship and a union of equals, for in our house there could be no dominant male or female place." When they divided responsibilities, they did it along no lines of gender but according to what was required of the moment. They also never lived in that symbiotic relationship of codependent togetherness, which our society so often upholds as ideal couple love:

> We were never dependent upon each other. For months at a time I would wander off across the world, and sometimes Elizabeth would travel in a different way, into preoccupations that were all her own. Though we were linked in such absences by a rapt concern with each other's happiness, translated frequently, and at vast expense, into transatlantic telephone calls or weekend flights, still we never begrudged each other our separate lives, only finding mutual affair more exciting when resumed.

It was apparent to Elizabeth sooner than to Morris that his manhood not only was meaningless to him but was a continual struggle for him to live with. And so it was with her help that he finally abandoned his attempt to "soldier on" as a male and took the first step toward his change of sex. That step was the ten-year hormone treatment. Midway in the treatment, when Morris looked neither particularly male nor female, he took to living almost entirely as a woman. This meant that he and Elizabeth had to devise a new public relationship. They decided on Mrs. Morris and Miss Morris, and became sisters-in-law so that both could retain kinship with their children.

At the end of the hormone treatment, Morris went away for surgery and returned as a woman. "Elizabeth welcomed me as though nothing in particular had happened," and professed it a relief to "be in my true company at last." Morris was desperately anxious that their children should not be ashamed of her. She reports that, if they were, they never showed it and concludes that it was because they had witnessed neither the collapse of love nor the betrayal of parentage; rather they had watched a person they deeply cared about finally achieve serenity. "I think they learnt from me, as I learnt from Elizabeth, the colossal constructive force of love, which can bridge chasms and reconcile opposites." Although the two officially are divorced, they continue to live much as they did before James became Jan, and they propose to "share our lives happily ever after."

The essence of their relationship as I see it is twofold. In terms of love, it is an almost literal affirmation of Shakespeare's beautiful idea of authentic love, expressed in Sonnet 116:

Let me not to the marriage of true minds
Admit impediments. Love is not love
Which alters when it alteration finds,
Or bends with the remover to remove:
O, no! it is an ever-fixed mark,
That looks on tempests and is never shaken.

In terms of gender and sexuality, it is an affirmation of my own contention that in connection is the erotic. That the essence of the erotic is based not on gender, and certainly not on gender polarity, but on the act of deep mutual recognition as I have described it. Morris describes their "passionate amity" this way:

Our intimacy was erotic . . . in a sense of arcane and ecstatic understanding, and sometimes a thrust of affection that came not, as it does in romance, like a lullaby or a spring scent, but like a blow between the eyes, a shock to the system, or a suggestion of tragedy—for there must be to all grand loves the perpetual secret dread of an end to it all. And a grand love our love has been. It has given nobility to my mostly frivolous life.

I find this love story profoundly moving. If we are to have great love stories, far better this kind than *The Romance of Tristan and Iseult*. It does not surprise me at all that two Harvard psychologists found this kind of love to have a positive effect on the body's immune defense system.[29]

Aspiring Passion

As I wrote this book I was frequently asked, "You're not going to take the romance out of love, are you?" If they mean romance according to the Myth of Romantic Love, my answer clearly is, yes. I think the real question here is, Can we salvage something of what usually is known as the romantic passion and incorporate it into a better model of love? Or, even better, Can we take back our passion from the Myth which has misappropriated it? To this question my answer also is, yes. This may smack of having your cake and eating it, too—and let's try for it.

I had serious doubts about this possibility while wading through the deep mystification created by the Myth. In his epic study of the Myth, Denis de Rougemont says of *The Romance of Tristan and Iseult* that in "raising up that image of the Dying Lovers which is excited by the disturbing and vampire-like crescendo" of the second act of Wagner's opera about them, his purpose is to bring the reader to the point of declaring frankly either that "This is what I wanted!" or else "God forbid!"[30] To which I consistently have been declaring frankly, in my verson of the second answer, "No way!" I stand by that. And yet I also searched for a kind of passion which I could include in love as I was trying to evolve it, both in theory and in the practice of my life. When I came across philosopher Martha C. Nussbaum's narrative essay, "Love and the Individual: Romantic Rightness and Platonic Aspiration,"[31] I found it. Here at last was a union of passion and authentic selfhood to which I could respond—as I did, out loud, at my kitchen table where I was reading—"This is what I wanted!" I call my version aspiring passion.

Is the path to love romantic? To the kind of love I'm advocating, no. The path to this love is better than romantic, it is genuinely passionate. Aspiring passion dazzles the mind with reality, instead of dazing it with illusions; it illluminates the core of being with direct perception, instead of obscuring it with love-blotting. It is passion that makes you feel more truly yourself, instead of like someone else. And, as a preamble to love, it has the further advantage that it doesn't stop. Because, unlike the romantic passion, this passion is of essentially the same nature as genuine love. This does sound like having your cake and eating it, too. Personally, I've always been in favor of this feat, and especially with respect to passion and love.

It is a maxim of the Myth of Romantic Love that when you "settle down" into loving, you have to say goodbye to passion (except in nostalgic "romantic moments"). That's why romantic fairy tales and Ideal Romances end just where they always do. The reason for this maxim has more to do with romance, however, than it does with passion. It is, I think, a misuse of the romantic passion to insist that it be the path to love. This kind of insistence inevitably brings about all manner of misery in people's lives, foremost among them the "end of the honeymoon" with its (quite literal) disillusionment. With aspiring passion, we have a different path to love, where disillusionment is not part of the deal. This is the paragon among passions to which I felt I had been introduced there at my kitchen table. And so I exclaimed with pleasure and resolved to explore it further.

To aspire is to be animated by an ardent desire for excellence. My characterization of aspiring passion is that it is that union of the knowing intellect with an intense visceral excitement which lifts me to my superlatives, such as I see them. Nussbaum expresses the view, after Plato's *Phaedrus,* that personal passion and rational aspiration are, in their highest forms, actually in harmony or even fused with each other; we do not really have to choose between the two. I've argued that romantic passion according to the Myth amounts to love-blotting and is therefore partially or totally blind to the true character of the beloved. In the *Phaedrus* Socrates counters this view by arguing that it is precisely *in* passion (not all kinds, true, but in this high kind) that one person is most truly able to know and to love another—to love what the other most truly is.

Aspiring passion begins with a recognition of values. Souls, says Nussbaum, are individuated by what they most deeply care about. For example, there is the type who cares most about philosophy and moral values, and who pursues these two together in life. To care about these values is the essence of such a soul. To love a person himself or herself, and not the accidental features of the person, is to love that.

The values that individuate a person are recognized in a way that requires passion. If you are of the type for aspiring passion, you are simply, mysteriously, struck by the splendor of the other, the "form truly expressing beauty and nobility." You are dazzled, aroused, illuminated. What you experience is nothing like cold respect or mere admiration. And yet it is crucial that in the beauty that arouses, you see a sign of the values you cherish and pursue. The beauty of the other is not, even in the beginning, seen as mere superficial attractiveness but as "the radiance of a committed soul." Awe and wonder are essential components of this passion.

Sexual attraction functions quite differently in aspiring passion than as mere physical attraction. The first person for whom I felt what I now would call aspiring passion, but at the time had no adequate description for, is someone who does not fit the current notion of "sexy." I was telling a friend about my passion for this person, whom I'll call "C," when she said, "But how can you feel sexually attracted?" My answer then was, "Who can say?" and I added that I thought this was the only fundamentally honest answer to the question in general. Now I begin to think that, in my case at least, maybe Plato can say. It's clear when someone merely fits the social stereotype of "sexy." That's observable intellectually, and sexual attraction to such a person is, in my opinion, suspect from the point of view we now are exploring. In the larger arena of what is attractive, I am of the opinion that one cannot separate mind and body. What struck me first about "C," for example, was a quality of mind. There was a sensuous elegance to the way it moved that I found enormously appealing. There were also what I might agree are accidental features (but which nevertheless also are important to me) like a quick and deep sense of humor, a straightforward gusto for the immediate (in this case, eating dinner and drinking wine), a sense of fun, a noncontrolling attentiveness, a love of music, and so on. But the overriding impact was very like the one modern physics makes on me: I was struck by a combination of elegance, scope, spirited integrity, nerve, and poetry, and I said, "Yes!"

Thus it was quite a non sequitor for me to be asked, tersely, "But how can you be sexually attracted?" and to have this question followed by a physical description of this person that was less than flattering. Not hideous, but not "sexy" in the conventional sense, either. Two things happened then. First came the realization that I had in no way thought about sexual attraction as I waxed enthusiastic, but that when the question came I knew I was attracted in a way that felt erotic to me. Second came the more surprising realization that I in fact did not really know what "C" looked like in precise physical terms ("Five-foot-two, eyes of blue"), even after we'd spent more than a few hours together. I resolved, upon the next meeting, to scrutinize the object of my passion. I did so, and then another interesting thing happened. I had to acknowledge that the physical description did in fact fit more or less as stated, but my awareness of this physiology vanished every time I did not consciously make myself think of it, and instead there emerged the "form truly expressing beauty and nobility." I think Plato says it exactly: it was the radiance of a committed soul. And this does indeed passionately attract a person of my type.

The point is, says Nussbaum to this type, you wouldn't *be* attracted if the other person didn't answer to your aspirations. Love and sexuality, at least in people like you, are themselves selective and aspiring. What excites your passion, makes you shudder and tremble, is the perception of something that answers to the desire of your soul. Your kind of passion loves *that*. It demands an object that is radiant with value. What you want with the other person, ultimately, is a mutual exchange of love and ideas that will be a seamless part of each person's pursuit of their central aspiration in life.

But you can't tell about the other when you first are struck. You go by the trace you see of the something that answers to your soul's desire and allow yourself, in considerable ignorance, to be melted. Aspiring passion is not detached and self-sufficient. In order to be moved toward value, you must be open and receptive. The crucial first step toward truth and knowledge about the other comes when the stream of beauty that enters the eyes is allowed to moisten and melt the dry elements of the soul. Only then does the soul begin to have insight into itself and its aims. And as time goes on in a context of intimacy, each of you follows up the trace in the other of your highest aspirations, coming to know one another, yourselves, and the true value at the same time.

The ABCs of Aspiring Passion

And they lived happily ever after . . . under the right circumstances. Can we promote some of these right circumstances? I think so. For example, it must be acknowledged that the radiance of that committed soul may dim for you with further intimacy and knowledge. Maybe not into utter darkness, but at least to fall beneath your level of illumination. Put bluntly, how can we make reasonably sure this isn't merely a fancy version of love-blotting? About being struck by that radiance, Nussbaum says, "Often I will know only that this person is beautiful and exhilarating in some way I cannot yet describe." Our key lies in that "yet." When we are struck by romatic love à la the Myth, we say, "I don't know what hit me." And the truth is, I think, that we don't *want* to know. The "magic" of this kind of experience lies precisely in the not knowing. We "just *know*." And to sober friends who might say, "But whatever do you see in him/her?" we respond, in effect, "Don't bother me, I want to indulge completely in this euphoria." Now, that surely is one way to go, and it has its compensations, ut it is not the way of aspiring passion. Here, we above all want to know—rationally, soberly, wisely—because this knowing is precisely what fuels such a passion. I'll use my own forays into passion as a means of elucidating my point. In the past decade there have been three such major ones, moving (I would now say) from gross romantic euphoria à la the Myth, to a mixed case of that and aspiring passion, to my first experience with what I now would call pure aspiring passion. In order to leave them quite anonymous, I am going to call them, "A," "B," and "C"—thus also giving a hint of a learning process, which indeed it was and is.

My passion for "A" was my Ideal Romance with my former hero. I became a Reverse Sleeping Beauty and fell asleep—to who I was and likewise to who he was, in and of ourselves, aside from whatever romantic or neurotic needs we might have been feeding in each other. I very consistently did not ask for information from friends and family that might have conflicted with my love-blotting. The result was a full-blown case of glowcoma and a loss of reality-testing so complete that even after five years I did not know with whom I had been having the pleasure.

This truth was brought home to me most bluntly by an old friend who said she had wanted to tell me what she had seen but had felt unable to do so, because it was evident that I could not hear her. Her observation was that it had been a case of "bliss-ninny" involved with "chicken shit." If your passion is of the aspiring sort, these are the intimates you deliberately seek out, because you know and value their insight about life's truths in general and therefore want it in this particular. In this manner you follow up on the "squirms" we explored in chapter 6 and try to ascertain exactly what it is they are telling you. That is one aspect of following up the trace of your highest aspirations as they manifest, or do not manifest, in the object of your passion.

"B" was a mixed case. I knew, even as I was struck, that it was the impact of both a knee-jerk reaction to a conventionally very "sexy" person and also what I now would call the radiance of a committed soul. The relationship that ensued, and which still is ongoing, consisted from my side of separating my romantic from my aspiring passion. I think this is a very difficult proposition, and probably the one that is most common in our passions, gender stereotyping rearing its muddling head as often as it does in our culture.

As I move toward aspiring passion, I still occasionally take a detour into a romantic relapse. The two feel decidedly different to me, so I call them by two different names. The one connected to my romantic passion I call "euphoria"; and the one I associate with aspiring passion I call "delight." Euphoria in its dictionary definition of the psychological meaning of the word is an abnormal feeling of buoyant vigor and health. Delight is a high degree of pleasure or satisfaction of mind. They both feel exhilarating in their own way, but I find the latter exhilaration of a more grounded sort—grounded to *me* as I think I know me, and grounded to what other people know of me. Since I tend to get easily enthusiastic and in my enthusiasm sometimes lose my bearings (which in any case, because of gender's muddling sway, are easy to lose), I use a friend's delicious comment to help me distinguish which of the two I'm actually feeling. In one of my outpourings of passionate enthusiasm over the attractions of "B," I noticed a slight reluctance in her response. I stopped and said, "A penny for your thoughts." She answered, "Everything you say sounds wonderful and I have nothing directly to say against it. Except I have the feeling whenever you talk like this, that . . . well, something like, your underwear is too tight." Her comment cracked me up, and I've used it ever since as an instant hit of reality testing. There's no getting around it: the feeling of too tight underwear is unmistakable when it exists.

In the matter of my aspiring passion for "C," also still ongoing, I've already talked about its nature. I can sum it up with a few general comments. The distinctive feeling that characterizes this passion for me is its affirmation. It says, "Yes!" to myself, to the other, and to life—all in the same breath. The passion comes from feeling the universe open up, offering more possibilities for being, because of the interaction with the other. And it comes from the feeling that this interaction brings out in me some of the qualities I strive for in myself, as I know them from other aspects of my life. In sum (applying here the two principle dynamic phenomena of systems theory as it intersects with my concept of autonomy) this interaction offers *self-renewal*—the ability of living systems continuously to renew and recycle their components while maintaining the integrity of their overall structure—and *self-transcendence*—the ability to reach out creatively beyond physical and mental boundaries in the process of learning, development, and evolution.[32]

I like to say that in connection is the erotic. By this I mean that I think the erotic is inherent in the act of connection itself. An erotic response isn't only something your body does when your erogenous zones are stimulated; in its larger scope, the erotic is a mental/sensual response to the experience of true connection between one's self and "out there"—be it with a person, a tree, an idea, music, or a sunset. For example, the passion I experience with "C" is akin to the passion I know in other moments of connection. Such as the passion I felt when the stream of beauty that is O'Keeffe's "Winter Road" first hit my eyes. I felt dazzled, aroused, illuminated; and when I say that the impact felt palpable I mean that I experienced it as erotic. My mind *and* my senses shuddered and trembled, in unison. I think what happens in aspiring passion is of this order. As, for example, with the man I mentioned earlier, whose intermittent withdrawal confused and upset me. He said, "I feel something, hear something from you, some idea or emotional insight, or emotion, and I say, 'Yeah! Wow!'"—and I think what made such moments so threatening to him that he withdrew is precisely that they were erotic in the total-mind-and-body sense I am describing and therefore especially powerful.

Taking back our passion from the single-minded grasp of the Myth of Romantic Love requires, among other things, that we begin to evolve a new language with which to describe what we are doing when we feel passionate, so that we don't automatically sigh, "How romantic!" As I've suggested, there is at least one other way to look at passsion than as romance, and one which is better suited to the kind of love we are exploring here. When I first began to look as soberly as possible at the blandishments of the Myth, it was with the idea that there must be a better way to love. To return to my astronomer simile, I predicted that a different mode of passion and love must exist, and with time I did in fact find it. First as a theorist; then as a person with new and quite different experiences in passion and in love.

When I found what I came to call aspiring passion, my first step was to realign my own perceptions of what I in fact was feeling and doing when I felt passionate, and under what circumstances. This step gave me the beginnings of a new language. This new language made possible new modes of behaving on the path to love, and new options in relationships.

I end this chapter on the note that began it, with worldviews. A person's concept of love does not exist in a vacuum but follows from that person's way of conceiving of his or her identity and its connection to others and to the cosmos. To the dominant worldview of the West, the kind of love and passion we have been exploring is seen as inconsistent with reality, absurd, and irrelevant. That's why so many of us feel we are working against the grain—the culture's and our own—as we try to live our intimate and especially our passionate relationships in modes different from the one prescribed by the Myth of Romantic Love. It is gratifying and encouraging to realize, therefore, that to the worldview that preceded the Scientific Revolution, love and passion as I have described and advocated them would not have seemed absurd or irrelevant. Nor would the statement "in connection is the erotic." Because according to this worldview, as historian Morris Berman tells us, "real knowledge occurred only via the union of subject and object, in a psychic-emotional identification with images," in a totality of experience characterized by a union of mind and senses, what Berman calls "the sensuous intellect."[33] This phrase seems to me to apply directly to Jan Morris's comment that "our intimacy was erotic . . . in a sense of arcane and ecstatic understanding." In fact, the "sensuous intellect" is a paradox only to the dominant materialist worldview. Those of us who can free ourselves of that hampering notion, the "objective observer" who knows something in the act of detaching from it, we know that this is not how the act of knowing *feels*. And certainly not the act of knowing in love.

As we continue to love "against the grain," we can therefore take heart—in all meanings of that phrase. We have going for us not only our personal experience but also the worldview of the past and of the future, as expressed by modern physics. This worldview tells us that we live in a participatory universe whose unifying principle seems to be relationship and whose "basic building block" is a continuous dance of energy connections. It is not our vision of love that is out of step with reality, but rather the worldview that tells us it is not True Love.

8. Love: Groundwork

One of the many pernicious aspects of the Myth of Romantic Love is its all-or-nothing approach to relationships. Thus, if we feel a connection to someone, we're constrained to say that we're "just friends" unless we can show that there is "something in it." That something is romance, and when it is "going somewhere" is when it is leading to the possibility of marriage. This single-minded approach is bad for marriage and bad for other important human relationships. In short, it's bad for love, because it drastically curtails the many loving interactions we can experience in our lives. In this chapter, let's try to reintegrate this variety of relationships into a broader base for love. We start with the most basic of all loving relationships, the one we have with ourself.

The Relationship with Self

Suppose I asked you to describe yourself in a way that would give you a good sense of who you are. Would you have an answer? Or are you like the 160 women Lillian Rubin asked in *Women of a Certain Age: The Midlife Search for Self?* Most of them had trouble coming up with an answer, and nearly a quarter of them could not answer at all. "In embarrassment," Rubin reports, "they finally said one version or another of: 'I'm blank. Maybe there just isn't much of a self there.'"[1] This is a rather sad statement to make after forty of fifty years living with yourself, and one that follows directly from the conventions of femininity that equate moral goodness with self-sacrifice. This socialization trains a woman to look away from herself or face the charge of selfishness. It leaves the well-socialized woman with the existential dead end that, to avoid the exclusion of others which is selfishness, she must opt for the selflessness that is the exclusion of self.[2]

We've seen the price men pay for having masculinity defined through separation: their sense of self is threatened by intimacy.[3] Since femininity is defined through self-abnegation in attachment, women's price is that their sense of self is threatened by separation. The result too often is a submersion of the self in others, to the point of losing sight of it. One woman spoke for many I interviewed when she said: "I, as a fifty-five-year-old woman, am so used to giving myself to other people and looking after other people first that if I start thinking of looking after myself I feel isolated, alone. Separate. And that is terribly painful."

There is, however, an alternative to the see-saw of always putting others first or being selfish. It's called taking others into account, and it implies including oneself among the people one considers it moral to take into account. Which in turn implies *having* a self to include, because to be a moral agent without a self to act from is impossible. It can't be done. To the injunction of the conventions of femininity we can therefore reply in the words attributed to Talleyrand: equating moral goodness with self-sacrifice is worse than a crime, it's a mistake.

This is the realization more and more women are coming to as they seek autonomy; and, though many women I spoke with talked like the woman above, I'm happy to report that many more talked like this one:

> Establishing a good relationship with self is not selfishness, it's a duty. It's *your* life, your life to try to shape. If you don't come to some conclusions about what your life should be, if you don't take responsibility for your life, you aren't really living. And I think if you don't have a good relationship with yourself, you can't have it with others.

I think it's true to say that the territory of a relationship with self is new territory to women; but, judging by the response I got to my questions, it's territory that fascinates us. Every woman I interviewed, without exception, made a point of thanking me for the opportunity to think about the subject. The woman quoted next is a good example. Like almost all the women, she asked for some questions to mull over first. We then met for dinner at a restaurant with the intention of doing the interview afterward. This plan went somewhat awry because we, who had never met before, found the occasion so enjoyable that we prolonged it while consuming a bottle of wine. Consequently, our interview was less sharp than it might have been. The next afternoon I found on my doorstep a carefully thought-out tape she had made for me. It ended with this "afterword," as she called it:

> This is a very new topic for me. I wanted to let you know that in thinking about these questions that you posed, the questions themselves have acted as a springboard for other sorts of thoughts, and I'm sure that this is going to continue to perk, as my daughter would say, and bear untold other kinds of fruit. So thank you.

What is the relationship with self? One woman put it well: "For me, it means becoming aware of an ongoing developing process of knowing who one is. Not in any intellectual kind of way, but in recognizing a pattern of learning and living, which seems always to have been there." I would call the relationship with self the most fundamental relationship we have, and the foundation for all others. A balanced and harmonious relationship with one's self is the basis not only for personal autonomy but also for love. It's been said often, and I think it's true, that if you don't love yourself—at least to the point of accepting the self that you are with reasonable affirmation and joy in being that self—then you can't love others. In this sense, establishing a viable relationship with self is homework at its most basic, not only as each person's life task but as a primary lesson in love. Because in taking responsibility for one's self, one leaves others free to take responsibility for their selves without pushing them around with one's needs, desires, or demands. This doesn't mean that one doesn't have needs, desires, and demands, it just means that one takes responsibility for them. And, as Carol Gilligan observes, to be responsible for oneself, it is first necessary to acknowledge what one is doing.[4] Anything else is, in fact, selfishness. Anne Wilson

Schaef's book *Co-Dependence* has much to say on this subject.[5] In an interview, she told me,

> I have found that the most selfish people and the most destructive people are the people who don't take care of themselves. When you honor you own process—when you go through the hard labor of finding your identity, your own reality—something happens almost by default: you honor other people; you don't have to use that other person to meet your needs. And so you have the option, then, of *relating* to that other human being. When you don't live your own process I fondly say that you puke it on other people.

I've said that the best way to know oneself is to love many things. I include the self among them. One acquires a sense of self by being recognized by others, but one must also learn to recognize oneself. For this process, I think solitude is essential. In solitude one learns the truth of the original meaning of the word alone—being all one—instead of the more common meaning of being bereft of company or cut off. Poets know this truth, even if our society generally doesn't. It is physically difficult to be alone in our society, especially if you live in a big city; it is also emotionally difficult. If someone wants to spend time with you and you say, "I'm sorry, I won't be able to do that because I have to work," that's considered okay. But try saying, "I won't be able to do that because I want to spend that time by myself." Not so okay. Yet being able to enjoy time alone is surely one of life's great blessings, just as being unable to do so is perhaps the most basic tyranny under which one can live. So I go with the poets. I especially like Wordsworth's notion of "that inward eye/Which is the bliss of solitude" and Milton's observation that "solitute sometimes is best society/And short retirement urges sweet return."[6]

Schaef calls this "alone time." She explained it to me this way:

> One of the things I think women learn when they have alone time is that they're *with* somebody. Most women don't know that. They'll talk about "being alone," and when they develop a relationship with themselves they find that when nobody is around they're with one of the most inter-

esting persons they've ever met. People who become more respectful of themselves need and insist on alone time.

Daily rituals are also a wonderful tonic for the self. Daily rituals are activities you engage in with yourself which give you pleasure. They can be anything from using a particular cup to drink from because it gives you fond memories, to making sure you every day engage in a new activity that enhances what Wordsworth wonderfully calls the bond of union between life and joy. Daily rituals are self-strengthening because they are self-chosen and reflective of oneself. They are also repeatable and can therefore be returned to at will. They don't need to cost any money, and they are portable in that they are adaptable to wherever one lives. They give a sense of being grounded that is especially powerful because no one else is needed to make them happen. They feel like a continuing meditation, or like being with an intimate and ever-available friend. I consider my own daily rituals among my more brilliant inventions. They remind me that life, as Coleridge says, is made of minute fractions, of the countless infinitesimals of pleasurable and genial feeling.[7] Certainly, much of this happiness comes from relationships with other people; but, equally certainly, much of it comes from the relationship with self.

I add that I decidedly am not of the "life is earnest struggle" school of thought. So when I speak of doing the work of establishing a solid relationship with self, I do so in the spirit of the anthropologist Ruth Benedict, who wrote, "I long to speak out the intense inspiration that comes to me from the lives of strong women. They have made of their lives a great adventure."[8] For me, no one epitomizes such a life better than the photographer Imogen Cunningham, who decided at the age of ninety-two to create a new body of work with which she was actively involved until she died at ninety-three. Her answer when asked to state her religion on a hospital form a few days before her death says much about her spirit. According to her son it was, "Haven't chosen one yet!"

Cunningham worked hard to make a living as a portrait photographer, but work and play were always synonymous to her. She lived alone for much of her life, never stopped working, and always claimed that her best photograph would be the one she would do tomorrow. "She seemed youthful to the last," says one who knew her, "because like the poet Emily Dickinson, she 'dwelt in possibility.' . . . We saw her striding around San Francisco, easily recognized by the beaded cap atop a fringe of white bangs and the black cape winging behind her intent little figure. The message she conveyed was hopeful and reassuring: that it was possible to grow old, working; to maintain interest in life; to be energetic; to be wholly oneself—in short, to love one's destiny."[9]

Just Friends

Some time ago I was on a long day's hike in the mountains with an old friend. We have known each other for more than twenty-five years, and our intimacy is based as much on the numberless small events of life as it is on some of the major life and death dramas we also have been through together. The weather turned grey and threatening in late morning. It became obvious that if we didn't pretty quickly find a spot to eat our lunch we would be eating wet sandwiches, so we chose a log under a large tree with a beautiful view and sat down. As I watched my friend huddle over her sandwich in the vain attempt to shield herself from the blasts of wind, a surge of pleasure and gratitute rose in me and I exclaimed spontaneously, "Aren't old friends wonderful?" She looked up without surprise, said, "Yes," and returned to her sandwich. There was no need for either of us to say anything else, and we didn't.

Old friends are indeed wonderful. It's especially when one thinks of them that the absurdity of the phrase "We're just friends" stands out. Considering the vagaries of the so-called sexual revolution and the vicissitudes of romance, it would often be more correct to say, "We're just lovers." One woman called friends "the emotional food of life," and that about sums it up. Staying with her metaphor, I would call old friends the staple of that food. Friends provide not only fun and variety; in their many-faceted comings and goings in our lives, they are the arena in which we can play out the largest scope of who we are as individuals. And old friends provide the emotional space in which we can make mistakes in the certain knowledge that they will still be there for us as friends, as we will for them. Friends provide a combination of constancy and variety in our lives, without the constraints usually found in relationships based on kinship, mating, or work. Debussy once said that his motivation for writing his music was that he wanted to sing his interior landscape. With friends we get the freest possible space in which to sing our interior landscape and to explore life.

Some writers have regretted the amorphous state of friendship in North America, one calling it "the neglected relationship"; and they have suggested various forms of codification and rituals to bring it into focus and put it on the map. For example, in *Just Friends* Lillian Rubin laments the fact that friendship in our society is a strictly private affair. "There are no social rituals, no public ceremonies to honor or celebrate friendships of any kind, from the closest to the most distant—not even a linguistic form that distinguishes the formal impersonal relationship from the informal and personal one." She calls friendship a "*non-event*" because it is "a relationship that just *becomes*, that grows, develops, waxes, wanes and, too often perhaps, ends, all without ceremony or ritual to give evidence of its existence."[10] She goes on to compare regretfully this lack of codification and ritual with those we have for kinship and marriage.

I say, leave friendship alone, we have enough trouble already with our institutions of kinship and marriage. One of the primary reasons why friendship is so uncodified in our society is that marriage is a monolithic institution. It appropriates to itself all manner of interaction that can and does happen elsewhere and calls it "of or leading to marriage" even when it doesn't or shouldn't. As one young woman exclaimed to me in annoyance,

"If you go to the movies with a man more than twice, you're already on the conveyor belt to marriage!" This is why single women are categorized as "premarital" and why "just friends" means "not really important." I find this an obnoxious way of streamlining people's lives, and the codifications and rituals of romance and marriage are prime causes of this streamlining.

Rubin regrets that it's practically impossible to know exactly what people mean when they call someone a friend, saying we should make this area of our lives more like kinship, where we have a comparatively large set of terms for distinguishing who is what. I say there are some obvious and appropriate reasons for distinctions among kin, which do not pertain to friendship. For one, kinship is fixed (an aunt is an aunt is an aunt), while the distinguishing feature of friendship is its fluidity. For another, "aunt" is the declaration of a formal relationship, regardless of affection, while "friend" is precisely the opposite. The problem inherent in trying to formalize relationships based on affection is epitomized by marriage. The terms "husband" and "wife" totter uneasily between public form and private affection. Unlike friendships, marriages may indeed start with a wedding and do end with death or divorce, but that is strictly speaking a formal statement only. Many married relationships end as vital interactions based on affection long before they are terminated by death or divorce. Rubin argues for making friendship more like marriage in terms of public ritual and codification; I argue exactly the opposite. Leave friendship free of the dubious benefits now accruing to couples because of the institution of marriage; make marriage less codified, less ritualized, and especially less institutionalized—in short, make it more like friendship—and it may finally get the chance to become an enduring relationship based on affection.

And, anyway, there is nothing to stop friends from making their own rituals to mark whatever they like to highlight in the process of their intimacy. I certainly do that with my friends, and I would not appreciate having the state involved one little bit in this. I think a relationship that gets to "just become"—to wax or wane, to end or not end—has much to recommend it. True, the evidence of its existence would not come from the fact that society had a bunch of rituals to mark its life. The evidence of a friendship comes from the knowledge of its existence by the people involved. My friends know who they are, they don't need society to tell them. Do yours? As you may have gathered, I intensely dislike authoritarianism. I think we have entirely too much official involvement in our private lives and I therefore become both vexed and alarmed when people try to tighten the straitjacket in which we already are constrained to live. It is perfectly possible to honor friendship without formalizing it officially, and let us try to do so now.

There are friends and friends. We don't need to codify in order to make some distinctions that keep in mind the fluidity which is the essence of friendship. I like this woman's distinction between friends of the road and friends of the heart:

> Friends of the road are people who pass through your life. You don't know them forever, but only for relatively short periods of time. When they're there, they're there. But you have to buoy them up. If you lose contact, you lose the friendship because it's the contact that keeps it alive and vital. Without it, it goes stale.
>
> But friends of the heart are different. You don't have to buoy the friendship up to make sure it'll be there. It's like family; they're both just there. They're friendships that are long-lived and continuous. There's absolute trust between the friends; the relationship is fully reciprocal; and you don't have to be there all the time.[11]

There is built-in movement in this distinction, which is all to the good. The particular friends of the road change with time as new ones replace old ones. Finding friends of the heart is likewise a changing process: If the potential for deep friendship is there, the process becomes simply one of increasing intimacy; if the potential is not there, the person is either dropped or moved into the friends-of-the-road group.

Friends of the road may be more shallow relationships than friends of the heart, but they have advantages because of this fact. They can provide a kaleidoscope of changing patterns, because this kind of friendship is understood to be ad hoc—it exists for a specific and often limited purpose. Such friends are in effect a deeper and more purposeful version of acquaintances. They offer quality and variety, while friends of the heart offer quality and depth. Each kind of friend has a distinct and proper function, and both are necessary to what we might call a full circle of friends.

It becomes interesting to speculate as to who among the people we meet becomes what kind of friend and why. Can we determine something about the nature of the process of moving into intimacy? I think so. The potential for deep intimacy between two people is either there or not there, and the process of moving into intimacy is the process of discovering this reality. Friendship and love is revealed, disclosed, found—with time, attention, and care by the parties involved. I first heard this view expressed by a woman in her late sixties, who claimed she had never had a really unpleasant surprise from someone she considered a friend. Few of us can say that, probably, so I asked her to elaborate:

> I think the reason is that I take my time. In the beginning, when you know that there is a possibility that this person may become a real friend, I look impartially on what happens. I feel open to whatever is ahead. I think that's the key.
>
> Life is like a wave that takes up stones and deposits them on the beach according to their weight and shape. I don't mean it as a symbol that some stones are better than others, it's more a matter of each one eventually finding its proper place. They end up where they fit in. People are as they can be; I am as *I* can be. Sometimes you fit, sometimes you don't. That's how it is, as far as I can see. So I would never hold it against someone that they turned out not to fit with me.

I agree. What separates one kind of friend from the other, or what makes a person not a friend at all, is a process as impersonal as natural law—even in the very personal realm of affection.

I discussed this concept with a physicist friend who soon

asked, "Have you thought of resonance as a unifying principle?" I had not and asked if she was thinking of harmonics. She said, yes, and recommended a book on the physical basis of music.

Resonance is the property possessed by all simple harmonic vibrators, of which musical instruments are more complex examples, of responding strongly to vibrations which occur at its own rate in any given time.[12] You'll know something of the phenomenon if you press the loud pedal on a piano, thus removing the damper so the strings can vibrate freely, and then sing a loud, clear note. Certain notes in the piano will respond weakly while only one note will re-echo yours to any extent. That note will come from the string whose natural frequency most closely matches that of the note you sang, and it will continue to sound for a while after your note dies down. That note resonated with yours, the others did not. Although human beings undoubtedly are very complex vibrating systems, I think the principle that ultimately draws or does not draw us to each other is the same: resonance. The existence or nonexistence of sympathetic vibrations on a profound level of our being.

Dr. Valerie Hunt's research into the human bioenergetic field supports this claim. She discovered that the human body emits continuous vibrations in the audible spectrum. We actually hear them, even though we may be unaware of doing so. These vibrations appear to manifest at the cellular level of our bodies, and they radiate from the body surface. So it appears that the human body both transmits and receives complex patterns of sound, and these sounds produced by our cellular vibrations are in fact perceived by us simultaneously with the vibrations which we hear as what we call normal sound. Dr. Hunt speculates that this human energy field also functions as a resonance membrane where mental phenomena are somehow assessed.[13]

I find this work fascinating, and I think it corresponds to our actual experience—remember the 1960s term "good vibes"? It seems reasonable to suppose than when we feel a sense of affinity for someone we meet, what we are feeling is literally "good vibrations" on a very deep level beyond our normal intellectual understanding. Similarly, if we feel nothing in particular, we could suppose we are encountering a person who does not resonate very strongly with us; and if there is a sense of active negativity, we may be facing a person who in effect is vibrating in direct interference with the pattern of our own vibrations. In these cases the body may know more than we think we have reason to know, and perhaps it would be wise to listen to its message and see where it takes us. This seems to me to be what Confucius was talking about in his commentary on a line in the *I Ching*: "Things that accord in tone vibrate together. Things that have affinity in their inmost natures seek one another. . . . Each follows its kind."[14]

Now let's apply the principle of resonance to the formation of friendships. I think the principle tells us this: the effect produced by the vibrations of our inner being on other persons is involuntary. Finding true accord with a kindred spirit can be voluntarily encouraged to develop, but it cannot be imposed if the basis for resonance is not there. The way to proceed is therefore to "sing one's note" in a clear, true voice and see what happens. If all goes well, as I remember it from my closest friendships, the process is one of increasing depth without the experience of serious friction.

But what happens if you move along and eventually realize that you may have reached a limit, that perhaps the deep resonance isn't there after all? I always remind myself at such times of George Eliot's dispassionate observation that "a difference of taste in jokes is a great strain on the affections."[15] At this point you are forced to consider whether or not to proceed into further intimacy and, if you choose not to do so, decide what to do about the other person. Again, I think the *I Ching* is directly to the point:

> We are often among people who do not belong to our sphere. In that case we must beware of being drawn into false intimacy through force of habit. Needless to say, this would have evil consequences. Maintaining sociability without intimacy is the only right attitude toward such people, because otherwise we should not be free to enter into relationships with people of our own kind later on.[16]

Sociability without intimacy: an excellent notion. Unless the action by the other person is truly egregious, we will not have to make a complete break but merely a shift in attitude. It's not necessary to become unpleasant or cold toward a person with whom we have reached a limit of resonance, it's only necessary not to invite further intimacy.

I mention all of this for two reasons. First, I believe this in fact is the basis for how affectionate relationships between people are formed. Second, being aware of this basis has at least two beneficial results. There is the general effect of throwing a certain clarity and even serenity onto the formation or nonformation of friendships. And there is the hope that this general effect can become specifically operable in the painful but hardly uncommon event of facing the end of a love relationship. Thus it may be possible (at least after the initial impact) to feel, not that you have been rejected and thereby hit in the solar plexus of your self-esteem, but rather that the accord in tone felt between the two of you was of a limited nature, that it was not after all an affinity based on your inmost natures. The break is in this sense propitious, because it leaves each of you free to follow your own kind.

What about jointly pushing limits when you reach them in a relationship with an intimate? This work of love involves being each other's critics, in the most positive sense of that word. So that whatever the limit is may be understood, its nature gauged with an eye to the possibility of transcending it, all with a nonjudgmental attitude toward the other and the ultimate outcome of what you are doing. Required for this work of love is what M. Scott Peck calls true listening, which in turn requires temporarily "giving up or setting aside of one's own prejudices, frames of reference and desires so as to experience as far as possible the speaker's world from the inside, stepping inside his or her shoes. This unification of speaker and listener is actually an extension and enlargement of ourself, and new knowledge is always gained from this."[17]

We tend to avoid this kind of confrontation because it is very difficult to do well. We may even convince ourselves that we are being considerate or at least polite in avoiding it. We're wrong. What's going on is not courtesy but a failure in caring. One great beauty of friendship is that it offers us the opportunity to learn this difficult work of love under conditions that are less loaded than those of the lover/mate relationship. In this, as in so many other ways, friendship is a lesson in love under the most favorable circumstances possible.

Amitié Amoureuse

"Can you mix companionship and sex?" asks Jessie Bernard in her landmark book *The Future of Marriage,* adding that the future of marriage rides on the answer.[18] So does the future of sexual love between people who don't marry. It's almost an axiom in our society that the answer to her question is, no. Be warned, says the axiom, if you mix friendship and sex, you will end up with neither a friend nor a lover. The underlying assumption here, as we see over and over again in the research on "attraction," is that companionship calls for similarities between partners, whereas sexual passion depends on differentiation between the sexes. In short, no *la différence,* no sex. That this view is myopic to the point of blindness is clear when we consider that all manner of people who do not have *la différence* between them in fact have all kinds of erotic commitments and feel plenty of attraction toward their lovers. It would be far more correct to say, *with la différence,* no sex—sooner or later. Because this arbitrary difference, which is foisted upon our erotic lives by gender polarity, carries with it the seed of its own demise. It is too rigid, too fixed, to carry life. And, with the waning of vitality comes the waning of sexual passion. What remains is boredom. Or, as one writer puts it, "a remorseless familiarity that leaves no solitude unturned, no radical difference intact" and that eventually erases the very knowledge of being in the two partners.[19]

This remorseless familiarity comes about because the very shallow field of difference that is *la différence* is fairly quickly mined; meanwhile, it erases whatever genuine differences may have existed between the partners. The result is a union that no longer is alive and vital, if it ever was. Life under such conditions gets boring because it produces nothing new. It merely repeats the similarity of facade-to-facade encounters à la sex roles. In short, *la différence* may indeed produce sexual passion initially for some people, but it has a built-in self-destruct of such passion.

If instead we meet face to face as authentic beings, I think exactly the opposite can happen. The inherent mixture of similarity and difference that is valued as such in the paradox of love is the best (and perhaps the only) guarantee we have of enduring passion, emotional and sexual. In this kind of love we can find the continual fascination with the familiar other that keeps a relationship vital, because he or she still remains separate and therefore always to some degree mysterious, always somewhat unpredictable and unknown. In this tension, and not in the artificial tension produced by the battle of sex roles, lies true passion as I understand it. When I say that in connection is the erotic, I mean that making genuine contact with a familiar yet separate other is like electricity: It produces a surge of excitement. My contention, as I have said, is that the surge of connection—when the mind and the senses are aroused and quiver—happens in any moment of real connection. And that the eroticism of this connection is the ground out of which grows authentic sexual passion with a partner. I think that when sexuality is removed from its conventional context there is a perfectly natural association between affection, love, sensuality, and sexuality. The erotic is there to be acted upon, or not, with any person to whom we feel a real connection.

We return to friendship, the free space in which we most easily can sing our interior landscape. And we look for the perfectly natural link between affection and sexuality. Which, we might speculate, comes from the sensed resonance with another on a deep level. What stands in our way as we look for this link? It's that conventional context again. Johanna Stuckey, the Canadian scholar who wrote an incisive treatise on the subject, explained to me the concept of *amitié amoureuse*:

Our problem is that we've tied sexuality to romantic love. Other cultures don't do that. They understand that this kind of love exists, but they don't see it as the only kind in which sexuality can occur. The French, for instance, have a concept of *amitié amoureuse*, a "sexy friendship."

So instead of seeing romantic love between conventional gender opposites as the thing that's going to give us the most fulfilling interpersonal relationship we're ever going to have, I think we should see it as something to dabble in, preferably when we're very young. And we should begin to look at intimate relationships between women and men—or women and women, or men and men—in terms of choosing a mate the same way you choose a friend. As someone for whom you develop esteem until slowly, over time, you love the person. You may even be sexually involved quite early, but without being "madly passionately in love."

The two men who wrote *Sexual Conduct* claim that without the proper elements of a script that defines the situation, names the actors, and plots the behavior, nothing sexual is likely to happen.[20] This seems only too true, and we know the conventional script. But fortunately this claim has an inverse: with new scripts we should be able to make something new happen in the way of sexuality. Many women I interviewed for this book are defining the sexual situation differently, and with it sexual attraction and sexual love. A woman in her early forties summed it up this way:

It's important that you find the person you love sexy in a variety of ways. But in the romantic love thing the sexual attraction is primary and the "love" follows from that. It seems to me that in a more mature love relationship the sexual attraction works in a more healthy way that says: I love you hence I'm attracted to you, and sex is an expression of that. It's the other way around, in other words.

Many women I talked with agreed that the sexual attraction that comes with the infatuation for a "real knock-out" in the sexual stereotype department feels qualitatively different from the sexual attraction they feel in what they call genuine love:

With infatuation, sexual attraction comes from surfaces and feels the way it's described—palpitations of the heart, weak knees, general agitation. With love, sexual attraction comes from the inside and feels sort of like sunshine—a warm and gentle sensation that starts in the solar plexus and spreads until it suffuses the whole body.

These women's distinction between two kinds of sexual attraction as they manifest with two kinds of love reminds me of the song that says, this can't be love because I feel so well, this is too sweet to be love. What a disheartening statement, and how entrenched it is in our culture. Like Johanna Stuckey, I refuse to believe that it has to be this way for love and for sex. Happily, new ideas about love and the experiences of many women suggest that it doesn't have to: that we can indeed mix companionship and sex, and that we can move into love on this basis. The passage may feel unfamiliar—it is, in our society—but it offers the possibility of simultaneously feeling passionate and sympathetic as two people become intimate. And the reason is, making another bow to Woody Allen, that at least you know you're in bed with a friend. A real friend, if you start with *amitié amoureuse* and take your time.

The two women whose stories follow did just that. The first story is a follow-up to the "sunshine girl" we met in chapter 5, who felt the need one fine day to choose between "their me" and "my me." "Her me" left behind the feminine act that had characterized her love life and opted for autonomy without gender polarity. We meet Rachel nine years later, in Ellen Goodman's *Turning Points*. She's now nearing another decisive moment in her life, brought on by her relationship with Alan:

[Rachel and Alan] became such good friends that she was sure they would never be lovers and so she let him know her.

When he finally stayed with her one night, "It was as easy as anything else. It was the only time I'd ever thought of sex as friendly."

Two years later, they still live separately, though they spend much of their time together. "Alan would like me to make a commitment to live with him. I'm not so sure. . . . It's important to me to be in charge of my own life. But on the other hand, I love being close with him. I don't mind that there's a 'we' creeping into my vocabulary. And I do think a lot about wanting to have a sense of family and even a baby."[21]

The second story is from a woman whose six-year marriage started with a friendship of several years during which both were romantically involved with other people—"We were luncheon buddies. We would make luncheon dates and cry on each other's shoulders about our romances." She is a professional dancer (and the person who coined the term sparkledust); he is a historian, and they are now in their early forties:

I don't remember for sure how our relationship began to move into the sexual. I do remember that we actually *looked* at each other and *said*, "Now what are we going to do? Are we going to take a chance of spoiling a wonderful friendship, or are we going to take the risk of making it a love relationship?" It was a rational decision rather than a passionate one.

And, as it happened, I got pregnant. The very first time. I felt stunned. I couldn't believe that I had, at my age—I mean, it was just like two teenagers. But part of me was very pleased. And he took it wonderfully. It gave us something very serious to get to know each other about, and we became very close very fast through that. I decided to have the child, even though we weren't going to get married because of this. He went off to Africa to do field work, and I started spotting. I had to stay in bed for a week, but I still lost it. I tried to get ahold of Sam in Africa. I called the police there, tried everything I knew, but he never ever got the message. But [pointing to her head] he got the message here. He phoned.

When he found out that I'd lost the baby he said, "Come *on* down." So I did. It was the only thing that helped me get over that.

We went together from then on, nearly inseparable, for the next year. He kept his place and I kept mine. We spent about every night together. There were times when he said, "I'm tired, I think I'll go home tonight" and I would get hurt. I never felt tired enough to go home. I just loved being with him. I felt happy and good inside from being with him. There was none of that draining, wrenching, awful stuff I was so familiar with. None of that now. Because it feels right, it all fits.

Do I miss that kind of palpitating passion I had with the others? Off the top of my head I'd say, Oh, God, no! Because what you remember is that driven, desperate feeling. *No,* I don't miss that. There's a certain fascination, a good side to all that torture, that's why you get pulled; but the torture isn't worth it. It feels so delicious—when it doesn't feel terrible. I don't have that heady feeling with him. I guess I don't think about it. Yeah, that's it: I don't think about it. I'd rather have what I have. There's a solid feeling inside. Everything is okay. I feel like a whole person. I feel I can relax and be me, and I don't have to worry about Who I Am, Am I Pleasing Him? Any of that *stuff*. It's like being with close female friends in that.

Together, the relationship with self and the relationships we have with friends provide the ground out of which rises the figure of the intimacy we experience in a love relationship. They are closely connected to the kind of love relationship we will find. And they are our best chance to experience love as a passionate union between two authentic selves. Having no viable relationship with self, we have no authentic self to bring to such a union. Having no important friendships in our lives, we have too little experience with intimacy and too few alternatives for intimacy, with the result that we overload the love relationship and probably sink it. In short, a good relationship with self and a good variety of friendships, sexual and nonsexual, are necessary for a full life. And they are essential as the basis for love.

9. Love: Practice

If we want to move toward love as I am advocating it, and if we want to do it by way of aspiring passion, we face the problem that romantic infatuation may still seize us occasionally and steer us off course. We can pardon ourselves for such wobbles, since our society is so saturated with the Myth of Romantic Love that we can expect it to run steady interference in our love lives, and since this passion functions in a manner that I call the tyranny of romantic love.

Love à la Mode

When you say, "I can't get him (or her) out of my mind," you are in a state of cognitive obsession. This endless thinking about the object of your passion is, most of all, intrusive and seemingly inescapable. It seems to be something that *just happens* instead of something you *do*. You awake in the morning, and there is the image of your inamorata in your consciousness, where it stays all day long until it ends up defining all other experience in relation to its perpetual presence.[1] "Having it bad" is to suffer what de Rougemont calls the impoverishment of a mind obsessed by a single image.[2] I call it mental tyranny. There may be times when we are of a mood to live in tyranny and can find pleasure in this kind of obsession. However, for those times when such is not the case, when we berate ourselves for not being in charge of our own lives, I offer here my suggestion as to why this tyranny is so powerful.

We know that romantic love thrives on obstacles. We also know that uncertainty is a major factor in this state, that the "romance game" usually is not up front but rather full of subterfuge and "not showing your hand" too soon. What we don't know and badly want to when under the influence is whether the person we're infatuated with returns the feeling. Much of our endless rumination is spent writing scenarios in the mind that reassure us: Yes, our inamorata does return the feeling. In short, more uncertainty. One woman spoke for all of us, female and male, when she described the condition: "It was something about the way Richard acted, feeding out just enough attentiveness to keep me on the hook, but never quite enough to let me relax. I don't say that was his intention, although at the time I even imagined that his unreliability was a deliberate plot."[3]

A person who is especially romantic is a person who is especially good at acting like Richard. This kind of behavior is what behaviorists call intermittent or partial reinforcement. Partial reinforcement is among the strongest known causes of behavior, and it works like this: When a given act is almost always reinforced, when we consistently get a positive response to this act, we are likely to continue to behave in the manner that produces this response. When we don't get reinforced, when we consistently get a neutral or even negative response, we are likely to stop acting this way, at least with this particular person. But suppose the response to our act is variable: sometimes nicely positive, other times neutral or negative. And suppose further that we can't predict what the next response to our act will be. Then what? Then we become hooked. It works with pigeons, it works with us. In the classic experiment the pigeon learns that a peck at a disc will get it a small quantity of grain. Then the reinforcement is changed: now the pigeon gets grain only once in a while and not very frequently. What happens? For an unpredictable reward of grain that averages twelve times an hour, the pigeon pecks at a rate of 6,000 times per hour.[4] How many times an hour do we think about our inamorata when we've "got it bad"? With the pigeon, we demonstrate it nicely: The characteristic result of partial reinforcement is that behavior is sustained over long periods of time with very little return.

There exists advice from behaviorists on how to break the enormous power of partial reinforcement over your mind. Remember this the next time you've "got it bad" and don't want it. Also remember that the romantic passion self-destructs eventually. You may feel, "I want you. I want you now, yesterday, and always," but people's experience, scientific research, and what we call our great love literature tell us that the prognosis is an average maximum of less than three years.[5]

A friend of mine used to say that falling madly in love is an emotional cry for help. I go along with him to the point of saying that it's an emotional cry, but a cry for the experience of wholeness as given to us by another. We fall madly in love with the kind of person who at the particular time looks as if he or she can give us that experience. Love-blotting tells us that we usually don't fall in love with a person. We fall in love with an image we build on the basis of that person; more specifically, I think, with an image built on the particular aspect of the person that we have a strong need for. Take the autonomous woman with her Magic Button, for instance, a woman who has endured social disapproval and the disapproval of men because of her unfeminine behavior. Her Magic Button is big, and it says, "Free me from the curse of unfemininity, tell me I am romantically attractive." The man who can push this button successfully, regardless of his total attributes as a person, is the man who will become her Mr. Wonderful. I asked a Reverse Sleeping Beauty I know, "What do you think made it happen?" referring to her romance with an otherwise unsuitable man. She replied, "Sex and fantasy," and I think that covers it quite adequately.

Learning to live with our romantic infatuations basically means learning to take them in stride without becoming totally addled. No one has expressed this delicate balance better than George Eliot: "Strange that some of us, with quick alternate vision, behold the wide plain where our persistent self pauses and awaits us."[6] This quote highlights the distinction I make between romantic and aspiring passion. Romantic infatuation usually is fueled by what Plato calls the accidental features of our love object, while in aspiring passion it's the person's persistent self that arouses us. Similarly, infatuation is fueled in us by our own accidental features and current urgencies, while in aspiring passion our persistent self is aroused. It doesn't have to pause and await us, because it is the core of such passion. We become more ourselves from going with it, whereas the result of romantic passion, and a great part of its appeal, was described by Romeo: "I have lost myself; I am not here; this is not Romeo, he's some otherwhere."

What shall we do with romantic passion in our lives? I have two suggestions. While the passion is upon us, I suggest enjoying it as knowingly as possible. Think of it as love à la mode: a delicious treat at its best, but you wouldn't make a meal of it any more often than you'd gorge on ice cream as your one and only dinner fare. When it ends, especially when it ends badly, I suggest taking the question, "How *could* I?" seriously—find out how. This is the time to turn love-blotting around and make it work for us as a mode of self-discovery and learning. Find out what qualified the Wonderful One for the job of making us feel whole. If, like my friend in chapter 1, we sigh, "It was Camelot," find out just what this lost Camelot means, and then see about getting it in a more self-reliant way than having it bestowed by another. Lucy Goodison makes an excellent point in her essay on falling in love when she says, "We use the term 'falling' in love which disguises the fact that we have chosen to leap and have abdicated responsibility for our experience. The feelings, fantasies and sensations that possess us are in fact our own. We say another 'makes' us feel unbelievable excitement, but actually the excitement is ours. If we can feel it in one situation, we can feel it in another."[7]

Treating romantic love as love à la mode seems to me to get the most out of it, both while it is going on and after it is over. However it plays itself out, this passion can have strong benefits in our lives if we enjoy its excitement, study it for what it tells us about ourselves, and then broaden the context in which we can feel those emotions. Knowing it for what it is, and especially for what it isn't, will loosen the grip of Maslow's Hammer on our love lives.

Moving into Intimacy

Now let's try to imagine what it would be like to meet someone, feel an authentic connection to him or her, and then follow the trace of that aspiring passion into intimacy. (We can take authentic connection to mean that each person feels his or her persistent self drawn to the other's.) What happens when we feel an authentic connection to someone and the feeling is mutual? First, there is a surge of excitement as the mind and senses are aroused. The subjective experience of this surge is that we feel, "Here is a person with whom I am more alive, more of a person, and in better contact with myself."[8] As one young woman wrote to me, "A sign I feel that tells me this is what's going on is when I find myself saying things to someone that I've never said *or understood myself* before. This is very wonderful and opening." At such a time there is a powerful pull to extend and expand the connection, and under optimum conditions both people will respond with enthusiasm to this pull. Jessica Benjamin calls it becoming alive in the presence of an equal other.[9] I would call this the first step into intimacy, and I think that whatever happens later, it is a positive step. As that young woman says, the step itself is expansive and illuminating. And joyful.

I define the process of moving into intimacy to mean the continuing activity of wishing to know and be known by an other. We might rephrase it in the image of Debussy's desire to sing his interior landscape: We are moving into intimacy when we mutually feel encouraged by the other to sing our interior landscape as it changes with time; and when that interior landscape is felt to be understood and valued by the other; and when there is complete acceptance that such a song will change, should be left free to change, and that this is good. Keeping Debussy's image, what can bloom in such a process is affection of the inmost heart.

The process of moving into intimacy is the process of discovering what the potential for deep intimacy is between two people.

The affinity will turn out to be there, or not there, and love can therefore not be imposed but is instead revealed and discovered. We can enhance the conditions for revealing it by being authentic and responsive and caring; but when we move into intimacy we are unavoidably moving into the possibility of finding inherent limits to the affinity that can exist between us. Some of these limits we may be able to live with amicably, some will require work and can then perhaps be lived with, some may prove insurmountable. These conditions of moving into intimacy seem to me simply a truth of existence, and I find it a very freeing truth. There is freedom in acknowledging what cannot be altered, and hopefuly therefore a lack of blame or guilt or recrimination. Tristan Bernard puts this existential principle in a nutshell when he says that "to live happily with other people one should ask of them only what they can give."[10]

In the spirit of this wise and loving observation, let's look more closely at the notion of inherent limits in intimate relationships, to see what can be said about them that will enhance the possibilities for loving. It strikes me that limits are to a personal relationship as limits are to the relationship of humans and the biosphere. We know there are inherent limits to how far we can behave as we please with respect to the biosphere. These limits have always been there, but they are only becoming really evident in our time. Until now, we could indulge ourselves without worrying too much about the globe, because there weren't that many of us and our technology was not yet dangerous. But now we can destroy ourselves and the biosphere if we don't learn what those limits are and respect them.

The same principle applies to all personal relationships and becomes most serious with respect to consequences in the most intimate relationships. The time humans have been able more or less to indulge themselves without thought for ultimate consequences on the biosphere corresponds in a love relationship to the beginning, where most things look open and possible because the inherent limits that may exist have not yet become evident. With time, however, they inevitably begin to emerge, and the degree to which they still can be transgressed without serious detrimental results to both parties involved becomes smaller. Some limits can be lived with, it's a matter of degree; but to the degree that the limit is of a truly central nature to either party, and if the limit is not agreeable to the other, there is a serious problem in the relationship.

I don't mean limit in the sense of inadequacy or limitation, I'm talking about the contours of a person's innermost self as they match or don't match with the contours of the other's innermost self. For example, some people welcome life with open arms, as it were, while some other people prefer to hold it more at arm's length. We might get fancy here (so as to cast no aspersions on either type) and call the former a Dionysian and the latter an Apollonian. My point is, were these two types to become mates we could expect serious problems because their basic ways of being in the world are so different. Probably the Dionysian would come to feel hemmed in, belittled for being "not serious," undermined; meanwhile, the Apollonian would feel more or less constantly at risk for an unwanted emotional roller-coaster ride and would long for some peace and quiet—which the Dionysian would see as monotony. And so forth.

There is no question of fault on either party's side here. The issue is one of facing a difference that may be irreconcilable and, if it is, of accepting what amounts to inflexible reality. When such a limit is reached, and the parties still continue to go on in the old manner rather than dealing positively with it, I think the result will be the same as it is for humans and the globe; namely, destruction—probably in the form of polluting itself and its participants to death psychologically. This is what I see happening in many couples, and it is a painful thing to observe. The most loving act under the circumstances is to try jointly to understand the nature of the particular limit and then to assess if it can be lived with in a life-enhancing manner. If not, dissolve the relationship before it becomes too polluted and has damaged each party too much. *And*—most important—do this without guilt feelings over so-called failure. Because this is a positive step, a loving step toward self and other in recognition of necessity, even if we might wish it were otherwise.

In other words, we should approach the question of limits impersonally. This is enormously difficult to do, of course, when love and thwarted love are the issue, and when we tend to have a belief that if love doesn't last forever it must not have been genuine love. We made a mistake, and we shouldn't have. So it's our failure as lovers instead of the meeting of inherent limits over which we have little or no control and for which we therefore cannot hold ourselves responsible. Especially not if, until the time of those limits' appearance, we have been open to the other person and seriously committed to having him or her grow and change and become more him/herself. Actually, I think if we truly are loving and responsive in a relationship, the limits that may exist will appear sooner than they will if we are obtuse and self-centered and, in short, unloving.

So, even under ideal circumstances of the best of loving we can end up facing limits that may be insurmountable, and we come to this difficult place innocently. If we fail to understand this important truth, we're liable to get tangled in an ugly mess of guilt and recrimination. And this will merely serve to embitter each party and poison the past between them, when they might have continued on as friends with a deeply shared past. To be friends with a former mate seems to me a very valuable thing and not one to be discarded lightly, with nary a "thanks for the memory." Were we to meet final limits in the spirit I'm advocating, we could gain both the freedom to follow our own kind and an intimate friend with whom we have a special bond.

Choosing a Mate

You know, it amazes me that love can be a subject as obsessive as it is in our society, and yet so few of us take it seriously in our own lives. Falling in love is not serious business, but becoming mates is. Very serious business indeed, since it involves making a major decision about how one is going to live one's life in the foreseeable future. Choosing a mate is probably the single most serious choice we make in terms of the subsequent quality of our life. It's a question not only of deepest values as they apply themselves out in daily experience, but also of preferred habits of everyday life—like, one sleeps with the window open and the other prefers it closed. Though not serious in terms of deep values and respect, these minor characteristics are important because they form the daily environment in which one lives with a person. (I, for example, would find it intolerable to sleep in a hot room with the window closed, no matter how marvelous I might find the person I was sleeping with.)

We know this with family and friends. We say, I love so-and-so and I could not (or would prefer not to) live with them. Such a statement does not deny the presence of love or attraction toward the person. It's often a statement of just such a presence, while also recognizing that this does not necessarily mean the person would make a congenial companion in one's daily home sphere. One of the people I love most in this world, have known intimately for two decades, find estimable and dazzling and illuminating in the highest degree, is a person to whom I've said for two decades: living with you would spin me right off my base. The feeling is mutual on all counts. And this is precisely *because* of the great affinity we feel toward each other's intense life energy—which, added to our own, would make for a home atmosphere so charged that we agree we'd both go bananas in fairly short order. It would be true to say that out of love for each other we stay apart. We leave it at that, except for a provisional and not entirely flippant agreement to take up the matter again when we reach our eighties.

The truth is, love is a necessary but not sufficient condition for living happily with someone as mates. All you need is love—plus some very important correspondences that range from the sublime to what may look like the ridiculous. In his book about love, psychologist Robert Sternberg presents the problem where two people who get together have different ideas of what love is, saying that he thinks this problem is much more common than people recognize.[11] How each person sees love in a mate relationship would seem to be a rather major question to explore with a potential mate, but how many of us do so? We may talk ad infinitum of Love when we're madly in love, but such talk is hardly likely to uncover genuine and especially problematic differences.

Sternberg makes the point I want to explore here: that what matters is not whether two people have different ideas of what love is, but rather what practical difference those ideas made. A simple and eminently sound distinction. As Eliza Doolittle sings, "Don't talk of love, show me." Beautiful sentiments of love notwithstanding, love is as love does. And the sooner we ask some very practical questions, the sooner we'll find love that does as we prefer.

I'm reminded of a cartoon that was said to characterize Reed College when I went there. Reed was fervently intellectual and the discussions in the dining hall were inevitably as high-flown as the food was abysmal. In the cartoon two students are sitting in a lovely flowering tree, books perched on a branch beside them. The young man looks entreating, the young woman serious. Caption: "That's very nice, John. Now, if by love you mean . . ." We have here an exceptionally wise young woman. I smile at her with affectionate esteem. She may even be a contender for aspiring passion. But she is definitely *not* romantic about love. Were she romantic, she would swoon, probably fall out of the tree, and certainly not ask bothersome questions at this magic moment. Most people don't do what she does.

I think Sternberg is correct—people tend not to confront what love means either to themselves or to their partner. Instead, we make assumptions and leave the reality of those practical differences in suspended animation, where we hope they will stay. Only they don't. They have a nasty habit of coming down to bonk us on the head sooner or later. I'll use myself again as a case in point.

As an error in love my case is, I think, quite common. I married my high school boyfriend halfway through college. We had been students together; each, as Plato has it, strongly individuated by what we most deeply cared about. In his case this was a passion for theoretical physics as it explored the deeper truths of nature, and in my case a passion for knowledge as it applied to social justice. Each loved the other primarily for this quality of passion, this devotion to something that was larger than ourselves and also larger than our feelings for the other. We must have looked like a stellar example of aspiring passion: what we wanted appeared to be a mutual exchange of love and ideas that would be a seamless part of our own central aspiration. That definitely is what I wanted and what I thought he wanted with me. For this vision I would have worked very hard, and I would have considered that work joyful. But I was not so wise as my Reed contemporary in that cartoon; I didn't ask bothersome questions, I merely assumed. And therefore these bothersome questions came back to bonk me with the practical results of our two views of love. Had I, instead of asking the abstract question, "What is your idea of love?" asked the far more practical one, "What do you see as the purpose and function of your wife?" I never would have been his wife. Suffice it to say, his answer would have been more like that of the couples in M. Scott Peck's group than like Peck's own. On the purpose and function of Bonnie we agreed so little that we in actual practice were fundamentally mismatched. He would have been far happier with someone of what I call the love-primary mode: a person who might take an active interest in work and the world, but whose central passion remained focused on him and the marriage. I would have been far happier with someone who actually wanted both of us to live in Plato's vision, a work-primary person whose passionate involvement with me was part of a larger vision.

All of this eventually became starkly revealed as the very serious limit it was, but by then it was the late 1960s and the women's movement was being started. We decided that we had a sex-role problem—and we certainly did. As far as his role was concerned, he still loved his physics and I still loved my vision, so I had little problem with this aspect of his behavior. As for my role, we were in complete accord on that one: I did not fit the role he had in mind for his wife, and I adamantly never would fit it. Since his notion of the proper function of his wife easily fell into the category of sexist, and since he did not like that one bit, we attempted to "work through" our problem.

I do not recommend a love relationship whose very substance is "working on the relationship." Some people see it as part of the struggle for a better world. I see it as a joyless way to live and a good way to kill love. For us, it became both. We managed to get rid of the sex-role problem, for which I commend us; but by that time we were both wondering what it was all *for,* this endless struggle between us. And, as the sex-role question faded, an even more fundamental obstacle to living together stood revealed. To this Himalayan limit, the foothills of sex-role conflict had acted as camouflage. I've described the limit already—a Dionysian was coupled with an Apollonian. Perhaps not surprisingly, it was the Dionysian who initiated the next move. The divorce, so we were told repeatedly by surprised lawyers, was a model of civility. We weren't surprised. Because, though all endings carry their own tribulations and regrets, we both knew that the split was in our best interests, and that it in effect was rectifying an error of omission made long ago. We should have known better than we did when we married. Perhaps even serious talking might not have revealed the Dionysian/Apollonian limit, especially since we were so young. But we would have known better than to marry if we'd asked the few and obvious questions that laid bare our striking practical differences about wifely love.

I've called the two modes at issue between my ex-husband and me the love-primary and the work-primary modes. Each mode seems to me to have its own value and meaning, but they are of a different order. What was true between us can be generalized: It doesn't really matter to which mode you belong, what matters is that the person you want to be mates with belongs to the mode you want in a mate—and vice versa. I think this is a major question for couples, and one that few seem to probe before they become enmeshed in each other's lives and find out the hard way if there is a mismatch.

Let's take the case of a mutual mismatch. Here we have two people in a couple, one of each mode, and both would prefer to be mates with someone of his or her mode. The result is that neither fits the other's preferred mode for a mate. As far as I can see, that spells big trouble in a relationship. What will happen? The delight of initial exploration as each follows the trace of illumination in the other will gradually diminish as restrictions begin to appear. For example, the work-primary person will feel increasingly boxed in, maybe even invaded, guilty (to the degree that he or she is guilt-prone) for "not doing enough" in the relationship. Worst of all for a person like this, the work that matters so deeply to him or her will be seen by the other as a rival, an interference, a self-indulgence–at least the strong devotion to such work will be seen that way when it interferes with Love. Eventually, a person of the work-primary mode coupled with someone who wants the love-primary mode will face the stark question: How far can I fetter myself in the name of love and still call it love? Even more stark for a person like this: How far can I fetter myself in the name of love and still do the work that matters supremely to me? Meanwhile, the person of the love-primary mode will feel unloved, unappreciated, probably always hungry in some deep and gnawing sense, resentful over doing "too much" in the relationship, and (to the extent that he or she feels righteous about "love first") feel that the other is getting away with murder in not doing enough while still wanting to call what he or she is doing love. This kind of person in this situation will eventually be faced with the stark question: How far can I starve myself in the name of love and still call it love? And worse, this kind of person with a mate of the other mode will run a grave risk of becoming increasingly demanding and possessive, out of sheer frustration, and will not see the other's mode of being as intrinsic to him or her and therefore to be respected, but rather as something to be corrected in the name of love.

If this incompatibility goes on long enough, each mate will tend to become what Sternberg calls a "punishing stimulus" because of his or her ability to evoke feelings that are unpleasant or even painful in the other.[12] I find that a very useful concept, and only too common in people's experience. Applying it here, what can we expect? The love-primary mate will increasingly come to be seen by the other as the prison warden—the one with the easy frown, the raised eyebrow, the strident voice, the ever-ready impatience or even contempt. The work-primary mate will come to be seen as the uncaring shirker—frivolous, self-centered, uncommitted—possibly even as incapable of love. I've seen friends grapple with solutions to this difference in modes, and personally I think it is a doomed enterprise. They may gain a temporary truce, laugh at their differences and try to live and let live, but I think that in the end a difference this deep and significant is corrosive no matter what symptomatic solutions we come up with. Because, even if the solutions ease the immediate tension, the underlying schism remains to undermine each person at the deepest level. It will be a case of the battle is over but the war goes on.

The acid test of love, to my way of thinking, is: Do you feel enhanced, in the overall, from being intimate with this person? Do you feel that his or her intimate presence in your life helps you to get on with living, or does it hamper that basic life thing? If both parties can't answer affirmatively to these questions, the relationship will become increasingly crippled. To the extent that people in such a relationship attempt to accommodate to limits that are alien to their deepest nature, to that extent will they cripple their own lives. And the reason is that in the name of love they will have allowed themselves, even forced themselves, to live their lives as someone they're not. Love, as far as one can call it that in such a relationship, will essentially consist of each mate's repeatedly seeking the other's forgiveness for the original sin of being herself or himself.

Toward Enriching Love

Fortunately, there are mates who happily can give what the other asks of them in relationship. They have enormous differences between them, but they are confirmation of the hope that differences do not *have* to manifest as serious and debilitating limits but can actually be an enrichment for each person involved. We will meet them later in this chapter. First, however, let's take a look at some experiences of people who are moving toward this kind of love—not via romance but via what they now are calling aspiring passion.

I had discussed with them my concepts about the process of intimacy and especially about the particular aspect of this process I call aspiring passion. I then wrote about the concepts, and they applied some of these concepts and reported back to me about their experiences with them. It makes me very pleased to be able to say that they found the concepts clarifying and empowering, especially as they tried to distinguish what they were doing from what they normally would have called romantic love. I do think this little sample augers well for those of us who want to try our own version of the nonromantic path to love.

Some of these respondents started all the way back in the friendship chapter: "The more I look at my many and varied relationships, the more I begin to realize the truth of that phrase 'each follows its kind' and of the stones on the beach analogy," commented one woman. "And I see that, in the main, all the people in my life are pretty well where they should be in terms of who they are and who I am. That is such a peaceful feeling." I agree. The more we can get away from our usual hierarchy approach to friends, where some are "better" than others up to "best friend," and instead find pleasure in each kind of intimacy as worthwhile in itself, the more firm our foundation will be for love. I don't mean to imply that intimate relationships other than mate-love relationships are a means to an end, far from it. To have a large variety of intimate relationships, each giving the participants what feels appropriate, and to value exactly the appropriateness of this state, seems to me the very best approach to all intimacy.

Making distinctions between romantic and aspiring passion was perhaps the major endeavor of my respondents. This potentially tricky business turned out to be much clearer for most of them than either they or I had expected. For example, one woman who told me about the "Boom!" of being struck and then wondering how to figure out whether she would call it romantic or aspiring passion made a neat distinction. She said, "I decided it was a very fine nonromantic version of Boom! Because I know what hit me. At the same time I also know that it isn't knowledge in other than a potential way: I may see that trace you talk about, and I may actually be a hundred percent correct in what I know—but I don't know that yet."

Another woman wrote about making the same distinction between romantic and aspiring passion as she moved along: "It feels like a slow movement through gently shifting patterns that are continuously moving, and I move through them while noting my steps to myself. Each step involves a careful sifting to see just what it is and also what it isn't. I'm discovering that what it *shouldn't* be is what is most familiar to me (old romantic stuff, lurching, leaping, being unreal, feeling alternately ecstatic and scared, etc.); and what it *should* be, and does seem to be, is what is most unfamiliar and yet what feels most right."

Most of my respondents talked about learning not to leap, as they were used to doing in romantic love. They seemed determined to walk into love instead of the usual falling. For example, "Yes, I would like all this stuff with Jim to move into everything that aspiring passion could be. At the same time I feel dispassionate about it in a decidedly nonromantic way. I feel no inclination to change my whole life around the way I know so well from of yore. *And* I don't feel that this is a sign of lack of desire or interest on my part, as I would have in the past. This is indeed progress!"

The two words I got most often in the "learning not to leap" department were time and space. One woman I interviewed said, "I've found it a wise procedure to include regular and sometimes lengthy absences while moving into intimacy. Distance. It's a great leveler. Makes you think, makes you stabilize. I think the hardest thing when you're going through transformation is that old patterns carry you forward *so* easily. So if you give yourself that space when you start to recognize those patterns you then have a chance to say, oops, I did it again, laugh at yourself and then retrace your steps and try it again in a new way."

A friend and I were discussing these concepts and our own experiences with them when she characterized the feeling of moving into intimacy via aspiring passion by this fine image: "It's like going down a river in a kayak—even with the rapids. If you leap at a rock too soon you get stuck. You just have to let the river take you and move with grace. Grace. That's a word I love. It has all that sense of dignity, timing, judgment, discretion, and also letting go of control. That's the way I want to move into love." I asked her what such a love would be like, if we did manage to move into it the way she described, and she answered without hesitation, "It would be like that poem by Rainer Maria Rilke: 'Love consists in this, that two solitudes protect and touch and greet each other.[13]' He's uniting separateness and love, which our society thinks of as a contradiction, and saying that they co-exist if it's genuine love."

I find the image of two solitudes protecting and touching and greeting each other most evocative as an image of love. It seems to reverberate with space and tenderness and my friend's word, grace. It also fits the love relationships we will encounter in the next part of this chapter. I always felt exhilarated when I came away from interviewing these separate (in the sense of individually distinctive as themselves) persons, who yet were connected to each other in a strong bond of love. I agree with Rilke about separateness, or what I call autonomy, and love; they do coexist if it's genuine love. In fact, I would say, you can't have one without the other.

Can This Be Love?

What would an examplary love story look like, in the mode of love that I am advocating? We start at the beginning. You meet someone and feel an authentic connection to him or her. The other person also feels that initial surge of excitement as the mind and senses are aroused by what I call aspiring passion. Both of you respond with enthusiasm to the trace you see in the other, that here may be someone who answers to the desire of your soul, and you both follow that trace into more knowledge about the authentic being of the other. You take your time, allowing the other to be his or her own self with you, instead of love-blotting or making assumptions. You probably become lovers; you certainly become friends. You manage to maintain that delicate balance between your immediate delight and your persistent self as you move cleanly and soberly, with passionate grace, into intimacy. Maybe with a few wobbles along the way, since who's perfect? You arrive at the end of this journey into love feeling reasonably certain that there are no major limits apparent between you—what each cares most deeply about matches with the other, and is cherished in the other as in yourself.

Now what? This is where fairy tales and Ideal Romances move their version of this journey into nothingness with the customary send-off. This is also where modern society leaves the travelers on this path in nothingness—or worse. Because not only is the journey ahead uncharted, it must make its pioneering way in our society through territory crowded with institutions and attitudes that, given less than half a chance, will hamper or even block its progress. How many of us know the kind of love I'm talking about from our own lives? Where each person says "Yes!" to the self, to the other, and to life, all in the same breath and into the future. I don't, and I doubt that I'm unique. I have wanted it and sought it, even as I detoured myself by binges of romantic love or poor choices in partners for such a journey. I know some strong hints of it from recent experience, and I can imagine more by extrapolating from these experiences in love. I have looked for evidence of this kind of love in the lives of others, especially while writing this book, and I have found such evidence. Not often, but often enough to sustain the vision. From among those people, I have chosen two couples who look to be going this route in love and who agreed to be interviewed. I also present a couple I "met" in a biography, who inspired me by the fact of their existence. Like the real life love story of Annie Oakley and Frank Butler, these stories are not romantic. Because they are real, they are full of difficulty and pain; because they are genuine love stories, they are also full of authentic passion and commitment and laughter.

Sandra Kelly and Keith Lerner

Sandy and Keith met as college students on a blind date on Valentine's Day 1969. Aside from that, little or nothing in their relationship is according to the Myth of Romantic Love. "We really liked each other," says Sandy, "and we hung out together for seven years before we decided to get married." They both finished college first, went on to graduate school, and then into their respective careers—his in biology and conservation, hers in public affairs and politics. While he was "working for conservation, trying to learn how to preserve the natural heritage of the State of California," she worked for a labor union. "I was the business agent there for ten years, and I would represent people in collective bargaining agreements, arbitration, whatever. It was a great job, a real pioneer job for women in those days."

They married during the second year of her job with the union, even though her hours were "unbelievable," with all-night negotiations a common feature. Keith sums up their life at the time: "We had two very, very interesting jobs and we both worked our tails off; I was trying to learn what to do and Sandy was learning what to do, and we had a pretty good time. We didn't see much of each other, though. But we always seemed to see a lot of each other, somehow."

I ask about housework. They look amused. "You gotta realize, we got pretty good at not doing it," laughs Keith. "But what housework we did, we shared. Once every three or four weeks we'd get in there and we'd share all the housework, except Sandy would cook and I would usually do the dishes." He muses, almost to himself, "We must have eaten out a lot." Sandy strikes a note I'll hear frequently, "We didn't really think, okay, you have to do this and I'll do that. It just happened when it had to happen."

Now she is thirty-six years old, he is thirty-seven, they have three children under the age of eight, and are in the kind of life crisis that puts your values, priorities, and relationships on the line. Keith and a number of colleagues have started a new and different international conservation organization that promises to deliver on their favorite ideas about global conservation. "It's very exciting," he says. "It's also very, very difficult and time-consuming." The result on the home front, where they have an avowed goal of joint parenting, is that "the balance has shifted dramatically," as Sandy ruefully puts it. She is a full-time mother at home, mostly on her own. He does what he can to equalize the parenting burden, but for the time being he can't do much because of the exigencies of the organization they both believe in.

"We're right in the middle of probably the toughest period of our marriage and our lives," they assure me; and I assure them, "That's why I'm here." I'm interested in how a stable and committed couple handles so difficult a situation; one which neither of them anticipated in their separate or joint scheme of things, yet also a situation in which there is no villain even though it is Sandy who is making the greater sacrifice.

"I've assumed more and more of the duties of total parenting over the past few years," she explains. "It's really difficult with three small children, because you not only have their physical needs, which are enormous, but also their emotional and intellectual needs. It was also difficult to decide that I was a homemaker and At Home. You have to have tremendous self-esteem to battle that image. Out there on the cocktail circuit they look at you as if you're not working when you say you're at home with your children; you have no role or worth in the economic sphere. At first it bothered me but then I thought, if we can't raise our kids jointly in these first years, then *I* want to do it. I have a way of looking at the world that I think is important. I want to get some values across to the kids, because what you leave unsaid is said somewhere else and often in a way that you don't approve of. So you really have to cover what's crucial to you. I'm doing something important and I want to be doing it.

"But the last few years have been more than I bargained for. Honestly, I reached my chaos level this year, and I had to ask myself, What am I going to do to make my life better? How am I going to function? It's really put me through the meat grinder to evaluate what is important." This deep questioning led her to join the board of a national educational nonprofit organization. She sees this as worthwhile in itself but even more as temporary relief. "It's wonderful to have that creative element as part of the other things I'm doing. I realized that I need to do things that keep my brain active and alert and validated. Fortunately, we've been able to get some help. We don't buy a lot of clothes and stuff, we use that money to get some spare hands, and that's helped a lot. Especially since the daycare situation is so poor here."

As Sandy is talking I become aware that the ambience between this couple is clean and peaceful, even while difficult things are being said. They often talk in unison, or they supplement each other when the subject is a joint one; yet there is never a sense that one disrupts the other. At times like this one, when she is talking out of her deep feelings, he keeps totally silent and just sits back looking interested and positive. "You know," Sandy continues, "the thing about this new organization is that it's a *new* organization. We have another newborn baby, that's basically how I look at it. It's like having a baby that needs to be fed every three hours, and you're just there all the time. You have to focus on that newborn, you can't just ignore it. I believe in conservation. If Keith weren't in it, I'd probably do it. As it is, I've become a spokesperson for this organization, so I not only approve of it, I feel a part of it in a way that's maybe kind of unique to our relationship. We're each part of what the other is doing."

At this point Keith interjects for the first and only time in the interview. "I must say this," he fairly blurts. "For the first time in my life, because of the pressures of trying to make this organization survive, trying to deal with the difficulty on Sandy, trying to deal with the pain in my kids—I'm really struggling with: Is it worth it to do this? Is it fair to do this?" He begins to act out what he's saying. The impression he makes is powerful and authentic. "I mean, I come home and look and see that Sandy is *gone,* mentally. She's had it, and here's the baby and here are the other two and you take over. So I do. I take over totally. Sandy either takes off someplace or finds a book or gets in the tub, and I go through the excitement of trying to tune in to the kids and give them a bath and get them ready for bed. And then get up early the next morning and start the whole thing over again. It's a meat grinder.

"I get lectured, too. The other day I got a lecture from our oldest daughter when I was leaving to go to Peru. She said, 'You are supposed to be here with *us*.' It was a very spontaneous, teary, angry outburst—because I'm not around. I show up and I have to work, and I leave, and it's been like that for the whole year. It's been just awesome." I ask him what he said to his daughter in response to her outburst. "I said, 'I understand why you're angry, and it makes me sad, too, and as soon as I get back from Peru we're going to be able to have a vacation. But you're right.' That's what I said. What else can you say?" You can tell her to shut up; lots of parents would.

Sandy joins in, "One thing about Keith, when he's there he's there one hundred percent. And the kids *know* it. He gets up with them in the morning and cooks them breakfast, hangs out with them, and then goes away to do whatever he's got to do that day. But when he's there, he's *on*." Keith smiles, "It just seems like the right thing to do. They're *fun* to be with, and they need it. I need it. We all need hugs and kisses and interaction. Do I get hugs and kisses? You bet! That's part of the deal."

He stops smiling. "Still, what do you do? I don't know the solution. I *really* don't know the solution. In the last hour the thought probably flashed through my brain—in fact, I know it did—that maybe what I ought to do is just resign. Or maybe I should turn over the reins of this organization to somebody else and be in a support position. You know, just as a flock of geese fly through the sky, there's always a shift as the new goose takes the front and guides away so they can kind of share the burden. Maybe it's time to shift."

With a look on her face that must have been familiar at the all-night labor negotiations, Sandy says to both of us, "Not just yet.

I do see this phase as easing up. Our youngest is two-and-a-half. She talks, she's starting to get trained; she's getting to the stage where she's easier. And I think we're past the crisis with the organization. Give it another year all around, and we should be in a better situation." Then she turns directly to me and continues, "The thing is, if you can keep the perspective as you go through every day that you're not a victim, you're not a martyr, that's just the way the chips fall right now, and you make your decisions accordingly and try to take the upper side—it really can work."

In a separate interview with her alone, I ask Sandy why she thinks it's working even under these strained circumstances. This is obviously something she has thought about. "One of the great strengths of our relationship, I think, is that Keith is very adaptable. He didn't get bothered when I made more money than he did, even though I did get a kick out of it and sometimes teased him about it; he doesn't mind now that I'm, quote, just a housewife. A lot of men today want their wives to be heavy-duty career people, still have kids, still be home and do all that stuff, and they don't realize that something has to give. Like the wife, usually. So I feel that's a real strength for me. I don't have anybody telling me, you gotta be this, you gotta be that. I can be what works at the time."

If I had to give the key to the success of all the various couples I interviewed for this book, I think it would be this phrase of Sandy's: I can be what works at the time. For all the differences between these couples, the people in them invariably gave each other the freedom and support to be whatever he or she thought worked at the time. This is the essence of nonstereotypic living and loving, which I think is why these relationships work so well even under the most difficult circumstances—perhaps especially under the most difficult circumstances—and also why I found them so exhilarating to be with.

I am convinced that aiding the other in being whatever works at the time is especially necessary today for people who want to break out of the old mold of stereotyped love relationship. Because what Sandy says about women like herself also goes for men like Keith: "I think women my age who are going through all this are the guinea pig generation. We've been helped by the feminist movement. When we got on the scene a lot had already happened, minds were opened. Now we're trying to figure out what the hell we're supposed to be doing and how we're supposed to be doing it. I don't think the old ways work for people like us. The question is, which ways do? I think one of our strengths, Keith and I, is that we don't try to figure out every angle. We just say, okay, let's try that. We ride the waves, and in the main it works for us because we trust the other to be there if the going gets rough."

I ask what she is planning to do when the present rough going eases up, and her face lights up. "I'm brainstorming with a friend about starting our own company. We would act as consultants in how to start a nonprofit organization—basically, how to start an idea. The name of our company is Start-Up. I have a few friends who have started major nonprofit organizations." She starts to grin. "We could have guest speakers—like Keith." Then, looking serious and excited, she concludes, "I think it would be great to do that. Just my kind of thing, and I'd even get to apply much of what I've learned from being involved in launching this newborn baby that's causing us so many problems right now."

Vera Jacobs and Martin Westerkamp

Seven years ago Vera Jacobs was on tour with her chamber music quartet in Germany. Back in New York, where she lived, she was also a freelance cellist doing everything from Bach to Broadway musicals; and she would shortly add to this crowded schedule a teaching job in a small New England arts college. As it turned out, she would also add a love relationship and motherhood. She was thirty-two years old at the time, an American Jew who was used to big city life and her own hectic pace. In Bonn, she met Martin Westerkamp, a German non-Jew from a small town who had thought about becoming a violist but had opted instead for law. He was still a law student, with good prospects but no current income, and he was twenty-four years old.

Vera certainly is not overstating the case when she says, "Our relationship didn't start off to be Permanent, Definite True Love. It had a very jagged graph at the beginning." To most outside observers their relationship looks, if not impossible, then at least highly improbable. By all usual standards of romantic love and the normal couple relationship, theirs should not be working. Nevertheless, it works—jaggedly and splendidly.

Vera, an unusually forthright person, looks at me with lingering amazement in her eyes and says, "When we first got together I did something I have never done before or since. I lied about my age. I thought to myself, well, I know he's younger than I am, I'd better say I'm thirty-one instead of thirty-two. So I did and then he said, 'I'm twenty-four.' I kicked myself and thought, oh, God, what did you do that for, you should have said you're twenty-eight." They both laugh, and Martin adds, "I have to say, when you are twenty-four, thirty-two or thirty-one doesn't make any difference." She says, whimsically, "But twenty-eight might have helped," and he responds with the bearing that would auger well for the judge's bench, "There was no help needed." Now thirty-one years old himself, with a mate of thirty-nine and a daughter, Anna, age two, he clearly means it.

Their differences are legion: age, nationality, background, language. Vera's German, though not totally fluent, was a great deal better than Martin's English, so their relationship was conducted almost exclusively in German for the first four years.

Then there's the Atlantic Ocean. "I figured it out," says Vera. "During the seven years of our relationship, we have flown across that ocean eighty-four times between us, and that doesn't include Anna's eighteen flights. I have the record short visit: I flew over on a Wednesday and back on a Sunday." In the United States she has two reasonably large apartments—one in New York, where we conducted the interview, and one "underneath a dorm at the college; I have kids living over me and next to me, and some of them love to baby-sit, isn't that great?" But in Germany—she shakes her head as she tells me—"the whole thing has been going on in Martin's one-room apartment; our lives got much better when we moved Anna out of the bathroom and into the kitchen area." One of the first presents she gave him was a telephone, which he did not have when they started.

They also have very different emotional fuses. "I have a short fuse that goes off fast and is a spectacular storm, and then it's gone very quickly. Martin sort of clouds over. Every once in a while there's a slight storm, but basically it's just a lot of dark clouds that you can't see through. Then eventually the weather changes, like the weather in Germany."

Martin is a social person who likes to eat dinner in convivial company when he has a free evening; her idea of a perfect evening is to spend it at home transcribing music for her students or (she sighs with bliss at the very thought as she tells me) read a book. She likes to read in bed before going to sleep, he doesn't; she gets up early, he doesn't.

And then there's the matter of money. He says, "I never have money." She says, "I always have money, because I work so hard that I never spend the money that I earn." He says, "I work hard, too, but you don't get much money when you're studying. At least during my internship I think I paid for all my side." She says, "When I play concerts in Europe (I never travel without my cello) or when I teach over here, I usually get paid in cash. So I just give Martin half of it, because his taking care of Anna while I'm working is worth exactly as much to the ongoing operation as what I'm doing." They agree, "We really don't care who has the money and who pays, it's not important." He smiles. "It's no problem for me that Vera earns money and I don't, that makes it easier on me." He stops smiling, adding with quiet determination, "The problem is just that I really want to *do* something in my profession, which is necessary for myself."

In the fourth year of their relationship, when Vera was nearing her thirty-fifth birthday, she started to think about having a child. She would have preferred to have it with Martin, but he did not feel ready to take that step. She then considered having a child with someone else. The issue of whether or not to have a child together brought them to what Martin calls "the point where the serious relationship started." It was still a ways from that to Anna. "Having a serious relationship and having a child was not the same thought. That came later. For Vera it was clearer faster, she felt more pressure than I did. Also, she was already working and in a stable position, and I'm still not in that position." Martin went back to Germany, and another year went by before the decision to have a child was made. He returned to the United States for the first three months of Anna's life, taking part of his internship at a law firm near Vera's college. Then, says Vera, "we had three-week periods where I would be a single parent, followed by two-week periods where we were together, on and off like that. We'd planned Anna's birth for when I had tenure and could take time off, and she obliged us."

They continued on as parents, again separated by the Atlantic Ocean. How does such an arrangement work? "It works about the way housework and money work," answers Vera. "When something has to happen, then it seems to. For example, when Anna was seven and a half months old I played in a summer festival with a very demanding schedule. I realized that nursing was going to become a big problem and that as much as I enjoyed it Anna didn't really seem to care whether she was eating one way or another, so I figured that I could stop nursing and that Martin might be in a position to take care of her. The job he was doing at that point was not really eight-hour days, it involved a fair amount of work at home. That is difficult with a baby, but she slept more then than she sleeps now." With some apprehension, he agreed to take Anna. "It was very hard. I had not much time for her. I never found a long-lasting solution, I relied on my friends for the time being. And my neighbors. Some even came after their work and asked whether they could take Anna, they really liked her. There was also a friend who had no work at the time, so she took care of her for pay. I knew in advance that this would be an important experience, and it was. It worked out fine, but it was still very difficult and it was still really a problem. And it was again the next time I had Anna."

The night before our interview there was a party in the New York apartment. By all accounts, it was a fine event highlighted by a fabulous cake created by the two hosts to celebrate the end of the transatlantic part of their union. "You're not going back to Germany?" I ask Martin. He smiles. "No. This is it. We have made the decision that we want to stay together as a family now." He has finished law school and came this time to the United States as a lawyer with a specialty in international administrative law. He's looking for a job. "Then you'll be one of those lawyers with twelve-hour days," I exclaim at the thought of this addition to their already convoluted schedule and lack of time. He looks more calm than I feel and merely says, "Yes." I turn to Vera. "You're continuing to go back and forth to the college?" She nods, "Uh-huh." I look around the somewhat crammed apartment. "And you would live here, all three of you?" He says, "Yes, probably," and then she adds what I am not prepared for, even after everything I already have heard. "The real undecided is whether we want to have another one of these things." She points to Anna, who is hopping concertedly between them on the couch, and adds darkly, "Right now, I am not leaning towards it." I simply stare at her. She shrugs eloquently, "Well, I'm the single daughter of a single daughter of a single daughter, and I kind of think maybe the mold should be broken." I turn to Martin. "What do you think?" "I would enjoy another one, too, but—well, there are a few things one has to think about first." He smiles the smile I am coming to like a lot. "It is the beginning, let's say, of the discussion."

Vera says, "I've been investigating the early childhood center up at the college, for Anna, because I think I don't have enough friends who have kids her age to give her the socializing she needs. Anyway, once she's in at least a morning care situation, I can imagine that there would be room in my life to take care of another kid and not feel like I'm neglecting everything." She starts to laugh. "You say this is boggling your mind. You know what's boggling mine? The thought of commuting in my little car with *two* of these monsters—plus my cello."

She goes off to put Anna down for her nap, and I turn to Martin. He is sitting with the quiet, self-possessed mien I am coming to like as much as I like his smile. "This is a really wild question." I hesitate, and he says, "Yes?" in an inviting tone. "I was just thinking. Here you are, seven years later and this sane but zany life is pulsating all around you. Is this what you had in mind back when you were twenty-four?" He shakes his head. "I had nothing particular in mind, and certainly not this. I had been considering music, but now I'm very content with my profession; and we can talk about music and also about law, and we both enjoy it. We are both interested in the other's profession, so it gives us more. I think one also cannot decide whether family or work is more important, they are both very important; somehow, it has to blend without really saying whether one or the other has a priority. I cannot imagine life—now, of course—without one or the other. Even the problems, the technical problems of making it all fit together, sometimes it's a crisis on your nervous system —can I say that in English? But we always have found a solution somehow."

After the interview I get a small taste of the commuting scene as we three and Anna—but minus the cello—pile into the car. They are hoping to bring some pictures from the night before to Martin's aunt, who is departing momentarily for Germany. Vera is driving. From behind me Martin explains, "Usually, Vera and the cello are in front when we go somewhere, Anna and I are in the back." We stop at a red light and Vera, who seems unperturbed by hurtling in and out of traffic, turns to me and says matter-of-factly, "Good. Now we have time for a hug." I get a big hug on the yellow light and am out the door on the green, but not before she has beamed at me a look I'll long remember and said, "I'm just so happy." It was a lovely moment.

Thinking of that happy look while writing up their story some months later, I feel an urge to phone them. Martin answers; Vera and Anna are at the college. "How is it going?" I ask and get the expected reply that all is well, he is now a lawyer with the twelve-hour days, the pace is as hectic as can be imagined. "How many kids?" There hasn't been enough time yet, but I can't resist. I can hear the smile in his voice. "One and a half," it comes back. "And amniocentesis tells us, a healthy child. We are planning to name him Erich."

Margaret Morgan and Charles Lawrence

Few of us get to see an exemplary love relationship up close over a really extended period of time, because few of us are as fortunate as the sociologist Sara Lawrence Lightfoot. She is the child of such a relationship, and she has chronicled it for all of us in the story of her mother's life called *Balm In Gilead.*[14] This biography of Dr. Margaret Lawrence, whose wish that her life should "make a difference" took her to the height of success as a child psychiatrist in Harlem, celebrates the human spirit at its best as it moves to carry out the vision of bettering the lives of others while finding personal fulfillment in work and love.

Margaret's dream of becoming a doctor began to shape her life when she was still a child. It took her from the deep South to Harlem, where "the negro girl from Mississippi" walked off at high school graduation with the top prizes in Greek and Latin, and with a full academic scholarship to Cornell University. She arrived in Ithaca in the fall of 1932 with nine dollars in her pocket and with the distinction of being the only black undergraduate in arts and sciences at the time. She was to repeat this kind of distinction throughout her life as she continued to break molds in pursuit of her dreams. Often, it was a costly distinction. At Cornell, for example, she had to work as a maid and general housekeeper for room and board, because blacks were not allowed to live in the college dormitories.

Margaret refers fondly to the summer of 1933, when she was nineteen, as the "Summer of Discovering Charles Lawrence." His vitality attracted her immediately. She was particularly intrigued by his worldliness and by the way he took ideas and turned them on their heads; and she "loved his seriousness *and* his laughter, one following the other, leaping through their conversations." Most of all, she remembers his capacity to love. He, in turn, was intrigued by her self-confidence, by the way she could "be alone with herself." Most of all he admired her "single-minded pursuit of her dream."

The beginning of their relationship, observes their daughter, was so easy and so nonadversarial that it almost didn't feel like romantic love; and, in fact, Margaret and Charles felt most comfortable calling it friendship. Margaret had had several romances before she met Charles, but they usually came to a quick end when the young man would propose marriage and she would feel "claustrophobia." She was afraid that marriage would get in the way of her becoming a doctor. With Charles, right from the beginning, she never experienced the panic that he would block her from what she wanted to do. Instead, the opposite happened: the connection between them was fueled by their wonderful, intense conversations and by a deep respect for each other's sense of purpose and vision. "How did Dad feel about your dream to pursue medicine?" asks Sara. Without hesitation her mother replies, "He immediately *joined* it."

They waited nearly five years to marry, finishing college and two years of graduate school while living hundreds of miles apart. After the wedding, Margaret returned to her third year of medical school at Columbia and Charles to his Ph.D. work in sociology at Atlanta University. They sustained and clarified their relationship in writing, by daily and sometimes twice-daily letters. Three months after the wedding, Charles wrote: "I am as proud of you as I have every right to be. I have exhibited the *Times* clipping until it's frayed and torn, yet I've protected it with all my heart." And the next month: "Congratulations on the fact that you have completed 'Fractures'! The way you have worked with this particular phase of your course causes me to agree—as I have always agreed—with the sentiments of the janitor who says that you 'will get somewhere in the world.'"

It was another five years until they had the first of their three children. The next two were born eighteen months apart while Margaret was the only woman physician on the faculty of Meharry Medical College in Nashville. She wanted to combine for her students the image of mother and teacher, and she did so graphically: As they studied pediatrics and learned about the development of babies, the students could follow the progress of their own professor's pregnancies. When Margaret returned to classes two weeks after each birth, "the students brought me roses." Chuck, Sara, and Paula Lawrence were born within four years of each other while both their parents maintained their careers. Margaret and Charles pulled off this difficult feat partly by becoming very good at juggling work and home schedules, partly by spending what free time they had with their children ("We did our work, but when we weren't working, whoever was born went out with us"), but mostly because they were equally committed to being parents. "Charles *wanted* to be the first to bathe Chuck. . . . You hear lots of fathers say that their children have to be walking and talking before they can feel involved. Not Charles. He was immediately *involved* with the babies." He was also known, if child-care arrangements broke down and Margaret had duties at the hospital, to take his small children with him to the university and carry on with his lecture while they were settled in the back of his classroom with books and toys.

Margaret and Charles were together for fifty years until his death three-quarters of the way through the time it took their daughter to compile Margaret's story, a project which he aided despite serious illness. The three Lawrence children grew up with an enlightening heritage. They saw, writes Sara, "a marriage defined by respectful and loving equality," a father who was vitally engaged in the world and yet always available emotionally, a mother who said without sentimentality, "I love my work." They saw two parents who cared passionately for the world and for each other, and who laughed together up to and including the day on which Charles died. Paula remembers "a living room full of instruments, and nights full of music . . . a family table groaning with food, lively with conversation, the stage for famous imitations of our teachers . . . the warmth of my father's fires that are the center of my childhood home and the spirituals he fell asleep singing to his wakeful children as he held all of us at once in his big chair." Sara remembers that "even as a young child, I knew both the passion and the reverence my mother brought to her work. At the dinner table, while protecting the privacy and anonymity of her patients, she would reenact the dramas of the clinic, providing enough details for us to get caught up in the story. . . . Her tales [were] long and skillfully dramatized, sometimes even by tears running slowly down her cheeks." The story of Margaret and Charles reminds us not only that genuine love enhances the lives of the lovers but also that it enhances, hopefully even inspires, the lives of their children. That we owe it to our children, as to ourselves, to find better ways of loving.

The three relationships I have introduced here are quite dissimilar, yet they have some significant things in common. By their singular vitality and integrity, I think they fire our imagination to life's possibilities. These are people who make of their love lives a great adventure. They are alike in their striking ability to cut through the misleading wrappings our culture puts around love, and to reach so unerringly the human core. Like Sandy, they feel free to be what works at the time, separately or together. People like them show us that autonomy and love are not opposed, but that out of a genuine love relationship can come support for us to engage life at its fullest and most direct. They show that it is, after all, possible to be wholly oneself as a woman and also find love with a man. And that if men take the chance to be wholly themselves instead of the partial human being called a "real" man, they can also love wholeheartedly. These love relationships tell us, in short, that our old divisions are the product of old scripts for women and men which we no longer have to endorse or follow. We can continue to live our love lives in the customary manner prescribed by patriarchal myths, or we can begin to write ourselves some new and better scripts for loving. For the first time in recorded history, the choice is truly ours.

Conscious Loving

Debussy wrote his music because he wanted to sing his interior landscape. I wrote this book because I want to optimize our chances to experience the kind of passionate love where each of us is encouraged to sing her or his interior landscape, *and* to have that song validated. Because without validation—by our self, by the other, and by society—our song is scattered to the winds.

In order for us to get this validation, certain conditions have to exist: we must be able to make conscious choices about how we wish to love, and we must have the freedom to exercise our ability to make such choices. We know that defusing the power of the Myth of Romantic Love by uncovering its unconscious aspects allows us to make conscious choices about them. And we've explored a mode of loving in which being passionate does not mean being "swept away" from our conscious self. We have a new image of the self in relationship, where love becomes a dance of passion and authentic selfhood between mutually caring peers—which is to say, it becomes conscious—and we've seen that it can indeed become reality in people's lives. Now we would like to see such love flourish in our own lives and in the world. So far, so good.

But a person's mode of loving does not exist in a vacuum. We are working against the grain when we choose to live our passionate love relationships in this mode, because it differs significantly from the mode prescribed by the Myth of Romantic Love and validated by our society. We can deal with the problem of working against our own grain; and we are, as we begin to flex those new psychological muscles and see our habitual mode of loving transform itself into a more life-affirming one. But our new mode of loving goes against the societal grain becuase it is inconsistent with our presently dominant worldview.

A worldview, as we've seen, tells us what is "real," what is "natural," what "makes sense," what "sane" people believe and do, and so forth. It also tells us what "real" love is and when we're doing it "right." Suffice it to say that, in this worldview, the kind of love we've been exploring does not "measure up." What we need is a new worldview, another way of perceiving reality and the self within it, a way in which love as a union of passion and authentic selfhood would be endorsed and fostered.

Fortunately, such a worldview is emerging in our time, inspired by the observations and discoveries of modern physics. What physics tells us is that we live in a universe whose unifying principle is relationship. And that the high value our dominant worldview places on separation and opposition is a serious error in perception of reality, because it does not reflect the harmonious interrelatedness physicists observe in nature. Nor do "the battle of the sexes" and "conquest and surrender." A mode of love based on concepts like these is so at variance with harmonious interrelatedness that it could be fairly called "unnatural."

The kind of love we've been exploring *does* reflect what physicists observe in nature. What physics tells those who want to see such a vision of love flourish in the world is that, though it does indeed go against the cultural grain, it does not go against nature's grain. The universe is behind us, even if our society isn't.

Actually, we can narrow that statement. *All* of our society isn't behind us, but a good part of it is beginning to be. New ways of thinking in an increasing number of areas are right in line with our new way of thinking about love. Prominent among these allies are: the systems view of life (as in "ecosystem" and "infrastructure"), the holistic sciences and holistic sciences movement, noetic sciences and the consciousness movement, humanistic psychology and the human potentials movement, ecology and the environmental movement, feminism and the women's movement. The emerging worldview is taking hold. A cultural transformation is underway, and what's lagging behind is the transformation of our major social institutions. Like the Myth of Romantic Love, these institutions stand between us and a better vision of love. Together, they fully validate only one kind of love relationship: romance-initiated, heterosexual, married, monogamous, sex role-based, child-producing, "'til death do you part." This is the pure form of what our dominant institutions uphold as "real" love and doing it "right." Deviations from this narrow and rigid mode are countered with sanctions and stigma, sometimes even with outright force. And still most of us do not conform completely. Despite the strong presence in our lives of these institutions, we manage to remain more human than that.

I agree with William James that real culture lives by sympathies and admirations. Let us try to imagine, then, what a society might look like if it truly reflected nature's harmonious interrelatedness. How would it treat the human activity of loving? First and foremost, such a society would be kind to that activity. It would evolve institutions that were harmonious with the evolution of love. Unlike the society we now live in, it would, in short, be pro-love.

A pro-love society would say that all people have the right to life, liberty, and the pursuit of happiness; and that the pursuit of happiness in love is therefore also a human right instead of a privilege granted by the state and revoked if not done in the one approved manner.

A pro-love society would not define people's love and sex lives for them, and then back that definition with sanctions and force. It would leave people free to explore for themselves these basic aspects of being human, so that they could define who they are as lovers in terms of their own reality.

A pro-love society would encourage sober questioning about the meaning of love, instead of insisting that it is "magic." And it would acknowledge and uphold human diversity, instead of claiming that sexual attraction is the work of "chemistry" between approved sexes.

In sum, a pro-love society would encourage us to feel that we have all possible options in our love lives, barring only infringement on the human rights of others, and then leave it to each individual to choose a way of loving that is true to his or her self.

On the happy day that we live in a pro-love society, it would in effect say to every one of us, "You want to engage in the all-important human activity called loving? Great. We need it. Here's a bunch of institutions that will support you on your path. Happy trails!"

That day may be approaching. The times are in our favor. Worldwide, from nation states to the domestic realm, old restrictive orders are crumbling, often in a surprisingly peaceful manner. We are living in the flux of a cultural transformation of global dimensions. After several thousand years under the sway of a patriarchal ideology that corrupted the very notion of relationship, we are now beginning to heal our connection to our self, to each other, to our earth, to the universe. Increasingly, all these relationships are becoming in tune with the harmonious interrelatedness of nature. Such a transformation is realistic in the truest sense of the word; it is also supremely practical. We who seek authentic passion and conscious loving are engaged in self-help of the most enlightened kind. For as we find new and more life-enhancing ways of loving in our private lives, we are at the very core of the transformation to a more life-enhancing and secure world.

Notes

Introduction

1. I am indebted to Isak Dinesen for the wonderful concept of "a direct relationship to life" as a description of what many modern women are seeking. See Judith Thurman, *Isak Dinesen: The Life of a Storyteller* (New York: St. Martin's Press, 1982), 235.

1. Once Upon a Time

1. For an analysis of the Ideal Romance, see Janice A. Radway, *Reading The Romance: Women, Patriarchy, and Popular Literature* (Chicago: University of Chicago Press, 1976), chapter 4, "The Ideal Romance: The Promise of Patriarchy," 119–56.
2. Shere Hite, *The Hite Report: A Nationwide Study of Female Sexuality* (New York: Macmillan, 1976).
3. ———. *The Hite Report on Male Sexuality* (New York: Alfred A. Knopf, 1981).
4. ———. *Woman and Love: A Cultural Revolution in Progress* (New York: Alfred A. Knopf, 1987).
5. Northrop Frye, in the introduction to *Abraham Rotstein, The Prospect of Change* (McGraw-Hill Company of Canada, 1965), xiii.

2. The Prince

1. From the 1983 survey by the Federal Reserve Board, quoted in William Greider, "Annals of Finance," *The New Yorker* (November 9, 1987): 62.
2. *Common Cause Magazine* (July/August 1987): 37.
3. Carol Tavris and Carole Wade, *The Longest War: Sex Differences in Perspective* (San Diego: Harcourt Brace Jovanovich, 1984), 19.
4. Sam Keen, *Faces of the Enemy: Reflections of the Hostile Imagination* (San Francisco: Harper & Row, 1986), 110.
5. For information about the archaeological revolution, see for example Marija Gimbutas and James Mellaart, in Riane Eisler, *The Chalice and the Blade* (San Francisco: Harper & Row, 1987), xv–xvi, 9–10, 42, 13.

   Why are we only now getting access to this hidden past? There are a number of reasons, which boil down to a previous lack of information and a misreading of what little information was available. Some of the misreading was predictable: Five thousand years of established patriarchy was bound to produce a certain myopia among the almost exclusively male scholars who have looked at our prehistory. This myopia is clearing significantly with recent feminist scholarship by women and men. It was not until after World War II that archaeology ceased to be what amounts to sanctioned grave-robbing (by European museums instead of local thieves) and became a science that sought to extract information rather than valuable objects from a site. Since then, thanks also to a technical breakthrough in methods of dating, archaeology has become an interdisciplinary science aimed at the systematic study of ancient sites in an effort to understand the life and thought of our prehistoric forebears.

I am presenting one currently accepted line of feminist argument about the creation of patriarchy. More scholarship is forthcoming on this subject. I am grateful to Dr. Johanna Stuckey for her knowledgeable aid.

6. *Ibid.*, 20, 32.
7. *Ibid.*, 44.
8. *Ibid.*, 251.
9. Gerda Lerner, *The Creation of Patriarchy* (New York: Oxford University Press, 1986), 8.
10. Denis de Rougemont, *Love in the Western World* (Princeton, NJ: Princeton University Press, 1983), 19.
11. Barbara Walker, *The Woman's Encyclopedia of Myths and Secrets* (San Francisco: Harper & Row, 1983), 290.
12. Lerner, *Creation of Patriarchy,* 196–97.
13. Helen B. Andelin, *Fascinating Womanhood* (Santa Barbara, CA: Pacific Press, 1963), 122.
14. Lerner, *Creation of Patriarchy,* 206–7.
15. *Ibid.*, 211, 10.
16. *The Summa Theologica of Saint Thomas Aquinas,* in *Great Books of the Western World* (Chicago: Encyclopedia Britannica, 1952), Vol. 19, 489.
17. Susan Sherwin, "Ethics: Towards a Feminist Approach," *Canadian Woman Studies 6,* no. 2 (Spring 1985): 21.
18. Quoted in Barbara Ehrenreich and Deidre English, *For Her Own Good: 150 Years of the Experts' Advice to Women* (New York: Anchor Press, 1978), 17–18.
19. M. F. Ashley Montagu, ed., *Man and Aggression* (New York: Oxford University Press, 1968), 5–6.
20. Keen, *Faces of the Enemy,* 134.
21. Donald H. Bell, *Being a Man: The Paradox of Masculinity* (Brattleboro, VT: The Lewis Publishing Company, 1982).
22. Keen, *Faces of the Enemy,* 19; and M. Scott Peck, *The Road Less Traveled: A New Psychology of Life, Traditional Values and Spiritual Growth* (New York: Simon & Schuster, 1979), 51.
23. Lawrence LeShan, *Alternate Realities* (New York: Ballantine, 1987).
24. Anthony Astrachan, *How Men Feel: Their Response to Women's Demands for Equality and Power* (New York: Anchor/Doubleday, 1986), author quoted in "The 'New Man' vs. the Old" by Glenn Collins, *The New York Times Book Review* (July 14, 1986): 18.
25. Robert L. Woolfolk and Frank C. Richardson, *Stress, Sanity and Survival* (New York: Signet, 1979), 57.
26. Naomi Weisstein, "Psychology Constructs the Female," in Anne Koedt, Ellen Levine and Anita Rapone, eds., *Radical Feminism* (New York: Quadrangle, 1973), 178–97.
27. Joseph H. Pleck, *The Myth of Masculinity* (Cambridge, MA: MIT Press, 1984), 7.
28. Quoted in Mark Gerzon, *A Choice of Heroes: The Changing Faces of American Manhood* (Boston: Houghton Mifflin, 1982), 6.

29. Pleck, *Myth of Masculinity,* 22, 34.
30. *Ibid.*, 139.
31. Ruth E. Hartley, "Sex-Role Pressures and the Socialization of the Male Child," *Psychological Reports* 5 (1959): 457–68.
32. Elizabeth H. Pleck and Joseph H. Pleck, eds., *The American Man* (Englewood Cliffs, NJ: Prentice-Hall, 1980), 424.
33. Joseph H. Pleck and Jack Sawyer, eds., *Men and Masculinity* (Englewood Cliffs, NJ: Prentice-Hall, 1974), 14.
34. Pleck and Pleck, *American Man,* 424.
35. Pleck and Sawyer, *Men and Masculinity,* 4.
36. Lillian Rubin, *Just Friends: The Role of Friendship in Our Lives* (New York: Harper & Row, 1985), 90.
37. Pleck and Pleck, *American Man,* 429.
38. Marc Feigen Fasteau, *The Male Machine* (New York: McGraw-Hill, 1974).
39. Pleck, *Myth of Masculinity,* 87.
40. Fasteau, *Male Machine,* 12–13.
41. *Ibid.*, 13.
42. *Ibid.*, 11.
43. *Ibid.*, 4.
44. O. William Battalia, and John J. Tarrant, *The Corporate Eunuch* (New York: NAL, 1974).
45. Fasteau, *Male Machine,* 15.
46. *Ibid.*, 15.
47. Nicolas Platon, quoted in Eisler, *The Chalice and The Blade,* 32.
48. Fasteau, *Male Machine,* 24.
49. Marabel Morgan, *The Total Woman* (New York: Pocket Books, 1975), 65.
50. Pleck and Pleck, *American Man,* 420–21.
51. Bell, *Being a Man,* 58.
52. Fasteau, *Male Machine,* 22–23.
53. Amanda Cross, *No Word from Winifred* (New York: E. P. Dutton, 1986), 30–31.
54. de Rougement, *Love in the Western World,* 47.
55. Gerzon, *A Choice of Heroes,* 225.
56. François, Duc de La Rochefoucauld, *Maxims* (1678), no. 312.
57. Pleck and Pleck, *American Man,* 39.
58. See, for example: Fasteau, *Male Machine,* 49; T. George Harris, in Elaine Hatfield and G. William Walster, *A New Look at Love* (New York: Addison-Wesley, 1981), 48–51; and Joseph Critelli, *et al.*, "The Components of Love: Romantic Attraction and Sex Role Orientation," *Journal of Personality* 54, no. 2 (June 1986): 354–69.
59. Critelli, *et al.*, "The Components of Love."

3. The Myth of Romantic Love

1. Joseph Bedier, *The Romance of Tristan and Iseult,* translated by Hilaire Belloc (London, 1913); quoted in Denis de Rougemont, *Love in the Western World* (Princeton, NJ: Princeton University Press, 1983), 15.
2. Jessie L. Weston, *The Story of Tristan and Iseult,* rendered into English from the German of Gottfried von Strassburg (London: David Hutt, 1970), introduction to volume I.

3. I have condensed the plot, as presented by de Rougemont, *Love in the Western World*.
4. *Ibid.*, 34.
5. Heather M. Ferguson (pseudonym for Johanna Stuckey), "Passionate Romantic Love," *Canadian Woman Studies* 4, no. 4 (Summer 1983): 97–98.
6. John H. Gagnon and William Simon, *Sexual Conduct: The Social Sources of Human Sexuality* (Chicago: Aldine, 1977), 1.
7. Northrop Frye, *Anatomy of Criticism* (Princeton, NJ: Princeton University Press, 1957), 136, 99–118.
8. Carol Pearson and Katherine Pope, *The Female Hero in American and British Literature* (New York: Bowker, 1981), 285.
9. de Rougemont, *Love in the Western World*, 52, 145, 16, 223, 24.
10. *Ibid.*, 312.
11. Iona Opie and Peter Opie, *The Classic Fairy Tales* (New York: Oxford University Press, 1980), 106.
12. Frye, *Anatomy of Criticism*, 116.
13. *Ibid.*, 153.
14. My analysis of the structural elements in these three fairy tales is based on V. Propp, *Morphology of the Folktale* (Austin: University of Texas Press, 1968); and on their first translations into English, as presented in Opie and Opie, *Classic Fairy Tales*.
15. de Rougemont, *Love in the Western World*, 18.
16. Andelin, quoted in Elaine Hatfield and G. William Walster, *A New Look at Love* (New York: Addison-Wesley, 1981), 162.
17. John G. Cawelti, *Adventure, Mystery, and Romance* (Chicago: University of Chicago Press, 1976), 9.
18. Margaret Ann Jensen, *Love's Sweet Return: The Harlequin Story* (Toronto: The Women's Press, 1984), 143.
19. Cawelti, *Adventure, Mystery, and Romance*, 34.
20. Jensen, *Love's Sweet Return*, 76.
21. Janice A. Radway, *Reading The Romance: Women, Patriarchy, and Popular Literature* (Chapel Hill: The University of North Carolina Press, 1984), see especially chapter 4, "The Ideal Romance."
22. Jensen, *Love's Sweet Return*, 119.
23. *Ibid.*, 85.
24. *Ibid.*, 118.
25. Radway, *Reading The Romance*, 147.
26. Jensen, *Love's Sweet Return*, 111.
27. In Radway, *Reading The Romance*, 129.
28. Jensen, *Love's Sweet Return*, 97.
29. *Ibid.*, 154.
30. *Ibid.*, 114.
31. *Ibid.*, 85.

4. The Princess

1. Colette Dowling, *The Cinderella Complex: Women's Hidden Fear of Independence* (New York: Pocket Books, 1981), 21, 14.
2. Marc Feigen Fasteau, *The Male Machine* (New York: McGraw-Hill, 1974), 43.

3. Nancy L. Peterson, *Our Lives for Ourselves: Women Who Have Never Married* (New York: G. P. Putnam's Sons, 1981), 202.
4. Doris Lessing, *The Summer Before the Dark* (London: Jonathan Cape, 1973), 47.
5. *Funk and Wagnalls Standard College Dictionary, Canadian Edition* (Toronto: Fitzhenry & Whiteside, Ltd., 1976).
6. Inge K. Broverman *et al.*, "Sex-Role Stereotypes and Clinical Judgments of Mental Health," *Journal of Consulting and Clinical Psychology 34,* no. 1 (1970) 1–7.
7. Clifton, McGrath, and Wick, "Stereotypes of Woman: A Single Category?" SEX ROLES: A JOURNAL OF RESEARCH in Joanna Bunker Rohrbaugh, *Women: Psychology's Puzzle* (New York: Basic Books, 1979), 163.
8. Judith Thurman, *Isak Dinesen: The Life of a Storyteller* (New York: St. Martin's Press, 1982), 235.
9. Dowling, *The Cinderella Complex*, 4.
10. Fasteau, *The Male Machine*, 69–70.
11. In Carolyn Heilbrun, *Reinventing Womanhood* (New York: Norton, 1979), 188.
12. Scenes 1–5: Mirra Komarovsky, "Cultural Contradictions and Sex Roles," *American Journal of Sociology* 52 (1946): 184–89. Scene 6: Marabel Morgan, *The Total Woman* (New York: Pocket Books, 1975), 62.
13. N. M. Henley, *Body Politics: Power, Sex, and Nonverbal Communication* (Englewood Cliffs, NJ: Prentice-Hall, 1977), 149.
14. Sue Cox, *Female Psychology: The Emerging Self* (New York: St. Martin's Press, 1981), 158–61; also Henley, *Body Politics, 180.*
15. Rohrbaugh, *Women*, 226.
16. Thurman, *Isak Dinesen*, 235.

5. The Dragon

1. Gloria Kaufman and Mary Kay Blakely, *Pulling Our Own Strings: Feminist Humor & Satire* (Bloomington, IN: Indiana University Press, 1980), 165.
2. In Rosabeth Moss Kanter, *Men and Women of the Corporation* (New York: Basic Books, 1977), 201.
3. *Ibid.*, 230–37.
4. Joanna Bunker Rohrbaugh, *Women: Psychology's Puzzle* (New York: Basic Books, 1979), 221.
5. Colette Dowling, *The Cinderella Complex: Women's Hidden Fear of Independence* (New York: Pocket Books, 1981), 172–73, 21.
6. Matina Horner, "The Motive to Avoid Success and Changing Aspirations of College Women," in Judith M. Bardwick, ed., *Readings on the Psychology of Woman* (New York: Harper & Row, 1972), 62–63.
7. Liz Roman Gallese, *Women Like Us: What Is Happening to the Women of the Harvard Business School, Class of '75—the Women Who Had the First Chance to Make It to the Top* (New York: William Morrow, 1985).
8. *Ibid.*, 16, 34, 29, 106.
9. Marge Piercy, *Living in the Open* (New York: Alfred A. Knopf, 1976), 71.
10. Gallese, *Women Like Us*, 79.
11. Stanley Berenstain and Janice Berenstain, *The Bike Lesson* (New York: Beginner Books, 1964).
12. Quoted in Rohrbaugh, *Women*, 221.
13. The information on the two Annie Oakleys comes from these sources: *Annie*

Get Your Gun, MGM musical starring Betty Hutton and Howard Keel, with score and lyrics by Irving Berlin (1950); Bonnie Kreps, "Annie Oakley's True Love Story," *Ms. Magazine* (January 1977); Annie Oakley Collection (Annie's private mementos and scrapbooks of clippings covering more than forty years), Buffalo Bill Historical Center, Cody, Wyoming; and Ellen Levine, *Ready, Aim, Fire! The Real Adventures of Annie Oakley* (New York: Scholastic, 1989).
14. *New Yorker* (May 20, 1985).
15. Komarovsky, "Cultural Contradictions and Sex Roles," 189.
16. Carol Cassell, *Swept Away: Why Women Fear Their Own Sexuality* (New York: Simon & Schuster, 1984), 116–17.
17. Susan Brownmiller, *femininity* (New York: Simon & Schuster, 1984), 221.
18. G. Stanley Hall, quoted in Mark Gerzon, *A Choice of Heroes: The Changing Faces of American Manhood* (Boston: Houghton, Mifflin, 1982), 143.
19. Psychiatrist Helene Deutsch, quoted in Betty Friedan, *The Feminine Mystique* (New York: W. W. Norton, 1963), 173.
20. Ellen Goodman, *Turning Points* (New York: Fawcett Crest, 1983), 76–77.
21. Margaret Ann Jensen, *Love's Sweet Return: The Harlequin Story* (Toronto: The Women's Press, 1984), 104.
22. Nancy L. Peterson, *Our Lives for Ourselves: Women Who Have Never Married* (New York: G. P. Putnam's Sons, 1981), 52.
23. Zick Rubin, *Liking and Loving* (New York: Holt, Rinehart and Winston, 1973), 78.
24. Marc Feigen Fasteau, *The Male Machine* (New York: McGraw-Hill, 1974), 69.
25. Rubin, *Liking and Loving*, 76–77.
26. *Ibid.*, 77–78.
27. Dorothy Tennov, *Love and Limerence: The Experience of Being in Love* (New York: Stein and Day, 1980), 21–22.

6. Life in The Castle

1. Barbara Gordon, *I'm Dancing As Fast As I Can* (New York: Harper & Row, 1979), 281.
2. Jessie Bernard, *The Future of Marriage* (New York: Bantam Books, 1978), 41.
3. See, for example, Myrna M. Weissman and Gerald L. Klerman, "Sex Differences and the Epidemiology of Depression," *Archives of General Psychiatry* 34 (1977): 98–111.
4. Silvano Arieti and Jules Bemporad, *Severe and Mild Depression* (New York: Basic Books, 1978), 365.
5. Marabel Morgan, *The Total Woman* (New York: Pocket Books, 1975), 80.
6. Arieti and Bemporad, *Severe and Mild Depression*, 367–68.
7. John Money, *Love and Love Sickness: The Science of Sex, Gender Difference, and Pair-Bonding* (Baltimore and London: Johns Hopkins University Press, 1981), 65, 71.
8. Jeffrey R. M. Kunz, MD, ed., *The American Medical Association Family Medical Guide* (New York: Random House, 1982), 194–95.
9. Dorothy Tennov, *Love and Limerence: The Experience of Being in Love* (New York: Stein and Day, 1980), 18.
10. M. Scott Peck, *The Road Less Traveled: A New Psychology of Love, Traditional Values and Spiritual Growth* (New York: Simon & Schuster, 1979), 85–105.

11. Marc Feigen Fasteau, *The Male Machine* (New York: McGraw-Hill, 1974), 32.
12. Stanton Peele, with Archie Brodsky, *Love and Addiction* (New York: New American Library, 1976), 70.
13. *Ibid.*, 113.
14. Sheila Graham and Gerold Frank, *Beloved Infidel* (London: The Book Club, 1959), 152, 187–88.
15. Lewis Carroll, *Through the Looking Glass* (1872).
16. Gregory Bateson, *Mind and Nature: A Necessary Unity* (New York: Bantam, 1980), 109.
17. Peele, *Love and Addiction*, 265.
18. *Ibid.*, 79.
19. Margery Allingham, *Crime and Mr. Campion* (New York: Doubleday, 1937), 101.
20. Carol Travis, *Anger: The Misunderstood Emotion* (New York: Simon & Schuster, 1989).
21. *Ibid*, 131–32, 144, 23, 47.
22. Peter Marris, *Loss and Change* (New York: Anchor Books, 1975), 24, 157, 132, 164, 42.
23. *Ibid.*, 36.
24. *Ibid.*, 12, 98, 37, 20, 41, 51, 29, 162.
25. Dorothy L. Sayers, *Have His Carcase* (New York: Harper & Row, 1987), opening lines.
26. Marris, *Loss and Change*, 163–64.
27. Peele, *Love and Addiction*, 102.
28. Alice Koller, *An Unknown Woman: A Journey to Self-Discovery* (New York: Bantam Books, 1983), 249.

7. Love: Theory

1. Definitions from *The Compact Edition of the Oxford English Dictionary* (Oxford University Press, 1982); *Webster's New World Dictionary of the American Language*, 2nd College Edition (New York and Cleveland, 1970).
2. Arno Gruen, *The Betrayal of the Self: The Fear of Autonomy in Men and Women* (New York: Grove Press, 1988), xv.
3. *Ibid.*, 127.
4. Jessica Benjamin, *The Bonds of Love* (New York: Pantheon Books, 1988), 23.
5. Leo Buscaglia, *Love*, (New York: Fawcett Crest, 1982), 11.
6. Morris Berman, *The Reenchantment of the World* (Ithaca: Cornell University Press, 1981), especially chapters 1–4.
7. B. A. Seyfried and Clyde Hendrick, "When Do Opposites Attract?" *Journal of Personality and Social Psychology 25* no. 1 (1973): 15–20.
8. Dr. Joyce Brothers, *What Every Woman Ought to Know About Love and Marriage* (New York: Ballantine, 1985), back cover.
9. Carol Gilligan, "Remapping the Moral Domain: New Images of the Self in Relationship," in Thomas Heller, Morton Sosna, and David Wellberry, eds., *Reconstructing Individualism: Autonomy, Individuality, and the Self in Western Thought* (Stanford, CA: Stanford University Press, 1986), 247.
10. Benjamin, *Bonds of Love*, 76.
11. Gilligan, "Remapping the Moral Domain," 243–44.

12. Benjamin, *Bonds of Love*, 191.
13. Gilligan, *In a Different Voice: Psychological Theory and Women's Development* (Cambridge, MA: Harvard University Press, 1982), 29–30, 158–63, 61, 79, 149.
14. Fritjof Capra, *The Turning Point: Science, Society and the Rising Culture* (New York: Simon & Schuster, 1982), 77.
15. Fritjof Capra, *The Tao of Physics* (New York: Bantam Books, 1977), 188.
16. *Ibid.*, 252.
17. *Ibid.*, 57.
18. *Ibid.*, 127–28.
19. Capra, *The Turning Point*, 269.
20. "Real culture lives by sympathies and admirations, not by dislikes and disdains; under all misleading wrappings it pounces unerringly upon the human core." William James, "The Social Value of the College-Bred" in *Memories and Studies* (1911).
21. Benjamin, *Bonds of Love*, 19–21.
22. M. Scott Peck, *The Road Less Traveled: A New Psychology of Love, Traditional Values and Spiritual Growth* (New York: Simon & Schuster, 1979), 166.
23. Benjamin, *Bonds of Love*, 221, 40.
24. *Ibid.*, 47–48.
25. *Ibid.*, 30.
26. Ursula K. Le Guin, "Is Gender Necessary?" in Vonde V. McIntyre and Susan Janice Anderson, eds., *Aurora: Beyond Equality* (Greenwich, CT: Fawcett, 1976), 130–39; Ursula K. Le Guin, *The Left Hand of Darkness* (New York: Ace Books, 1979).
27. Benjamin, *Bonds of Love*, 218–22.
28. Jan Morris, *Conundrum* (London: Faber & Faber, 1974), 146, 59, 22, 56–57, 57–59, 60, 145, 152, 162–63, 165, 60–61.
29. David D. McClelland, "Some Reflections on the Two Psychologies of Love," *Journal of Personality* 54 (June, 1986): 2; also: Daniel Goleman, "Psychologists Pursue the Irrational Aspects of Love," *New York Times* (July 22, 1986): C1, C8.
30. Denis de Rougemont, *Love in the Western World* (Princeton, NJ: Princeton University Press, 1983), 25.
31. Martha C. Nussbaum, "Love and the Individual: Romantic Rightness and Platonic Aspiration," in Thomas Heller, Morton Sosna, and David Wellberry, eds., *Reconstructing Individualism: Autonomy, Individuality, and the Self in Western Thought* (Stanford, CA: Stanford University Press, 1986), 253–77.
32. Capra, *The Turning Point*, 269.
33. Berman, *The Reenchantment of The World*, (1981), 73, 76.

8. Love: Groundwork

1. Lillian Rubin, *Women of a Certain Age: The Mid-life Search for Self* (New York: Harper & Row, 1979).
2. Gilligan, "Remapping The Moral Domain: New Images of The Self in Relationship," in Thomas Heller, *et al.*, eds., *Reconstructing Individualism: Autonomy, Individuality, and The Self in Western Thought* (Stanford, CA: Stanford University Press, 1986), 250.

3. Gilligan, *In a Different Voice: Psychological Theory and Women's Development* (Cambridge, MA: Harvard University Press, 1982), 8.
4. *Ibid.*, 82–83.
5. Anne Wilson Schaef, *Co-Dependence: Misunderstood–Mistreated* (Minneapolis: Winston Press, 1986).
6. William Wordsworth, "I Wandered Lonely as a Cloud," stanza 4; John Milton, "Paradise Lost," IX 1.249.
7. Samuel Taylor Coleridge, "The Friend. The Improvisatore." (1828).
8. Carol Pearson and Katherine Pope, *The Female Hero in American and British Literature* (New York: Bowker, 1981), 3.
9. Imogen Cunningham, *After Ninety*, introduction by Margaretta Mitchell (Seattle and London: University of Washington Press, 1977).
10. Lillian Rubin, *Just Friends: The Role of Friendship in Our Lives* (New York: Harper & Row, 1985), 1, 4, 5.
11. *Ibid.*, 106.
12. Arthur N. Benade, *Horns, Strings, and Harmony* (New York: Anchor Books, 1960), 43–44.
13. David Dunn, "Synchronisms: Toward a Phenomenological Science," *IS Journal #1* (1986): 6.
14. Richard Wilhelm, trans; translated into English by Cary F. Baynes, *The I Ching: Or Book of Changes* (Princeton, NJ: Princeton University Press, 1967), 9.
15. George Eliot, *Daniel Deronda*, II. 15.
16. Wilhelm, *I Ching*, 38.
17. M. Scott Peck, *The Road Less Traveled: A New Psychology of Love, Traditional Values and Spiritual Growth* (New York: Simon & Schuster, 1979), 128.
18. Jessie Bernard, *The Future of Marriage* (New York: Bantam Books, 1978), 157.
19. Michael Vincent Miller, review of James B. Witchell *Forbidden Partners* (New York: Columbia University Press, 1986), in *New York Times Book Review* (January 18, 1987): 7–8.
20. John H. Gagnon and William Simon, *Sexual Conduct: The Social Sources of Human Sexuality* (Chicago: Aldine, 1977), 19.
21. Ellen Goodman, *Turning Points* (New York: Fawcett Crest, 1983), 97.

9. Love: Practice

1. Dorothy Tennov, *Love and Limerence: The Experience of Being in Love* (New York: Stein and Day, 1980), 33–35.
2. Denis de Rougemont, *Love in the Western World* (Princeton, NJ: Princeton University Press, 1983), 145.
3. Tennov, *Love and Limerence*, 52–53.
4. See: B. F. Skinner, *About Behaviorism* (New York: Alfred A. Knopf, 1974), 57–61; and Ernest R. Hilgard, Richard C. Atkinson, and Rita L. Atkinson, *Introduction to Psychology* (Harcourt Brace Jovanovich, 1971), 198–200.
5. See, for example: Tennov, *Love and Limerence*, vii, 247; Sydney L. W. Mellen, *The Evolution of Love* (Oxford and San Francisco: W. H. Freeman, 1981), 139–41; *The Romance of Tristan and Iseult*; John Money and A. A. Ehrhardt, *Man and Woman, Boy and Girl* (Baltimore: Johns Hopkins University Press, 1972), 191.

6. George Eliot, *Middlemarch*, quoted in Amanda Cross, *In the Last Analysis* (New York: Avon, 1981), 67.
7. Sue Cartledge and Joanna Ryan, eds., *Sex and Love: New Thoughts on Old Contradictions* (London: The Women's Press Ltd., 1984), 63.
8. Jane Pearce and Saul Newton, *The Conditions of Human Growth* (Secaucus, NJ: The Citadel Press, 1980), 218.
9. Jessica Benjamin, *The Bonds of Love* (New York: Pantheon, 1988), 221.
10. Tristan Bernard (1866–1947), *L'Enfant Prodigue Du Vesinet* (1921).
11. Robert J. Sternberg, *The Triangle of Love: Intimacy, Passion, Commitment* (New York: Basic Books, 1988), 283.
12. *Ibid.*, 280.
13. Rainer Maria Rilke, *Letters to a Young Poet*, M. D. H. Norton trans. (New York: W. W. Norton & Co., 1963).
14. Sara Lawrence Lightfoot, *Balm in Gilead: Journey of a Healer* (New York: Addison-Wesley, 1988), 86, 94–96, 106, 108, 151, 157, 109, 212–13, 260, 263, 18, 7, 302–3, 107.

Bibliography

Alberoni, Francesco. *Falling in Love*. New York: Random House, 1983.

Andelin, Helen B. *Fascinating Womanhood*. Santa Barbara, CA: Pacific Press, 1963.

Arieti, Silvano and Jules Bemporad. *Severe and Mild Depression*. New York: Basic Books, 1978.

Astrachan, Anthony. *How Men Feel*. New York: Anchor Books, 1986.

Bateson, Gregory, *Mind and Nature: A Necessary Unity*. New York: Bantam, 1980.

Bell, Donald H. *Being a Man: The Paradox of Masculinity*. Brattleboro, VT: Lewis Publishing Company, 1982.

Benjamin, Jessica. *The Bonds of Love*. New York: Pantheon, 1988.

Berman, Morris. *The Reenchantment of the World*. Ithaca: Cornell University Press, 1981.

Bernard, Jessie. *The Future of Motherhood*. New York: Penguin, 1975.

———. *The Future of Marriage*. New York: Bantam, 1978.

———. *The Female World*. New York: The Free Press, 1982.

Broverman, Inge K., *et al*. Sex-Role Stereotypes and Clinical Judgments of Mental Health. *Journal of Consulting and Clinical Psychology 34* (1970): 1–7.

Brown, Gabrielle. *The New Celibacy*. New York: McGraw-Hill, 1980.

Brownmiller, Susan. *Femininity*. New York: Simon & Schuster, 1984.

Callahan, Roger with Karen Levine. *It Can Happen to You: The Practical Guide to Romantic Love*. New York: Signet, 1983.

Capra, Frijof. *The Tao of Physics*. New York: Bantam, 1977.

———. *The Turning Point: Science, Society and the Rising Culture*. New York: Simon & Schuster, 1982.

Cartledge, Sue and Joanna Ryan. *Sex & Love: New Thoughts on Old Contradictions*. London: The Women's Press, 1984.

Cassell, Carol. *Swept Away: Why Women Fear Their Own Sexuality*. New York: Simon & Schuster, 1984.

Cawelti, John G. *Adventure, Mystery, and Romance*. Chicago: University of Chicago Press, 1976.

Cox, Sue. *Female Psychology: The Emerging Self*. New York: St. Martin's Press, 1981.

de Rougemont, Denis. *Love in the Western World*. Princeton, NJ: Princeton University Press, 1983.

Dodson, Betty. *Sex for One*. New Jersey: Harmony Books, 1988.

Dowling, Colette, *The Cinderella Complex: Women's Hidden Fear of Independence*. New York: Pocket Books, 1981.

Ehrenreich, Barbara, Elizabeth Hess, and Gloria Jacobs. *Re-Making Love: The Feminization of Sex*. Garden City, NY: Anchor Press/Doubleday, 1986.

Eisler, Riane. *The Chalice and the Blade*. San Francisco: Harper & Row, 1987.

Fasteau, Marc Feigen. *The Male Machine*. New York: McGraw-Hill, 1974.

Ferguson, Heather M. (pseud. for Johanna Stuckey). "Passionate Romantic Love," *Canadian Woman Studies* 4, no. IV (Summer 1983): 97–98.

Friedan, Betty, *The Feminine Mystique*. New York: W. W. Norton, 1963.

Frye, Northrop. *Anatomy of Criticism*. Princeton, NJ: Princeton University Press, 1957.

Gagnon, John H. and William Simon. *Sexual Conduct: The Social Sources of Human Sexuality*. Chicago: Aldine, 1977.

Gallese, Liz Roman. *Women Like Us: What Is Happening to the Women of the Harvard Business School, Class of '75—The Women Who Had the First Chance to Make It to the Top*. New York: William Morrow, 1985.

Gerzon, Mark. *A Choice of Heroes: The Changing Faces of American Manhood*. Boston: Houghton Mifflin, 1982.

Gilligan, Carol. *In a Different Voice: Psychological Theory and Women's Development*. Cambridge, MA: Harvard University Press, 1982.

———. Gilligan, Carol. "Remapping the Moral Domain: New Images of the Self in Relationship." In Heller, Thomas, Morton Sosna, and David Wildberry, eds. *Reconstructing Individualism: Autonomy, Individuality, and the Self in Western Thought*. Stanford, CA: Stanford University Press, 1986.

Goodman, Ellen, *Turning Points*. New York: Fawcett Crest, 1983.

Gruen, Arno. *The Betrayal of the Self: The Fear of Autonomy in Men and Women*. New York: Grove Press, 1988.

Hatfield, Elaine and G. William Walster. *A New Look at Love*. New York: Addison-Wesley, 1981.

Heilbrun, Carolyn. *Reinventing Womanhood*. New York: Norton, 1979.

Henley, N. M. *Body Politics: Power, Sex, and Nonverbal Communication*. Englewood Cliffs, NJ: Prentice-Hall, 1977.

Hite, Shere. *The Hite Report: A Nationwide Study on Female Sexuality*. New York: Macmillan, 1976.

———. *The Hite Report on Male Sexuality*. New York: Alfred A. Knopf, 1981.

———. *Women and Love: A Cultural Revolution in Progress*. New York: Alfred A. Knopf, 1987.

Horner, Matina. "The Motive to Avoid Success and Changing Aspirations of College Women," in Bardwick, Judith M., ed. *Readings on the Psychology of Women*. New York: Harper & Row, 1972.

Jensen, Margaret Ann. *Love's Sweet Return: The Harlequin Story*. Toronto: The Women's Press, 1984.

Kanter, Rosabeth Moss. *Men and Women of the Corporation*. New York: Basic Books, 1979.

Keen, Sam. *Faces of the Enemy: Reflections of the Hostile Imagination*. San Francisco: Harper & Row, 1986.

Koedt, Anne, Ellen Levine, and Anita Rapone, eds. *Radical Feminism*. New York: Quadraugle, 1973.

Koller, Alice. *An Unknown Woman: A Journey to Self-Discovery*. New York: Bantam Books, 1983.

Lightfoot, Sara Lawrence. *Balm in Gilead: Journey of a Healer*. New York: Addison-Wesley, 1988.

LeGuin, Ursula K. "Is Gender Necessary?" in Vonde McIntyre and Susan Janice Anderson, eds. *Aurora: Beyond Equality*. Greenwich, CT: Fawcett, 1976.

———. *The Left Hand of Darkness*. New York: Ace Books, 1979.

Lerner, Gerda. *The Creation of Patriarchy*. New York: Oxford University Press, 1986.

LeShan, Lawrence. *Alternate Realities*. New York: Ballantine, 1987.

Lessing, Doris. *The Summer Before the Dark*. London: Jonathan Cape, 1973.

Levine, Ellen, *Ready, Aim, Fire! The Real Adventures of Annie Oakley*. New York: Scholastic, 1989.

Marris, Peter. *Loss and Change*. New York: Anchor Books, 1975.

McClelland, David D. "Some Reflections on the Two Psychologies of Love," *Journal of Personality* 54 (June 1986): 2.

Mellen, Sydney, L. W. *The Evolution of Love*. Oxford and San Francisco: W. H. Freeman, 1981.

Money, John and A. A. Ehrhardt. *Man and Woman, Boy and Girl*. Baltimore: Johns Hopkins University Press, 1972.

Money, John. *Love & Love Sickness: The Science of Sex, Gender Difference, and Pair-Bonding*. Baltimore and London: Johns Hopkins University Press, 1981.

Montagu, M. F. Ashley, ed. *Man and Aggression*. New York: Oxford University Press, 1968.

Morgan, Marabel. *The Total Woman*. New York: Pocket Books, 1975.

Morris, Jan. *Conundrum*. London: Faber & Faber, 1974.

Nussbaum, Martha C. "Love and the Individual: Romantic Rightness and Platonic Aspiration." In Thomas Heller, Morton Sosna, and David Wildberry, eds. *Reconstructing Individualism: Autonomy, Individuality, and the Self in Western Thought*. Stanford, CA: Stanford University Press, 1986.

Opie, Iona and Peter Opie. *The Classic Fairy Tales*. New York: Oxford University Press, 1980.

Pearce, Jane and Saul Newton. *The Conditions of Human Growth*. Secaucus, NJ: Citadel Press, 1980.

Pearson, Carol and Katherine Pope. *The Female Hero in American & British Literature*. New York: Bowker, 1981.

Peck, M. Scott. *The Road Less Traveled: A New Psychology of Love, Traditional Values and Spiritual Growth*. New York: Simon & Schuster, 1979.

Peele, Stanton with Archie Brodsky. *Love and Addiction*. New York: New American Library, 1976.

Peterson, Nancy L. *Our Lives for Ourselves: Women Who Have Never Been Married*. New York: G. P. Putnam's Sons, 1981.

Pleck, Elizabeth H. and Joseph H. Pleck, eds. *The American Man*. Englewood Cliffs, NJ: Prentice-Hall, 1980.

Pleck, Joseph H. *The Myth of Masculinity*. Cambridge, MA: MIT Press, 1984.

Pleck, Joseph H. and Jack Sawyer, eds. *Men and Masculinity*. Englewood Cliffs, NJ: Prentice-Hall, 1974.

Propp, V. *Morphology of the Folktale*. Austin: University of Texas Press, 1968.

Radway, Janice A. *Reading the Romance: Women, Patriarchy, and Popular Literature*. Chapel Hill: University of North Carolina Press, 1984.

Rohrbaugh, Joanna Bunker. *Women: Psychology's Puzzle*. New York: Basic Books, 1979.

Rubin, Lillian. *Women of a Certain Age: The Mid-Life Search for Self*. New York: Harper & Row, 1979.

———. *Intimate Strangers: Men and Women Together*. New York: Harper Colophon, 1984.

———. *Just Friends: The Role of Friendship in Our Lives*. New York: Harper & Row, 1985.

Rubin, Zick. *Liking and Loving*. New York: Holt, Rinehart and Winston, 1973.

Salk, Jonas. *Anatomy of Reality*. New York: Praeger, 1985.

Sanford, Linda T. and Mary E. Donovan. *Women & Self-Esteem*. Garden City, NY: Anchor Press/Doubleday, 1984.

Schaef, Anne Wilson. *Women's Reality*. Minneapolis: Winston Press, 1981.

———. *Co-Dependence: Misunderstood—Mistreated*. Minneapolis: Winston Press, 1986.

Schachter, Stanley and Jerome Singer. "Cognitive, Social, and Psychological Determinants of Emotional State." *Psychological Review 69*, no. 5 (September 1962): 379–99.

Skinner, B. F. *About Behaviorism*. New York: Alfred A. Knopf, 1974.

Starhawk. *Dreaming the Dark: Magic, Sex & Politics*. Boston: Beacon Press, 1982.

Sternberg, Robert J. *The Triangle of Love: Intimacy, Passion, Commitment*. New York: Basic Books, 1988.

Snitow, Ann, Christine Stansell, and Sharon Thompson, eds. *Power of Desire: The Politics of Sexuality*. New York: Monthly Review Press, 1983.

Tavris, Carol and Carole Wade. *The Longest War: Sex Differences in Perspective*. San Diego: Harcourt Brace Jovanovich, 1984.

———. *Anger: The Misunderstood Emotion*. New York: Simon & Schuster, 1989.

Tennov, Dorothy. *Love and Limerence: The Experience of Being in Love*. New York: Stein and Day, 1980.

Vance, Carole S., ed. *Pleasure and Danger: Exploring Female Sexuality*. London: Routledge & Kegan Paul, 1985.

Walker, Barbara. *The Woman's Encyclopedia of Myths and Secrets*. San Francisco: Harper & Row, 1983.

Weissman, Myrna M. and Gerald L. Klerman. "Sex Differences and the Epidemiology of Depression." *Archives of General Psychiatry 34* (1977): 98–111.

Zee, A. *Fearful Symmetry: The Search for Beauty in Modern Physics*. New York: Macmillan, 1986.

Index